BY THE SAME AUTHOR.

(Leisure-Hour Series.)

AROUND A SPRING.

BABOLAIN.

LEISURE HOUR SERIES

AROUND A SPRING

TRANSLATED FROM THE FRENCH

OF

GUSTAVE DROZ

BY

MS.

SECOND EDITION REVISED

NEW YORK
HOLT & WILLIAMS
1873

MIDDLETON & CO., STEREOTYPERS,
BRIDGEPORT, CONN.

AROUND A SPRING.

A FEW years ago, the village of Grand-Fort-le-Haut was totally unknown .to the outside world. Lost among the defiles of the mountains, perched like a raven's nest amidst the branches of an old walnut tree, it was far removed from all progress, a stranger to political emotions, unmoved by social changes. The pretty road, adorned with side walks, gas-burners and tiny fountains, which now leads to it, turning and winding like a braided ribbon, did not then exist, and the only communication possible between the valley and the village was a rough, sunken road, encumbered by stones which the melting snows and heavy rains yearly deposited, and so steep that nothing but ox teams could ascend.

About half way up this picturesque, but almost impassable road, may be seen on the left, nearly concealed by briars, a fine old bridge, which, spite of its great age, boldly arches the deep ravine, and abuts upon a dark old doorway almost as ancient as itself, filled with clefts, surmounted by a large escutcheon, and studded with enormous nails. This was the entrance to the château of Manteigney, whose slender towers, pointed roofs, narrow, strongly-barred windows, and thick, reddish walls, covered with moss and ivy, may be indistinctly perceived through the foliage. It had been deserted fifteen or twenty years ago, and the sight of the old feudal manor, rising in stately solitude from the ravine, and silent as a tomb, was indescribably mournful to a Parisian eye; so, after a hasty glance, one would continue his way without a second look, until he gained the first houses on the outskirts of the village, which soon appeared, and instantly effaced the impression produced by the château.

Nothing can be more bright and cheerful than these pine huts, with their tall brick chimneys mingling with the foliage, large, flat, reddish roofs overshadowing cracked, propped, disjointed balconies, covered with creepers and wild eglantine, little low doors, and tottering staircases which would creak under the weight of a bird. They stand steeped in the sunlight, scattered hap-hazard on both sides of the road, keeping their balance tolerably well on the sharp slope, among the gnarled chestnut trees which shelter them with their huge branches, uphold them with their gigantic roots, and seem to make a part of their structure.

I well remember the flock of ducklings which, startled at my approach the first time I entered the village, fluttered about among a number of half-naked babies lying on a clean white cloth, like Homer's phoci on the shore of the sea. The picture is as perfect as ever in my mind. The screaming babies and bewildered ducklings tumbling about among the fat legs and dimpled arms, an old grandmother with outstretched, wrinkled neck surveying the scene through her spectacles, and threatening the rebels with her distaff, and a stout man engaged in cutting poles, laughing till he shook from head to foot. It was a pleasant incident both to eyes and heart; one felt that one was in the midst of worthy people. Even the sun, which flickered through the foliage as if it were an immense skimmer, had a specially friendly, cordial aspect, and seemed to delight in sending a thousand rays to play over the scene; here, lost in a mass of fair hair, and yonder in the folds of a blue apron; now gliding over a ploughshare, and now glittering, not without malice, on the scarlet kerchief of a young girl talking to the shoemaker, who appeared as if framed in his narrow window, between two pots of wall-flowers, laughing, jesting, attractive, irresistible. One could not help noticing the sun, for it was everywhere flashing on the little round glass panes in their leaden casing, adorning with brilliant colors the scraps hanging from the balconies here and there, or converting a long bit of straw from some roof into a golden thread that glittered in the shadow. What a pretty collection of brilliant hues, and how charming to the eye was the glimpse of the interior of the blacksmith's shop, with its warm rich tones which please the eye as much as the fumes of a good ragoût delight the gourmand. The innumerable spider-webs looked like a milk-white cloud against the smoky rafters of the roof, and while the brawny neck of the Cyclops assumed tints of gold and purple beneath the caress of the sun's rays, the fire in the forge grew pale and dim.

Spite of the delay, I wish to make one remark here. Let those who are in a hurry glide over it rapidly. Phœbus is not merely the handsome, pompous youth, curled *à la* Louis XIV., blessing the world from his gilded chariot, and whirling through space as fast as his four coursers can çarry him. He likes to peep through the vine branches and pry into little corners without caring for decorum, or thinking of his plumes, visit poor people, and thrust his laughing face into attics. If a place pleases him, he forgets his astronomy, and without the least ceremony interests himself in botany, and plays with the children.

It must be confessed that in dull weather, Grand-Fort-le-Haut is sombre, gloomy, rough, and poverty-stricken; but I first saw it under a cloudless sky, when all was merriment, all seemed rich, and songs echoed from every dwelling; the villagers were hammering pounding, working together in the middle of the rough road, over which no carriage ever passed. The carpenter's axe flashed like the sword of the archangel; the wheelwright turned his huge screw, pressing his stout form against it with many a grunt; and from time to time, farther on, merry rogues sat cracking their whips astride the greasy machine for shoeing oxen, which might have been taken for some unknown tool of the Holy Inquisition. The recollection of the little scene is still firmly impressed on my memory.

To conclude, Mayor Baravoux was a grocer, and his assistant kept the little inn, whose fir boughs might be perceived in the distance. The spit was seldom turned within its walls, for very few persons came there; no one, to tell the truth, except the forest-keepers who sometimes stopped while on their rounds.

After passing through the whole village, a little, irregular, grass-grown square appears, at one end of which stands the humble church, worn by time and the winter snows. Its modest belfry scarcely overtops the lofty chestnut tree growing near the porch. An unpretending belfry we might well call it. Imagine a noisy child striking a Dutch oven with a pot ladle. The most remarkable thing about it is, that the quavering of its faint voice has a simple, hearty sound by no means inappropriate to the surroundings. On approaching nearer and looking at the porch, whose timbers are worn by friction as far as the height of a man, one can see the great ladder and fire buckets, the bier on which the dead are borne to the grave, and the round shelf containing the consecrated bread, stored away in the roof. The floor is flagged with tombstones, whose inscriptions and sculptured ornaments long since disappeared under the tread of the congregation. The door is charming with its triple row of crumbling columns, and single arch carved as elaborately as a Byzantine bracelet. Spite of its decay, the keystone of the arch still revealed traces of a fiend tempting and Christ in the act of benediction. God had wholly disappeared, and nothing was left of the devil but an enormous tail, twisting about between the alternately raised and hollowed squares which surrounded the whole arch. Who could the skilful artist, angel or fiend, have been who carved so exquisitely in this wild place? These surprises are by no means rare in France. In the most out-of-the-way wretched corners, may sometimes be found some delicate fragment of art, the forgotten relic of a lost civilization, a mute witness of a feeling which must have sprung up and died in this solitary place: but to continue.

On the left of the ancient church, and resting against it, was a little house built of round stones, cemented by grayish mortar, and surmounted with a red roof. It was an humble dwelling, only one story in height, with a little blooming garden about ten yards square at most, in front, and overlooking the ravine in the rear. If you passed it early in the morning, you would probably see a tall man, clothed in a black robe, perched on a ladder, pruning-knife in hand, training his grape-vine. The little house was the priest's dwelling, and the man in black no other than Abbé Roche, curé of Grand-Fort-le-Haut.

He was about thirty-eight or nine years old, tall, stout, firmly built, broad shouldered, and possessing the easy carriage and bold, free step which in society is most frequently only an acquirement obtained by certain modes of life, but with him was the natural result of an upright mind and vigorous health lodged in a robust well-balanced frame. His clear, searching glance was that of a man who, having nothing to conceal, looks people in the face wishing to understand them, and only asking to be understood in return. The prominent muscles of his jaw, contracting at the slightest emotion, indicated rare energy, which was confirmed by the strong white teeth slightly curving inwards. His hair was thick, somewhat rough, and cut very short.

In character he was benevolent, generous, and good; but his smile, however frank, always had a somewhat sad expression, and even in his acts of kindness he was grave, and might easily have been considered proud and haughty. The true reason was that Abbé Roche had never known either father or mother, and submitted to the common law imposed upon those poor children who, having always been ignorant of familiar caresses and the frank affection of home, feel themselves strangers at every board, and maintain a constant reserve. Such children are long in unfolding their characters; it seems as if an endless regret was weighing upon them. Kisses are to childhood what the warm sun is to the young buds of spring. Plants and men droop sadly in the shade.

Although he cultivated his garden himself, was a great player at bowls, and had a decided liking for physical exertion, his sunburnt hands were delicate if not white, his fingers beautifully formed, straight, supple and strong, and his nails well shaped. He did not have the wan, soft hand that is frequently, and often incorrectly, associated with churchmen, but rather that of a gentleman who has handled a sword in a leathern glove. He should have been seen facing the wolves that were driven into the village by the snow, or at the fire in 1859, when three barns were in a blaze almost at the same time; the whole man seemed completely transformed. His face assumed a strange expression of determination and courage when confronting danger; he threw off his robe, his eye kindled, his voice became so loud and sonorous that he might have been taken for some adventurous leader charging into the midst of the mêlée, and his orders were obeyed without comment or hesitation.

He himself was the first to rush forward, raising enormous beams, and using his axe like the infuriated wood-cutter in the ballad. One would have said that danger attracted him, and he took delight in wrestling with it. Was it a thirst for self-sacrifice, or an effort to pour forth in a single burst all the pent-up fire of his nature? It was impossible to say; for the danger passed, he regained his customary calmness and re-assumed his every-day manner, accepting thanks reluctantly, repelling praise, and ashamed of having been caught *in flagrante delictu* of heroism. He was indeed very hard to understand, and one might almost believe there were two natures in him. He lived simply and humbly, but with a steadfast, unvarying purpose, and would boldly give his last sou to help some one poorer than himself, or throw his cloak in a winter night over some beggar's shivering shoulders with the greatest joy that he could render the poor wretch some service; but his pleasure was equalled by pride in the thought that he was conquering himself and disdaining the cold feared by so many others. In mid-winter he ventured out into the deep snows with as much eagerness as he had shown in battling with the conflagration, and when one saw him returning, holding in his hand an immense staff cut in the forest, with his robe raised to his waist, his limbs protected by huge woollen stockings, his nostrils reddened by the cold, dilated, and quivering as he inhaled the frozen air, his game-bag on his back, and his jaws set, he had a noble intrepidity of expression that commanded respect. He was held in high esteem for his strength, skill, and charity, and if by chance any difficulty arose, was instantly sought for, as in all circumstances he was known to be morally and physically a solid man on whom one could rely; but at the same time, his parishioners felt that he had a nature which was not akin to theirs, and loved him with reserve, and at a respectful distance.

Abbé Roche was born among the mountains, but the exact place from whence he came no one knew. Nursed by a peasant woman, and received and educated among the nuns, he had naturally passed from their hands into those of the priest's, who had soon noticed his keen intellect and good conduct. He had grown up among these surroundings, the authorization rendered necessary by his birth was obtained, not without difficulty, and one day he entered the seminary without either distaste or enthusiasm, as a child born in a regiment enlists under the flag that has served him for swaddling clothes. He knew nothing of the life outside the vessel that had received him; supposed it to be full of pitfalls and storms, and was glad to be in a place of safety.

The years spent in the seminary were the only ones in which he breathed the air of a great city, but he only caught a glimpse of the world by stealth and with a thousand scruples, and on leaving his adopted family, became a curate in a poor parish in the Landes, where he remained only a short time. His ecclesiastical superiors esteemed him highly; his position as an illegitimate child, which had been a serious obstacle to his taking orders, was now a claim to the especial consideration of his chiefs. While he was still very young, they appointed him curé of Grand-Fort-le-Haut, where we find him, after a residence of fifteen years, forgotten, but perfectly contented. What had taken place in his heart during this long period? A few of his locks had grown gray, his eyes were sunken, and his face perhaps retained some trace of mental struggle, but all storms seemed to be forever lulled to rest in the calmness of a regular, simple, and busy life.

II.

The manor of the counts of Manteigney, of which we caught a glimpse just now among the trees, dates back for several centuries. Each generation had added something, left some trace of its presence, and as the site was rather restricted in its limits, the result was a confused pile of incongruous buildings. It was here that for centuries the lords of the country had held their powerful sway. Possessing the whole valley as far as the market town of Virez, which commanded its entrance, masters of immense forests, pasture grounds, and estates which covered the side of the mountain, they had always considered the village of Grand-Fort-le-Haut, which lay at the door of their dwelling, as a dependence of the château. It was then a mere collection of huts in which the count's shepherds and wood-cutters were tolerably well lodged under the protecting care of their master. By degrees these few huts had increased in importance, while the château lost its authority, until, aided by the great revolution, all active life concentrated in the village; and the manor, sombre, ruined, inert, appeared to be utterly defunct, leaving in the country only the memory of the legends connected with its ancient stones, and a sort of mysterious reverence.

Among mountains, memories and impressions are most tenacious. Ideas are like clouds; they settle and lodge in crevices, and the tempests which pass overhead must blow a long time ere they succeed in uprooting the old beliefs which rest in the clefts of the rock. Just as the impulses of thought give a man a quicker gait, so slowness of motion entails dullness of mind. There is a remarkable connection between physical and mental activity, between the manners of a country and the condition of its roads. Birds, which move so swiftly, ought to think quickly also; the circulation must be equally rapid in all parts of their organization. They say that imagination has wings. I like to fancy that everything winged possesses imagination. For instance, look at an ox moving along; must not ideas be tardy in forming within him, and sensations slowly digested in the brain of the worthy beast, which is supplied with four stomachs? The ox is conservative, and so is the mountaineer. It is enough to see the latter ascending a path among the slippery stones, with measured, regular tread, economical of strength, and lavish of time, to understand that that man has no feverish brain. The snow that shrouds the country for five or six months does not merely imprison plants and rocks in its hoary mantle, but huts, men's ideas, and traditions which put forth the strongest, most gnarled roots in this interval of silence and concentration. Thus in these regions the ideas of the past cling to man as man clings to the earth, and the old moss-covered pines cleave to the rocks.

Hence it was not very extraordinary that the château of Manteigney should have retained the prestige of former days. It presented an imposing aspect, spite of having been abandoned for twenty years. True, its weather-cocks were on the point of falling, and its pointed roofs in a most pitiable condition under their veil of moss, but the old walls were still strong enough to withstand a siege. The most ancient portion of the château was the left-hand tower, which flanked the principal entrance. It dated from the beginning of the fourteenth century; and although at a much later period narrow windows with stone mullions had been inserted, the ground floor—a low hall which was reached by two well-worn steps, proved, by the ogive moulding of its ceiling and the shape of its huge chimney-piece, the correctness of the date just mentioned.

This ground floor had been occupied for more than twenty years by père and mère Sappey, to whom the care of the château had been entrusted. They lived there like mountaineers; had as much wood as they wanted, the whole chestnut harvest, a cow and a goat; what more could be desired? During the first few years after they were installed, they occasionally aired the rooms, swept them at rare intervals, and dusted a few articles of furniture; then finding that it became very difficult to open the windows, their consciences readily absolved them from the duty, and the spiders took up their abode in the lofty rooms, which no one ever entered.

There was, however, one very curious portion that was occasionally visited when some tourist or travelling agent wandered to Grand Fort. This interesting out-of-the-way corner, was the upper portion of a tower, to which the old relics from the arsenal had been banished. It was reached by a little winding staircase, lighted by large loop-holes, through which the wind whistled with a doleful sound. The bats and screech owls fluttered away at your approach, and one really felt relieved of a great weight when once fairly out of the narrow space. Then, in the midst of a chaos of scattered fragments, might be seen two culverins belonging to the former counts, three or four guns which had been mounted on the ramparts, notched sabres, a cresset with two burners, postillion's boots, a spear, half of a cuirass, a fragment of a helmet, a goodly number of empty bottles, and one of those huge, broad-backed, old-fashioned armchairs formerly universally seen in our ancestors' bedrooms, but now discarded by modern luxury.

On leaving the tower, a broad terrace extends to the left, from which the whole valley can be seen, and upon which opened in former days the wide folding doors of the state drawing-rooms, and the picture-gallery with its long lines of plumed, cuirassed, and curled chevaliers, majestic and terrible in their worm-eaten frames. In confronting these imposing, highly-colored, haughty, and determined lords, one would need to have a very firm will not to be sufficiently awed to remove one's cap. The sight of such a past, still triumphant even beneath its veil of dust, leads one to think of the present and the future, and one would ask involuntarily what had become of the heir, the young Count, Robert Pierre Jean de Manteigney, the direct descendant of these haughty lords, and the sole hope of his race? It was known that he was not dead; and the imagination pictured him as strong and vigorous like his ancestors, a great hunter, a hard drinker, also, gay and careless in his bearing, bold, intrepid, and perhaps very gallant to the fair sex. The latter was one of the characteristics of his family, at least so several old women with hooked noses coquettishly pretended to remember. Numerous conjectures had been made, and were still formed, concerning the young count, who was as interesting as an enigma, mysterious as a legend. Where did he live, what was he doing? He had left the castle, with tearful eyes, just after his mother's death, when a lad about ten years old, and had never returned.

The truth was that the orphan was found to be too poor to make a good figure in his ancestral home, and also receive an education in accordance with his rank; therefore a portion of the domain, long since shrunk to very meagre proportions, was sold, thus obtaining some little capital with which he might seek his fortune elsewhere, and the poor child went to his maternal uncle's, the Marquis de Vernac, who was henceforth to supply a father's place.

This marquis, who lived with the utmost economy on the remnants of his fortune, was a very peculiar person. He resided in Paris, Rue des Lions-Saint-Paul, on the second floor, looking out upon the court-yard. This was not all; he was excessively thin, pale, and as closely shaven as a Carthusian friar. There was something in his personal appearance suggestive of the sacred Ibis of the Egyptians. Why, how! I should not know how to describe it, but there *was* a resemblance. A perfect gentleman in every respect, one felt at first attracted towards him, but on perceiving at the top of the tall figure a microscopical little skull, shining and polished as a billiard-ball, one wondered where the poor marquis kept his thoughts. The truth is, that want of room had always prevented his obtaining any very large store of them. He had few ideas, for he always used the same methodically classed, carefully arranged, and strung one after another like the beads in a chaplet, so that when he threw off his night-cap in the morning, he began his first *pater* and went on from *ave* to *ave* until evening without the least emotion or fatigue but a calm conscience, and the feeling that he had done his duty under the protection of the laws and the eye of God.

He was, in truth, the last person in the world to need a description, had it not been for his resemblance to the sacred bird, and an unfortunate mania for rearing pheasants in his dressing-room, which gave him some little individuality. When Count Jean reached Paris, the marquis was electrified by the thought that he was to occupy a father's place to the last of the Manteigneys. The old gentleman, clad in his sky-blue coat and nankeen pantaloons, visited every college in Paris, and at last, worn out by these expeditions and anxieties, which disturbed his usual mode of life, placed his nephew at the College Saint Louis, in memory of the crusades. It was quite time, his head was bursting! Thenceforward, his task completed, the thought of the lad's education was like another bead to the chaplet in the marquis's cranium, and every day, at a certain hour, he fell into the habit of saying: " Thanks to my truly paternal solicitude, my nephew, Robert Pierre Jean, is receiving an excellent education under the patronage of the best of kings, Louis IX., surnamed St. Louis. 1215."

The marquis's surroundings were not such as to excite the imagination of young de Manteigney, or make him dream of any thing beyond his quiet life; on the contrary, a Sunday spent in the Rue des Lions-Saint-Paul was sufficient to make the collegian joyous for a week. The class-rooms appeared to him to be comfortable, sweet and clean; the court-yards, where their leisure hours were spent, green and airy, in short, he thought it a model school; but when the first down of his mustaches began to darken his lip, his mind became burdened with a heavy sorrow. The change was a rapid one. He had suddenly remembered that he was a count; he saw again, as if in a dream, the picture gallery at Manteigney, hung with the portraits of his ancestors; the plumes, the glittering breast-plates and magnificent wigs, began to whirl through his brain, and as he thought of his schoolmates, principally the sons of merchants and petty shopkeepers, he felt heart-broken. The idea that he was to take his bachelor's degree on equal terms with this herd, made the blood mount to his brow; the uniform, a livery he had worn for seven or eight years without thinking of complaint, now seemed unendurable, and he felt an intense desire to shake off these surroundings, and attest his noble birth by outward signs; which was, in truth, a most natural feeling.

Doubtless he succeeded in borrowing money on the fortune which was soon to come into his possession; for one fine morning he appeared before his uncle in a white vest and brown pantaloons, armed with a gold-headed switch, curled, perfumed, and most elegantly attired. Upon this the marquis, taking it for granted that his nephew's education was fully completed, thanked Heaven, embraced the young man, slipped a note for five hundred francs into his vest pocket to assist him on his entrance into society, and gave him his blessing.

During the following year, the last of the de Manteigney's became totally transformed; he was seen at the races and the theatre, entered the ranks of those amiable youths who are met with everywhere, frequented riding and fencing schools, became an *habitué* of the Bois de Boulogne, gave rise to various gossiping tales, and to complete his reputation as a man of fashion, began to seek for a mistress. Once embarked on this course, he commenced to drain heavily on his property, and opened the campaign with the little fortune of which he became absolute master on attaining his twenty-first year. Thus the last fragment of the old domain was squandered, and if to this be added the modest estate of the Marquis de Vernac, who died one morning as he was giving his pheasants their breakfast, the extreme skill with which the youth manœuvred, and the tact and prudence he displayed in the difficult art of aristocratic living, his mode of life will be understood, as well as the reputation of being a thorough leader of fashion which he so long enjoyed among the brilliant circle in which he moved.

III.

But none of Count Jean's exploits had ever reached Grand Forte, and the mountaineers, although deprived of the presence of their lord, had lived in peace for twenty years under the shadow of the old château, when suddenly a report well calculated to excite curiosity, spread through the valley. If public rumor was to be believed, the last of the de Manteigneys, whom all the men of fifty remembered having seen when a child, had just made an extremely wealthy marriage in Paris, and was preparing to return to his ancestral home in triumph. Already strangers had been seen wandering through the valley and visiting the village. A benediction, a heavenly dew, a golden rain was about to fall. The château was to be repaired and splendidly furnished ; all the estates belonging to the domain were to be purchased, and it would soon be restored to its original dimensions. All this must be true; for the notary from Virez, dressed in a white cravat and red as a turkey cock, had been seen in twenty places at once, and had even been galloping through the fields, an event hitherto unprecedented.

While these interesting pieces of news were in circulation, commented and enlarged upon by every one, an architect arrived; the doors and windows were thrown open, and the workmen began their task. Soon nothing was spoken of in the mountains but the count and countess, the splendor of their surroundings, and the wonderful improvements of which the château was to be the object. The noble couple must have been in haste, for the work was pushed on with the greatest eagerness. An army of laborers, hired in the neighborhood, plied pickaxe and shovel day and night to make the horrible road that was mentioned, passable. Nothing was to be seen but slaters, suspended by ropes from the roof, painters busily occupied with the window-sashes and railings, gardeners arranging the flower-beds on the lawn, carpenters and joiners repairing the stables. Every day huge carts drawn by four oxen came into the courtyard, and large crimson arm-chairs, with gilt feet, upholstery hangings, and hosts of beautiful things were unpacked. At the end of a few months the château was placed in a suitable condition to receive its master, and the people of Grand Fort were thinking of preparing a reception for the count and countess equal to the grandeur of the occasion. Already a triumphal arch, fireworks, speeches, and baskets of flowers were discussed, but the arrival of a letter destroyed all their magnificent plans.

M. de Manteigney expressed, in a few words, a very decided preference for entering his château without any flourish of trumpets, as if he had left it only the day before. To be doubly certain, he refused to mention the time of his intended arrival. Whenever that was to be, a vanguard of servants in red small-clothes and gold-laced caps now took possession of their own quarters, the stables were filled, and the old kitchen chimney sent forth a noble volume of smoke. The excited villagers and their agitated mayor waited all one week, then a second passed away, and wearied by the delay, each resumed his usual occupations. On Sunday evening after vespers, the lovers of bowl-playing—and they are passionately fond of it in those regions—who usually joined the curé, having assembled under the great trees in the enclosure, Abbé Roche unbuttoned the lower part of his cassock, seized his two balls, and the game began. It had continued about half an hour, when the curé, returning after a splendid hit, found himself face to face with a singular little personage, who had just entered the enclosure unseen by the players.

This puny little man, with narrow, sloping shoulders, was dressed from head to foot in white flannel trimmed with blue braid. His long, thin neck, rose from a turned-down, yellowish shirt-collar, whose points were adorned with dogs' heads. A pink and blue cravat was knotted under it, and among its folds glittered a gold scarf-pin, the design of which represented a horse's saddle and two dangling stirrups. His pants were extremely tight, and fitted closely over his microscopical boots with their very high heels, covered with sky-blue cloth, ornamented with large pearl buttons, and embroidered with wonderful skill, stitched, embossed—they were certainly jewels of boots. Two locks of curled red hair fell below the hat, which shaded a weary, worn, sallow face, furrowed by the sickly wrinkles which are not caused by old age. Add to the picture a pair of red mustaches coquettishly twisted at the ends, and gloves, the color of blood, thrust half way into one of his pockets.

Standing proudly with his legs stretched very far apart, the little man held a wonderfully tiny cigar-case of Java straw in his white, well-kept hands, and by dint of making a most hideous face, kept a square eye-glass without setting or cord in one eye, and looking smilingly at the good curé, who was gazing at him in astonishment, said: "The deuce take it, but you have a strong wrist, Monsieur le curé. You certainly hurled that well!"

Abbé Roche felt the flush that mounted to his very temples, and finding no answer for the moment, allowed his grave, searching glance to wander over this singular person, who still smiled with the most perfect indifference. The other players had stopped in amazement.

"Go on with your game, this is Sunday, I believe! Your roads are in a pitiful condition," continued the person in white flannel, looking at his precious boots, which were slightly soiled, after which he placed a cigarette between his lips, took a little silver-gilt tinder box from his pocket, and carefully arranged the red wick with as little embarrassment as if he had been alone in his sleeping-room.

"Do you belong to this part of the country, sir?" asked the curé, who began to be somewhat irritated by this excessive self-possession.

The smoker slowly lighted his cigar, turning it between his thumb and finger, then having poured forth a huge cloud of smoke through his nostrils, replied, with the most perfect sangfroid: "Yes, I live in the château yonder on the right, about ten minutes walk from here."

"Is it possible that you are Count Jean de Manteigney?"

"Jean de Manteigney, as you say. Then you know me?"

"Excuse me, M. le comte, I—"

And so saying, the curé dropped the ball he was holding, while all the mountaineers bared their heads as if at church. "Excuse you for what?" rejoined the count, "pray continue your game, my dear curé, I am no spoil-sport!" And he pushed back his little hat with a gesture both patronizing and familiar, carelessly thrust his hands into his pockets, and began to hum, still smoking and balancing himself on his heels. "Tell them to go on, my dear curé. I like to see these honest fellows play. There is a splendid looking one, he has the strength of a bull. And then they are all looking at me—it is impertinent."

"Come, Bernard, it is your turn to play," said the Abbé, and then added: "Is it long since you arrived, M. le comte?"

"Only three or four hours, and I began by taking a walk in this direction. I like the country very much, it is pleasant and pretty. And the wine, how is the wine? Do the vines promise a good harvest? Faith! that is an important matter."

"Yes, M. le comte. Just now the—"

"Ah! I am delighted to hear it. People ought to remember that wine is the traveller's staff and the old man's milk. Stop, there is that young bull throwing his ball. A fine fellow! How old is he?"

"Twenty, at most."

"It is wonderful. And the chestnuts, my dear curé, what about the chestnuts?"

"They will be very plentiful," replied the curé, biting his lips.

"That is capital; better and better. Chestnuts are not to be despised! It is your turn to play, curé."

Abbé Roche took his position carefully, and

hurled the ball, but, a most unusual thing with him, missed his aim. He was confused by the gaze of that grey eye twinkling behind its tiny glass; and the careless ease with which the little man addressed him redoubled his embarrassment.

"Ah! you have missed your stroke, my dear curé."

"Yes," replied the priest, who was holding his second ball in his hand, and saw no cause for smiling.

"That is unlucky. Ah! I was forgetting to tell you that the countess talks of nothing but you—she is really wild to see you. It is, 'My curé! where is my curé?'—You are expected."

"I will pay my respects to the countess to-morrow."

"This evening, if you like. You will be welcome whenever you come; for my part, I don't like ceremony. You see I am perfectly frank. Farewell, don't trouble yourself to attend me to the gate."

And, as a child finding himself in the way, stared at him with wide open eyes, he exclaimed: "What are you doing there, little rogue, instead of going to school? Ah! to-day is Sunday! Stop, here is something to buy gingerbread," and tossing two or three silver coins into the little one's lap, he went away whistling.

When he was fairly out of sight, all the mountaineers looked at each other as people gaze after some accident has happened. This was evidently not the count they had expected. It seemed to them utterly impossible that this little, thin, puny man, with his scanty reddish mustaches, could be the true lord of the château; the rightful descendant of the rude counts of former days. In regions where every one toils and struggles, physical weakness easily passes for infirmity, and a sickly appearance is considered something worthy of ridicule. As to the curé—was it on account of his herculean frame?—He had never found any thing but compassion in his heart for frail bodies and pallid faces. Good Christian as he was in other respects, certain familiarities annoyed him extremely; he felt at such times as if a tempest were raging within him, and if any one had ever dealt him a blow, it is very probable that the person would have been instantly knocked down; never would he have dreamed of turning the other cheek.

Besides being personally wounded by the count's manners, they had rudely dispelled his illusions; Abbé Roche had always respected the nobility, not because he believed that moral virtue and physical beauty were the exclusive heritage of a certain class of men; but there was something of the poet and artist within him, and he found it consoling to think that there were certain families, ennobled by time and placed above all ambition and poverty, who were the depositaries and guardians of certain special virtues. He did not reason upon these ideas, but believed in them instinctively, and enjoyed them.

IV.

It was not without a certain degree of embarrassment that our curé prepared to visit the château the following day. He spread out on his narrow bed his Sunday cassock and a new band, and looked at the big silver watch destitute of chain and key, which he always carried in his pocket.

He did not wish to reach Manteigney until after dinner, in order to avoid the invitation they would have been sure to give him, and which he greatly dreaded. He remembered how he had been wounded by the count's words: "Once for all, my dear curé, there is a seat at table for you." That was not the only sentence which recurred to his mind as a disagreeable recollection. "The countess is wild to see you. My curé—where is my curé?" Surely there was no reason that this great lady should be so extremely anxious to make his acquaintance. Perhaps she expected to find this curé, who had never left his mountains, a half savage, a boor, who had not a word to say, and doubtless wished to amuse herself at his expense. What other explanation could be given to words which bordered upon impertinence, "My curé! where is my curé?"

While carefully shaving himself, a multitude of thoughts passed through his brain, and he became so vexed at his own agitation that he was on the point of putting on his old cassock, merely as a protest against the weakness. He was thoroughly ashamed; yet at the same time thought of the hour. "They must dine at five or half-past; it is more than probable, because the mayor and notary of Virez have dinner at that hour. Now by arriving at half-past six I shall find them in the drawing-room, or else walking on the lawn—or perhaps sitting in a group—sitting in a group!"

And this Hercules, who would not have trembled if a bear had stood in his path, shivered at the thought of all those eyes bent upon him. How would they receive him, how could he endure the curious, mocking gaze of the countess, when she should at last see the curé of her dreams?

At that moment some one knocked at the door.

"Who is there?" said the priest, without turning.

"Tell me, M. le curé," replied mère Hilaire from the next room, "are you going to wear your silver buckles?"

"Why should I? Is to-day Easter?"

"Bless me, you can do as you like, M. le curé, but I would wear them if I were in your place. Nobles are accustomed to have people spruce up a little when they go to visit them."

"Well, do as you please."

"Have I vexed you, M. le curé?" said the good old woman timidly from behind the door.

"No, my good mother. Get the buckles ready, get them ready, if you think it best: but make haste."

This mère Hilaire was a little, plump old woman with very bright eyes, quick, active, energetic, trotting about with little short steps, rummaging, searching everywhere, and adoring her curé. She lived in the next house, but was very rarely found there, so busy was she in taking care of the priest's dwelling, preparing his meals, mending his linen, and putting patches into his cassocks when they needed it, which was very often. She worked with so much skill and patience, tenderness one might almost call it, that it was almost impossible to see the traces of her labor, and Abbé Roche had never perceived them. She did not wish any one to be able to say: "Monsieur le curé wears patched cassocks." People can have self-respect, if they are not rich. She also kept the accounts for the priest, who paid no attention to them, and merely took his money without looking to see how much remained in the little drawer, into which, more than once, the good old woman had slipped two or three of her one-crown pieces, without any one's being the wiser. Yet she had a warm affection for her poor crowns; but the most important matter was that M. le curé should not be restricted in his almsgiving, and that no poor people could say that, they had knocked at his door and been sent away with empty hands.

Mère Hilaire's affection for Abbé Roche, and the familiarity with which she addressed him, may be explained in a few words: the old peasant woman had been the nurse of the foundling who afterwards became curé of Grand Fort. She had filled a mother's place to him; and when he left her to be under the charge of the nuns, wept almost as bitterly as if her own child had been taken away. Other griefs, still heavier than that, had afterwards afflicted the good woman: she lost her only son, and five years after, her husband was killed by the fall of a pine tree which he was in the act of felling. She was thus left alone in her old age, in the tiny house at Virez where she had always had the society of her family; she had striven to endure her solitude, and had borne her fate for several years; but when she learned that the only being that was left to her, the child of her adoption, was settled as curé three leagues from Virez, at the other end of the valley, she quickly set out for Grand Fort, saying to herself: "I shall not die alone, one of the three who were lost to me is restored." She pictured him as the child whom she had seen in former days, playing before the house and dabbling in the mud with the ducks, or as the tall stalwart youth who had met her when she went to visit him before he entered the seminary. She hastened to Grand Fort, agitated by these recollections, but when, having knocked at the door, she found herself face to face with a full grown man of grave demeanor and serious expression, she stood still in amazement, knew not what to say, and felt the tears rushing into her eyes. Her dream had vanished, her milk pail was dashed into a thousand pieces. Yet she could trace the features of the child and youth in the austere countenance of the priest; there was the thin, prominent nose, broad noble forehead, and kind, frank glance. She recognized them all, and said to herself: "If he would only smile, I should see the little dimple near his mouth—I am sure it is still there."

But he did not smile, did not even recognize her, for the old woman had been terribly changed by grief. After an instant's pause, she made a great effort and said:

"I am mère Hilaire, Monsieur le curé; mère Hilaire from Virez."

Ah! there was no hesitation! She felt herself

suddenly raised from the ground and clasped so closely that she could scarcely breathe, and murmured: "Monsieur—Monsieur le curé! you will — you will crush me, my boy."

And Abbé Roche, kissing her on the forehead, said softly:

"Dear, dear mother, is it really you? Oh! my dear good mother!"

He no longer looked grave; great hot tears flowed from his eyes, and yet at the same time he was smiling so happily that the little round dimple in his cheek appeared once more, to the great delight of the good woman.

"And what brings you here, mère Hilaire?" said the abbé after a moment's silence.

"Well! Monsieur le curé, it was the pleasure of seeing you, and then,—it is stupid, I know, but I dare not say more!—I must tell you that God has left me all alone; my boy is dead, and my husband was killed by a pine tree that fell and crushed him ten years ago on the eve of Saint John. You did not know that, Monsieur le cure?"

"Why no, no. What a sad misfortune!"

"Yes, indeed, it is terrible! You do not remember when père Hilaire used to take you to gather faggots, and the tricks you played upon him. Excuse me, Monsieur le curé, I am talking of things that happened so long ago."

"Go on, my friend, you see that I like to listen."

"Since that time I have had no one; but the good God has restored you to me! Well, I said to myself: He has no one—and—and people who are all alone—it is natural—sometimes take pleasure in living together—and then, if Monsieur le curé had no servant, I—"

Abbé Roche looked at the peasant with an expression of such deep emotion that she cast down her eyes.

"Then you love me?" asked Abbé Roche.

"Have I not nursed thee, tell me; have I not brought thee up? Do I love him? It makes no difference if thou art curé, and a strong man, and much nearer God than I, of course thou art still my boy. You must not mind my talking, Monsieur le curé, I cannot help it; I do not know how to express myself very well, I keep saying thou. Oh, dear! I have called him thou! but I will take great care in future."

"Speak to me as you have always done, I entreat you."

She suddenly burst into tears, and clasping her hands, exclaimed: "Oh! Lord, is he not kind, and not at all proud. Well, Monsieur le curé, it shall only be when there is nobody here, and we are all alone in a family circle, because now only we two relatives are left. Ah, no! he is not proud."

She said all this rapidly, with deep emotion, stopping in the middle of her sentences to take breath. "But when anybody is present, we will no longer be relatives. He must keep his station, that is only right; and when they are gone, ah! indeed, then I will say: 'thou'—when you like, Monsieur le curé, but if ever you are disturbed by it, you shall say: 'Hush, mère Hilaire,' and I will be silent; it will not vex me in the least, my boy, my son. I have nobody in the world but you! Let me kiss your dear, beautiful hands. Heavens, what a strong man! and how good he must be, not to show me to the door after talking to him in such a way. A curé! my boy a curé!"

Abbé Roche understood the loving delicacy of the good woman's words, in thus constantly alluding to the imaginary ties of relationship which united her to him. The poor man experienced a most tender emotion, all the more profound because, while recalling certain private sorrows of which he had never complained, she applied the most efficacious of all remedies; but his vigorous nature rarely gave way to tears, and the sobs died away in his throat, rising and falling like the bubbles of air on the surface of water.

"Now, Monsieur le curé," continued the old woman, whose face was radiant with delight, "your house is very convenient, but it must be set in order, and you have no time to see to it. You must have curtains at the windows, and who will put them up? Well, and the clothes to wash, and everything to be taken care of, and the soup to be made. You will say that you are going to have a servant; that is all very well. But servant-maids are an article in which there is great choice—a very great choice: one breaks everything, another does not know how to do anything, and a third asks for forty crowns as one would ask for a glass of water. This is not all; you must not have a very young person. It is all nonsense to say that God does not interfere in these matters, and that He has nothing to do with what goes on here below. In short, this is enough; you, Monsieur le curé, do not want a young girl. I have been thinking over the pros and cons of the matter before I came, and I don't believe you could find any one who would suit you as well as I. Besides, there is another thing about it, I don't ask anything, but give my services; I have a little competence, and have no need of the forty crowns you would pay another person, so we save that much. I am an old woman; it will amuse me and occupy my mind to take care of the house; I will sell my property at Virez, and buy a little cottage close by you, with a bit of a garden and a small shed for my donkey—and then I shall be sure of dying near you, Monsieur le curé."

Thus mère Hilaire became the abbé Roche's housekeeper; and the reason she just urged him so perseveringly to wear the silver buckles, was because she had given them to her curé on the tenth anniversary of her coming to his house.

V.

When he had completed his toilet, the curé of Grand Fort set out on his way to the château. The sun, already low in the heavens, was glittering on the icy peaks, outlined against the horizon like airy festoons of silver lace. For the first time in many years, he passed on without even casting a glance upon the majestic scenery. The door of the château stood open. The priest, having entered its arched portal, stopped for an instant at the room occupied by père and mère Sappey, by no means sorry to delay his visit a few moments. The two old people were in gala dress, sitting side by side in one corner of the apartment on an old bench, blackened by use. It was the only piece of their old-fashioned country furniture that still remained. The ground floor of the old tower was wholly changed in appearance, and now resembled the lodge of a well-trained concierge. It contained two large arm-chairs of grayish wood in the Louis XVI. style, covered with lemon-colored Utrecht velvet. A square mat was carefully placed before each seat. The mountaineer's chest had disappeared, and was replaced by a commode of wrought copper, on which stood two superb candlesticks, one on each side of a clock, representing the temple of Love resting on a globe. Surrounded by this cast-off splendor, selected hap-hazard from the ancient furniture of the château, père and mère Sappey seemed to have lost their individuality; their whole expression was one of mingled surprise and sorrow, which might be taken for joy or despair, as one pleased.

On perceiving the curé, who also had not his ordinary manner, instead of going to meet him and inviting him to enter, as usual, they both rose with a little company smile and stood motionless, almost as yellow as the velvet arm-chairs.

"Well, père Sappey, are you happy?"

"Oh! certainly, Monsieur le curé," replied his wife, without raising her voice, "certainly, of course he is."

"You are no longer alone, and your room has been very handsomely furnished."

"Oh! bless me, yes, Monsieur le curé, bless me, yes. And our masters belong to the very best society. The countess's papa—ah, how affable and pleasant he is to everybody! Only—take care how you walk on the mats," added mère Sappey, addressing her husband, who had made a step forward, "you will flatten them, and then you will have a quarrel with the steward. Ah! Dufour is no joker, you know that very well."

"You told me that you were very well pleased, mère Sappey," continued Abbé Roche, "but you added *only*. What is it that you lack?"

"Nothing at all, Monsieur le curé. They give us everything we need. M. Dufour does not even wish me to make my husband's soup. He says that if I cook, it would make an odor—what in the world did he call it? Oh! he says that it would make an infectious odor; I don't know exactly what he means by that; but we are supplied with food, and well supplied, I can tell you! Too well, for we have nothing to do. It is so tiresome to do nothing!"

"Hush! you have been told that we are paid for doing that," said the mountaineer, gravely.

"I'm not saying any harm, only it's tiresome to stay here, sitting still all day long. It gives one a pain in the back—but we are very well off all the same; only—"

"There is your *only* again, mère Sappey," said the curé. "Tell me, quickly, what is the matter?"

"Well, this is what troubles me; you needn't wink at me—I can tell Monsieur le curé. Well, then, the steward said—he meant well, of course—that père Sappey must not be dressed in this way any longer; that—in short, a quantity of things; and they are going to put my husband into red clothes like the others, and it has such an effect upon me! It is just as if they said, 'You must be married to another man.'"

The old mountaineer muttered: "How silly these women are. Good Heavens, how silly they are!"

"And the Lord knows that the men are vain enough! It is because there are brass buttons, and gold lace around the pockets that he wants to wear that coat. He is dying to get it on."

"Why, mère Sappey," said the curé, "no one can compel your husband to wear a livery against his will. You are anxious without cause. Are the count and countess in the château?"

"Yes, Monsieur le curé, you will find them on the lawn with the others."

As the priest left the tower, the good woman turned to her husband: "There, you have again forgotten to pull the handle. Don't I tell you that you will get us into trouble?"

She rushed forward, striding over the little mats, to a copper button which projected from the wall, and the ringing of a bell was heard in the court-yard. A footman in small-clothes and white stockings instantly appeared at the head of the stairs, and walked on before the priest, who began to regret that he had not left the huge cane he was in the habit of carrying, in père Sappey's charge.

While he was crossing the ante-chamber and the splendidly decorated drawing-room, he could not help observing the superb lackey who was leading the way. He was a noticeable person, and moved with striking ease and dignity of bearing. His complexion was pale, his expression grave; his carefully arranged hair was powdered, his stiff, light whiskers brushed back on either side of his noble countenance, and the shining pumps he wore had such delicate soles and were so handsomely shaped, that on looking down at his own shoes, which left much to be desired in point of beauty, the curé felt an involuntary sense of mortification—even heroes are not exempt from such follies—yet he was well pleased. The glittering ornaments, the suits of armor resting against the walls, the hangings, embroidered with the count's armorial bearings, the stately portraits, proud witnesses of a venerable past, even the valet, who had acquired something of the characteristics of the aristocracy while in their service—all was a fitting expression of the majesty by which he wished to see the nobility surrounded. The apartments had an air of grandeur and magnificence, and were, in truth, an appropriate residence for these noble counts with their imposing appearance.

The valet opened a glass door, which admitted them to the lawn, and the priest, advancing, heard such shouts of laughter as sometimes rise from the grounds of a boarding-school during the hours of recess. In the centre of the lawn seven or eight persons, dressed in light colors, were playing hot cockles with the most total absence of restraint. The curé, somewhat bewildered by the unexpected sight, turned involuntarily towards the dignified footman, who was perfectly calm, grave, quiet, and impassible. On finding himself in the presence of people whom he had surprised in more or less ridiculous attitudes, and who were clothed in strange, fantastic costumes, the priest suddenly and completely regained his self-command, his face assumed its usual grave expression, and he descended the flight of three steps like the statue of the commandant.

"Ladies and gentlemen," cried the Count de Manteigney, twirling round on one foot, "allow me to present our beloved pastor." This sally produced a very different effect from what he had anticipated, and at the glance which Abbé Roche cast around him, the laughter died away, the eye-glasses dropped, and the gentlemen bowed courteously. The ladies welcomed the new-comer by a slight motion of the head, leaning back, almost reclining in their huge arm-chairs. One of them—the young countess—who seemed almost lost among the flounces and puffs of her white dress, raised a beautiful arm which looked almost bare in its transparent sleeve, and familiarly, as one convent friend would greet another at the préfet's ball, held out her little gloved hand to the amazed Abbé Roche. It was the first time in his life that he had encountered such an apparition. On certain days, when his mind was disturbed, he had perhaps caught a glimpse of attractive, tempting images in some fleeting dream! but the charms of this countess, whom he saw with his own eyes, could even touch with his own hand—for she extended hers—surpassed all that his imagination had ever pictured.

She did indeed possess a singular, most unusual style of beauty, whose wonderful brilliancy the priest could only explain to himself by attributing it to the influence of a heavenly soul, which was faithfully mirrored in the fair face. Her hair arranged in a multitude of light curls, and most skilfully knotted together, was of the light red and golden hues that one sees in a field of wheat when the sun is setting. And while her face was of the pure, creamy whiteness that one would not suppose the human skin could possess, her eyebrows were extremely dark, almost black, and as if traced by an artist's pencil, formed a most perfect arch and ended in a delicate line at the temples. Her eye had a deep, searching expression, caused by the dark tinge that surrounded it and gave it a mysterious glance, though without diminishing its brilliancy. The lashes increased this effect: they might have belonged to some Indian woman adorned for a sacrifice; unusually black, fierce looking, yet soft and curved so that the tips, of remarkable length, almost touched the extreme point of the wonderful eyebrows and seemed to mingle with them. She was most beautiful, but appeared like a vision, so that one was both uneasy and attracted. In spite of one's self, one strove to understand the secret of these charms, and could not take one's eyes from the living enigma. Abbé Roche, who was less acquainted than most men with the tricks and stratagems of modern coquetry, felt, in spite of his apparent gravity of demeanor, an irresistible curiosity. Was this an angel descended among us for a moment? was it some renowned fairy, escaped from an ancient legend; or perhaps the countess was angel and fairy in one—such phenomena are sometimes seen.

"Ah! my dear good curé, how glad I am to see you!" She spoke very rapidly, and made a thousand little gestures, most charming in themselves, but wholly unnecessary to convey the meaning of her words. "The count must have told you that you are never out of my mind; I have dreamed of you constantly; do not make excuses, but give me your hand. Oh, you shall not escape me, rely upon it; give me your hand. Pardon me if I cut short the introductions, there is nothing more stupid."

Then hastily removing her glove she waved her little hand, pink and white like her face, full of blue veins, and loaded with rings, around the circle, saying: "The Count de Manteigney you already know; Mme. and Mlle. de Rougeon, of whom I am very fond; Monsieur de Rougeon, with the black mustache, husband and father of the two ladies, whom I also like — sometimes; don't interrupt me, M. de Rougeon, I see you want to propose an amendment. Let me see, who else? ah! papa, whom you see yonder in a white waistcoat, he's rather stout, poor papa. He is talking just now with young Claudius, one of our Parisian beaux, with the curled whiskers, blue cravat, etc., a horrid creature—I say so because he isn't here."

"I hear you, countess," said Claudius, who was standing at some five or six paces distance.

"Then I will add that I like him very much, all the same, and he plays hot cockles as if he had invented it. By-the-way, wouldn't you like to play a game, Monsieur le curé? You see we are very unceremonious."

"Oh! my dear," murmured Mme. de Rougeon, waving her little fan with an expostulating air.

"Well, what! my dear friend? Is there any game less objectionable than hot cockles? Besides, I don't insist upon it. People need not play unless they wish. Monsieur le curé, put your little switch in a corner, and sit down here near me. I am so anxious to have a serious conversation with you. There are many poor people to be helped in your parish, are there not?"

"Some few, yes, Madame, but—"

"Well, I had taken it into my head that there were more; it is a settled idea. I shall visit the mountains myself from top to bottom, on a pretty little white donkey that I shall keep expressly for that purpose, with scarlet rosettes under its ears. How should one spend one's life if not in charity, and for what will God hold one accountable, if not for the good one can do!"

Abbé Roche was deeply moved by the last words. Was it not evident that they were those of a noble soul? Let us add that they fell from the countess's lips with a most musical intonation, and that her voice possessed delicate shades and unexpected modulations, whose charm would be felt by any ear, however uneducated and unsympathetic it might be. So sweet a voice must be the expression of moral beauty. And yet, if this young woman was an angel, as every thing tended to prove, why were her arms almost bare in the gauze sleeves which merely seemed to idealize their beauty? Perhaps it was on account of the heat: it was, certainly, extremely warm. Was it also a matter of chance that the upper part of the waist of her dress had no lining, and revealed the outline of her figure, which irresistibly attracted the gaze. Wherefore this display of charms, which were useless to a person who wished to devote her life to the relief of the poor? What a strange mystery! Was it also by accident that, while engaged in conversation, she thrust out her foot until a large portion was visible of her white silk stocking with its open-work embroidery, so open that the white became pink, either from shame at being observed, or because the limb it covered without concealing, appeared through its thousand accommodating meshes? Was it a matter of accident that the young woman tapped her little foot with an impatience for which there was no apparent cause, attracting the attention with innocent or most consummately artful carelessness, to a tiny pearl gray boot, which might have belonged to a child, with heels so high and narrow that it would be impossible for any thing but a bird to keep its balance on them. The priest was thinking of all this, while the countess was talking.

"And how can one conceive of the lives of these poor mountaineers, who spend half their time under the snow?" she continued. "And, oh dear! they rear children, notwithstanding all this:—it is an unheard of thing!" A general burst of laughter roused the curé from his abstraction, and he smiled without having comprehended a single word.

"What is there so very extraordinary in what I said?" asked Mme. de Manteigney, without showing the slightest embarrassment. "People must have no heart to laugh at such misfortunes; but tell me, my dear curé, is there no way of melting this dreadful snow or sweeping it off, or — we must find some means of removing it, for your situation is frightful."

At that moment the two wings of the glass door were thrown open, and a steward, dressed in black from head to foot, like a lawyer, announced that dinner was served. Abbé Roche felt his color rise. Doubtless they would think that he had chosen the dinner hour intentionally as the time to pay his visit; but how was he to suppose that the meal was served after seven o'clock.

"Come, let us go in to dinner, my dear curé, we shall be able to talk better there." Abbé Roche's embarrassment was always manifested by a chilling reserve, which would naturally be misunderstood by those who were not thoroughly acquainted with him. He excused himself in a very few words, and in such a manner that no one attempted to press the matter. The countess, after making a pretty little grimace, cried: "Ah! well, this is only the beginning. So you will not stay. I want you to visit us, Monsieur le curé, and as you are so fond of ceremony, I will send you an invitation to dinner on handsome, enamelled paper."

While Abbé Roche was returning home, with downcast eyes, thinking of what he had just seen, the inmates of the château took their seats around the large table.

"Do you know, my curé is very good looking?" said the countess; "he's not at all the kind of person I expected."

"He looks like a magistrate on the bench," murmured the count's father-in-law, blowing upon his spoonful of soup; and Mme. de Rougeon, who had the stiff manners one might attribute to some carven saint, replied: "It would be desirable that all magistrates had his noble, unaffected bearing and face. The curé of this village is a magnificent looking man, who must be remarkably dignified at the altar: one in whom Saint Thomas Aquinas would take pride, it is no exaggerated praise to say that."

"That is exactly like ladies," sighed Monsieur de Rougeon, " they judge a priest by the—what shall I call it? by the beauty of his form, if I may dare to say so."

"I should not have dared to say it, papa, and that is the way papas disturb young girls' minds by not being sufficiently guarded in their conversation."

"Angèle!"

"Papa."

"If you were not such a lively child, your—I don't know exactly how to express myself—your badinage would be embarrassing, little mischief. It is by the moral virtues that you should first judge a man of *caractère sacré.*"

"Good! papa is swearing."

And placing a tortoise-shell eye-glass on her little retroussée nose, Mlle. de Rougeon, with a saucy air, cast a merry glance at the guests, who all laughed heartily.

"As for me," said the count, addressing his wife, "I was by no means pleased with your curé; he is a pedant, and I should be surprised if this carabinier in disguise turned out to be any better than a simpleton."

"Faith, perhaps you are wrong my dear fellow," observed M. Claudius; "but it is my firm intention to make him my intimate friend. He will help me in my researches in this region, and I am sure that there are wonderful things to be collected, especially rare china—I already scent old china. Ah! by-the-way, I have put aside a little red copper kettle, adorned with the Manteigney arms. It is an exquisite thing—pure Louis Quinze. The savages were going to put it on the fire. If you are willing, we will make an exchange. I know that this Vandalism with regard to relics is the most common thing in the world, but it always vexes me. You have seen my Henri Second corkscrew?"

"Certainly, it is at Cluny?"

"Not yet; they are such obstinate people! We have been at a stand-still for six months about twenty-five louis. They offer me a hundred, but I want a hundred and twenty-five."

"You are making a good bargain, my friend."

"Certainly I am. I paid a little more than two francs for it, in an out-of-the-way inn near Orleans."

A general laugh again resounded through the room. "Claudius is a singular fellow. What a faculty he has for collecting curiosities. Nothing escapes him!"

And Claudius, as soon as silence was restored, began the story of the Henri Second corkscrew, relating with much wit and animation the numberless stratagems to which he had been compelled to resort in order to obtain the precious treasure.

VI.

Viscount Claudius was a gentleman who belonged to the most fashionable society. He was born—at least so he said—with soft fair hair, a very keen intellect, and great worldly experience. He also possessed principles of most unbounded liberality, and had, besides, unlimited credit at his tailor's. He was wonderfully accomplished and gifted. Nature lingered over her finishing touches to this young man, correcting the contours, retouching the half-tints, covering her work with delicate strokes, caressingly shaping the outlines. Unfortunately she had forgotten the frame, and the young viscount, on attaining years of discretion, had instantly realized the imperative necessity for a gilder who could supply what was wanting. There is no slight difficulty in making a fortune when the traditions of a majestic past, real or imaginary, compel you to accept only from divine liberality the wealth that others procure by regular, daily labor. This handsome youth thus found himself on leaving college, like many of his associates, strangely embarrassed by being confronted with numerous pursuits, into which the common herd rushed eagerly, while he could not even cast a glance at them without disgust. He remembered that chance had always been Providence *incognito*, and played a little at baccarat to recall himself to the memory of his Heavenly Father. His first efforts were successful; the louis rolled into the pocket of his pretty vest; he looked around him with more confidence, and perceived numbers of fair-haired gentlemen as charming as himself, who were in the same situation. Naturally he adopted their mode of life, observed their means of procuring money, and was soon convinced that the improvement of the horse was the only door of safety in which a man of rank could take refuge with any advantage. He therefore studied the crossing of the breeds with great assiduity, became familiar with the most famous horses, and, finding more and more pleasure in the pursuit, and also being gifted with great quickness, soon became known as a judge of horse flesh, and was quoted as an authority whose opinion was second in value to none. It was at this time that his intimacy began with the great duchess of Blanmon, who was a little—fond of horses.

The viscount's presence in the family circle at Manteigney may be very easily explained. Count Jean and Claudius had met in the upper circles of Parisian fashionable society. They had easily understood each other, and had become very intimate friends. It was to the viscount's tact that Jean de Manteigney owed the wealthy marriage that had regilded his escutcheon.

The two young men were leaving the Opera

House one evening. As they stepped under the awning over the entrance, they began to yawn, and the taller of the two, drawing his watch from his pocket, exclaimed: "Twenty minutes past twelve. What are you going to do this evening, de Manteigney?"

"Nothing, my dear fellow. I was thinking of looking in at the club, but it is of no consequence. I will go wherever you like."

"Well! that is just the thing; let us go to the club." He made a sign; a tiny coupé, about the size of a bureau, drew up, and both entered. After a moment's pause, as the little affair was whirling rapidly over the boulevard, Claudius said to his companion: "My dear Jean, lend me a hundred louis."

"Willingly, my friend, if you will first advance me two hundred."

"Ah! that is how it is."

"It is exactly as I have the honor to tell you."

"Then it is a serious matter?"

"Extremely so! And you?"

"Oh! I'm in the same fix, precisely."

And they both hummed a few moments, after which Claudius exclaimed, striking his friend on the knee, "What do you intend to do?"

"There are always the pontifical zouaves. What would you have?"

"Something better. You must make a wealthy marriage, and you won't find a fiancée there. May I ask you frankly just how much you have left?"

"I confess that the question coming from any one else would be extremely impertinent. I have—some credit, and an old house in the mountains, total—"

"What sort of a house?"

"A little old, black, sombre château, a perfect eagle's nest, concealed under the chestnut trees."

"And its revenues?"

"Can you ask such a question?"

"What is the name of the château?

"Manteigney, of course! It is our family château."

Claudius's face suddenly changed, and he exclaimed, speaking with comical emphasis: "What a child you are! you complain, and yet have all the trumps in your own hands! Ah! if I only had a château that bore my name! Will you place your fate in my hands? The deuce take it, we must make a bold push."

At the same moment Claudius let down the front window, spoke to his coachman, and the carriage turned in another direction.

"Are we not going to the club?"

"Certainly not, we are going to spend a quarter of an hour at friend Vernon's. There will probably be a crowd there this evening, on account of its being the first night of the *Varieties*— A feudal castle! Was there ever such a chance?"

"What are we to do at Vernon's?"

"Look up the father of the charming creature whom you are to marry in less than three months, if you play your cards well."

"Has she a—decent fortune?"

"Indecent on the contrary, colossal, monstrous. Are you satisfied?"

"And what sort of a person is the father?"

"Very fair, a very good sort of person. He is a manufacturer. You know what those kind of people are—very fair."

"A manufacturer—but a manufacturer of what? a lamp-maker, or a tinman?"

"Oh! he must have been a worker in tin, I won't conceal anything from you; he was a dealer in spouts, but they were excellent spouts!"

Both burst into a shout of laughter, in the midst of which Count Jean said: "I cannot keep such low company as that. Come, be reasonable, my family is of no mushroom growth."

"Neither is mine; and yet I assure you that the spout dealer's daughter would suit me perfectly. I will even tell you that I wouldn't give her to you, if it were not impossible to get her myself. I will add, my dear fellow, that your father-in-law gave up his spout business long ago."

"Ah! he has given it up. He did right; and what has been his occupation since then?"

"He is satisfied with being one of the great capitalists in France, in originating and sustaining colossal schemes, owning the mines and forges of Lamar, being the sleeping partner and associate of—of the—"

"Ah! do you mean père Larreau?"

"You have hit it exactly."

"Oh! why didn't you tell me so at once? You made my back creep with your spouts. He is not at all an out-of-the-way person. M. Larreau is well known—relatively. He is a financier, my dear fellow."

"Who said that he wasn't? Then he is in active life; has been in our society—in short, is very influential—a friend of the ministers."

"As to that, I care nothing about it. Does this Vernon fellow live far away. It is vexatious that he should have sold— What did you say that he sold? What singular commencements there are to some careers!"

"I said spouts, my good friend."

"There are so many chattering simpletons ready to say that we sell our names—fools, who will not understand—"

"The demands of the society in which we live; but, thank Heaven, we are in a position to choose our wives where we like, if it were from a back shop, without lowering ourselves by it. She will bring an immense dowry. Well, that is the least she can do; after having taken the dear little thing for nothing, and polished her up beautifully, should you be also at the expense of coloring! That makes me furious. What, my dear fellow, these people have pillaged, robbed, ruined us, enriched themselves at our expense, like footmen, by selling our cast-off clothes, and we are not to have a right to recover some little portion of our property, by marrying their daughters, whom we remove from them. The deuce! you must imagine that it was by stealing the lead from your gutters that M. Larreau succeeded in making his first spout, and becoming what he is. Well! now you say to him: 'I wish to marry your daughter; you shall be the father of a countess, robber, but restore my gutter.' That is how I understand the situation. Oh! I have a very clear head for these matters."

"How perfectly reasonable your remarks are, my dear Claudius."

"Good Heavens! suppose all these people, who have become suddenly rich, should humble themselves a little and place their daughters and their money bags at our feet, do you see any great harm in that? Does it not very much resemble a necessary restitution?"

"Yes, necessary, fortunate, providential."

"Certainly providential. For seventy years these people have blocked up all the roads, plundered and soiled everything, until in our noble country of France, a gentleman, who does not wish to soil his boots, is, deuce take it! forced to walk on his hands, or shut himself up in his cellar, and should not justice be done at last! Empty your pockets, Jean Bonhomme, give us your daughter, and return to your duties."

At that moment the carriage rolled over the gravel, and stopped before the door of a fine mansion, which belonged to Vernon, a historical painter by profession.

I deeply regret that respect for private life should have prevented my writing the curious volume about Vernon and his studio, which they both deserve. It would be to such a book that I should now send the reader, instead of spoiling a capital subject by a sketch which is of necessity too hasty. These are the facts, briefly told. From his early youth Vernon, the historical painter, had served in the heavy cavalry. He was a bold-spirited fellow, endowed with a very keen intellect, and exuberant gayety. He had a soldierly carriage, hooked nose, piercing eye, and moreover, was the legitimate son of the nurse of a person who occupied a very high station.

These circumstances procured him numerous and warm protectors; but he was worthy of fortune's favors both as cuirassier and artist, being in the one profession brave as his sword, and having also proved his vocation as painter by executing numbers of charming little pictures in oil and water colors, since his admission to the regiment. This taste and varirious other reasons induced Vernon, already a rich man and major of cavalry, to sheath his sword and devote himself to the cultivation of art. He bought a house, had a large studio built, and under the influence of the maternal star, became almost insensibly the most popular of hosts, and most renowned of the artists employed in taking the portraits of the dignitaries of the country. Although his two pupils, who greatly assisted him, could sketch and color, the works of this master are not chefs-d'œuvre. This is readily admitted by all, even while loudly praising his unique effects of light and shade, and the wonderful finish of his accessories.

Whether with or without reason, the portrait-painter, who had quickly become famous, found himself overwhelmed with orders. To sit for one's picture in his celebrated studio, was one of the most delightful of occupations. All the floating rumors in Paris centred there; the journalists came for news, and a constant succession of people of all kinds came and went from morning till night. The pleasant evening receptions that Vernon organized gave the finishing-touch to the popularity of his mansion. It was a favored spot, a sort of neutral ground, where, thanks to the unceremonious style of living natural to one half artist, half soldier, he succeeded in creating relations and friendship between people who would otherwise never have known each other. Men of pleasure, bankers, journalists, politicians, capitalists, and racing men met each other there, while Parisian exquisites, the flower of French aristocracy, fell into the habit of taking it as a place to exhibit their graces and elegance. This truly Parisian circle was naturally the fashionable coutisse for aristocratic curiosity-seekers. The studio contained wonderful rarities, magnificent furniture, jewels, and splendid tapestry, which came from nobody knew where, and were constantly renewed.

"Here is something I have found," said Vernon; "what do you say to it?"

"It is very elegant, gentlemen, exquisite enough!" murmured Claudius in a low tone, turning the article thoughtfully around, then raising his voice: "Vernon, you don't know what you have there."

"And who told you I didn't? It is a beautiful ivory carving, a hunting-horn belonging to the sixteenth century, adorned with the arms of France, neither more nor less."

"Vernon, my dear fellow, a hundred louis," grunted fat Marsoff.

"Ah! the deuce! I will take it at that price," cried Claudius. "Will you make an exchange?"

"No, I assure you that I do not care to give it up, my good fellow. You are very kind, but I don't want to part with it."

"But, if one offered you—"

"Ah! faith, if I was offered—"

"Three hundred louis, Monsieur Vernon," said Lord ——.

"You overwhelm me, your lordship. How can I

resist you? Oh! my poor ivory! At least be grateful to me, my lord!"

One thing Vernon had not thought of, the attention that his famous receptions must necessarily attract among fashionable women. If my memory is correct, it was the Duchess of Blanmon who first expressed a desire to enter the cuirassier's studio. The duchess was not a woman to relinquish a plan she had long meditated, or one easily daunted by difficulties. By the help of Claudius, the artist's sleeping-room was transformed into a little parlor, which communicated with the garden by an outer staircase; the door leading into the studio was replaced by a curtain, and one fine evening about midnight, the duchess arrived, wrapped up like a conspirator, and followed—by three of her friends. All passed off smoothly; unfortunately the frolic of these aristocratic ladies became noised abroad, and two days after, eight curious persons arrived, coming directly from the Stabat of the Italiens, where they had agreed to meet. The following week, the little parlor was as full as an egg and scented like a perfume case. All the ladies, listening eagerly, were grouped before the curtain, which they drew aside by imperceptible degrees. They pressed and crowded on each other as if in the vestry of a church at some wedding, restraining their bursts of laughter with great difficulty, and whispering questions to the master of the house, who did not know how to reply, and found himself amid these surroundings like a lady-bug buried in a bouquet of flowers.

"My dear Vernon, you say that the tall blonde yonder, talking to the ambassador, is Amélie Saintonge? Well, to be just, she is extremely beautiful Ah! there is the famous Tambourine. Good Heavens! my husband is kissing her hand. Oh! oh! ladies, just see my husband kissing that horrid Tambourine's hand, and with such an air!"

"Dear me—what a pretty creature! Ladies, I wish I were a man, only— It is funny to see all these jades. When one thinks—"

"That they are as pretty as we."

One evening, by the merest chance, the famous curtain was drawn aside almost half-way and remained so. A few timid women, who had no strength of character, vowed that they would never again set their pretty feet in Vernon's studio, while others, bolder, and avowed lovers of progress, accepted the fusion, a very discreet fusion, be it understood, skilfully managed, without embarrassment or confusion, and protected by the artistic element which pervaded the whole circle.

It is undeniable that Vernon's studio had a very considerable influence upon the manners of the times: not that the ex-cuirassier was a man of genius; he was entitled to no other merit than that of following his own impulses and taking advantage of events just at the right time. The Duchess of Blanmon, who is by no means wanting in sense or intellect, said a capital thing in regard to this. One evening, in a circle of intimate friends, when Vernon alluded to certain matters, and seemed disposed to claim an importance in the political world which he did not possess, she turned to him, and in the picturesque language she was fond of using, said: "Be quiet, my good little friend, you are a convenient tool, nothing more."

Such was the famous studio in which Count de Manteiguey was to meet the father-in-law he so greatly needed. For the rest, Claudius had, as usual, given proof of most excellent judgment in selecting Larreau.

VII.

The ex-spout-maker was rather inclined to obesity; but as he was no fool, contrived to turn his stout figure to good account, and, aided by the prestige of being a millionaire, might be said to have a stately presence. His high, bald forehead was apt to become easily flushed. At the extremity of his little short arms, which looked like a pair of fins, were two plump, dimpled hands, which were usually held clasped together on his white waistcoat. His whole person expressed the most charming good-nature. His smooth face, rosy, and well shaven, invited confidence, and his right eye, with which he beamed on society, was overpoweringly benevolent, if I may so express a charm which is exceedingly difficult to describe. True, the left eye somewhat belied its comrade's excessive affability; but he very rarely opened it—never, except when occupied with business matters. This eye, which was generally moist, shone like a diamond, was sharp as a needle, and I do not think it would be possible to find one more keenly observing, or better calculated to search the most secret thoughts of another. It was doubtless from motives of precaution that he yielded its remarkable virtues under the shadow of his heavy eyelids, thereby imitating those skilful surgeons who conceal their instruments in a case, and do not draw them from their covering until it is time to operate upon the patient.

Only a very small number of persons, comparatively speaking, were thoroughly acquainted with the capitalist's left eye; so that people in general felt most irresistibly attracted towards him. They were touched by seeing a man of such enormous wealth and immense influence remain so simple and affable in his manners to every one, conceal nothing of his laborious past, and, most remarkable, carry his self-denial so far as not to change his name. They said to themselves: "Here is a financier of the old school, such a man as one does not see now-a-days." When in society, his honesty, nice even to intolerance, was displayed by constant outbursts. If the name of some famous banker or well-known merchant were pronounced, even in a low tone, he would exclaim, interrupting his game of whist, "That man? he is a rascal!"

And his brow would flush so suddenly, he would utter the condemnatory word in such a sonorous voice, that the rudeness of the expression was pardoned out of respect to the virtuous wrath which inspired it. Yet he was not naturally quick tempered. Gifted with intellect, calm and watchful in the midst of the whirl of modern ambitions, terrified by nothing, he was capable of accepting all progress, whether forward or backward, provided his mind and capital found an opportunity of taking part in it. In all sincerity, he was both democrat and legitimist, no one could be more liberal, and yet at the same time a most inflexible ruler. He would have held up both hands to vote for compulsory instruction, would have voted that the gendarmes should compel every Frenchman to buy a grammar and A B C book, but on the express condition that he, Larreau, should have the monopoly of the sale, and become, without any possible competition, the sole and only bookseller in his country. You see that in saying: "Here is a financier of the old school, such a man as one does not see now-a-days," people judged only by appearances; scarcely any one could boast of being more a man of the times than he.

Certain people, to whom Larreau's operations had not been favorable, asserted that he had no principles, an accusation all the more dangerous because it must necessarily be vague, and leave a field for every variety of comment. The absence of a standard principle, which might serve for rule and measure, being generally felt, each judges his neighbor's by his own, and great is the confusion which results. Far from being destitute of principles, Monsieur Larreau possessed many on which he could rely; for he had carefully tested them all, lest he might have some occasion for regret. Nevertheless, if any one had compelled him—which would have been no easy matter—to express, in a few words, his firmest convictions, he would have replied: "I am a legitimist and a Catholic." These opinions had come to him by degrees, without his making the slightest effort, and very slowly. As his fortune increased, and he acquired position and importance, he felt the pressing necessity for surrounding himself with a more substantial barricade, placing the structure of his prosperity under the divine protection and associating Providence in his plans, a natural feeling, which has led many souls into the path of safety.

Claudius thoroughly understood the wealthy capitalist; so, when he perceived him among the throng that filled Vernon's studio, he did not attempt to find a plausible reason for speaking of Count de Manteigney, but went directly up to him, and having drawn him aside into a corner, said abruptly:

"My dear M. Larreau, do you wish to have your daughter married?"

"Certainly, my dear Monsieur Claudius, when I find a son-in-law who will suit her—who will suit us, you understand."

"I have one to propose."

The rich man half opened his left eye.

"One of your friends, my dear Monsieur Claudius?"

"The person of whom I speak is certainly one of my friends, and is utterly ruined."

"That is truly a great recommendation! you are in high spirits this evening, my dear friend. You say that he is utterly—"

"Oh! there is not the least possible doubt about it; but that is not all."

"Make haste, I am dying of impatience."

"My friend has a great reputation in Paris as a man of fashion—fine manners, great attractions—"

"That will do afterwards, Monsieur Claudius, afterwards; you are drawing your own portrait."

"Confess that I could not make a better beginning. Let me go on. My friend is sole heir—"

"Let us sit down, my dear Claudius, we can talk so much more comfortably."

"Sole and only heir of one of the noblest names in France, and still possesses the castle of his ancestors, the cradle of his race, with towers, precipices, draw-bridge, loop-holes, fortifications, court-yard—a real feudal manor, partially in ruins, I confess; for I will conceal nothing from you. The estates have been sold, but they can be bought back again. Here is an escutcheon to re-gild, and you could not find one more worthy of—restoration. In one word, I am speaking of the count de Manteigney."

The capitalist could not restrain an expression of pleasure, and his left eye, which during the short conversation had been constantly opening and shutting, became perfectly quiet.

Claudius presented the two gentlemen to each other that very evening. Four or five days after, Count Jean received an invitation to a ball at the house of M. Larreau, who, after studying the map of the country and the *Guide Joanne*, set out the following morning for Virez.

M. Larreau made his inquiries with skill and prudence, visited every part of the country, and found means to pursue his investigations for three days without arousing public curiosity; in short, he returned delighted, and showed himself willing to push matters forward rapidly. He had met his beau-ideal of a son-in-law. In the meantime the count discovered that the capitalist's daughter was wonderfully charming, in which he was perfectly right, and two months and a half after, to a day, the future couple signed the contract. If M. de Manteigney had been less eager to escape as soon as he decently could, from a situation which threatened soon to become unendurable, it is probable that he would have thought twice before signing. The capitalist, in short, gave his daughter, by the marriage settlements, the most absolute control over her dowry, which was sixteen hundred thousand francs, six or eight of which, by the aid of the Virez notary, were invested in a portion of the estates belonging to the ancient domain.

" By this means, my dear count," said the rich man, " the estates of Manteigne are almost wholly restored, and will descend intact to your children, by the deed executed by their mother and yourself. The portion of the valley I have purchased in my own name, and retain, will return to the original domains after my death. I adore my daughter, and hope soon to win your affection. You see that I am already an old man, and I have cherished the hope that it might not be disagreeable to you to have me for a neighbor. I shall have erected on the reserved estate—and it is the secret of its purchase—a little house, hut, châlet, no matter what, where I can end my days in the shadow of your château. My tastes are very simple"—After a short silence, he continued: " Unless you would receive me in any of the wings of your own dwelling—in which case, my dear son-in-law, I should beg you to allow me to defray all expense of the necessary refitting. Perhaps by uniting our incomes, we could maintain an establishment more worthy of the name you bear. It would make me very happy, I confess; it would be a real pleasure to me in my old age to be present in some corner, and witness the splendor of the princely style in which the arrangement I propose would enable you to live. Do not hasten to answer either yes or no, my dear count, reflect upon the matter."

Mlle. Larreau embraced her father with tears in her eyes. The young man, dazzled by the vision of the elegant style in which he might be able to live; intoxicated by the realization of a dream which flattered all his tastes; persuaded that he would soon be able to control a father-in-law who seemed so full of good nature; impatient to have done with the life of expedients which he had led for ten or twelve years, appealed to on the ground of his gentlemanly instincts, accepted everything, signed everything, and was married with the utmost cheerfulness. There was nothing better to be done.

VIII.

Yet when Abbé Roche had returned home and exchanged his new cassock and handsome silver buckles for his every-day dress, he experienced a sensation of great relief. His mind was disturbed, like that of a man who has just awakened from a confused dream. Everything about his visit to the château appeared strange and incomprehensible, and occupied his thoughts more than he could have wished. Therefore, when mère Hilaire questioned him about the welcome they had given him, he said nothing, except that he had been well received, and the good woman kept silent.

At times he imagined that there was an impassable gulf between these gentlemen, whom he had scarcely seen, and himself; he experienced an instinctive repugnance towards them, which he regretted so much the more because it seemed to be in direct contradiction to the profound respect with which he had always regarded the nobility. On farther reflection, he asked himself whether this impression was not, on his part, the result of undue pride; whether the surprise of suddenly finding himself in contact with scenes of comfort and luxury, which made his own life appear more narrow and humble by the contrast, had not rendered him too severe in his judgment upon these people of aristocratic birth, whose only crime, after all, was playing hot cockles without caring what people might say about it. Although he clearly perceived that his first impression was the correct one, he argued against himself with a species of obstinacy. Did he wish these ladies to dress exactly like the girls and women of Grand Fort? Why was it surprising that the countess should treat her curé with ease and freedom, or that she should be as curious as a spoiled child to make this half savage talk, and amuse herself by witnessing his embarrassment? What was there so very strange about her careless chatter? She was young, rich, and noble enough to allow herself to act her own pleasure before a poor, unknown priest. It is certain that she was wonderfully beautiful, and very singularly dressed; but what did he know about customs and fashions, and since when had ladies of high rank been forbidden to be remarkably beautiful? Besides, why had he, the curé of Grand Fort, noticed all these things with so much interest and curiosity? Was it in accordance with his position as a priest to linger around these earthly charms, which God had commanded him to pass by with indifference? Was he then so weak, so extremely impressionable, that a woman could disturb his mind and occupy his thoughts? He told himself all this, was humiliated, dissatisfied, indignant with himself; then wishing to obtain an exact knowledge of his weakness, in order to correct it the better, recalled one by one the impressions he had felt; and all the details of what he had seen passed once more before his eyes, while in the depths of his soul, some unknown voice murmured: "You have humiliated yourself enough before the memory of these people. You are more noble than they, even in your shabby cassock; you will soon read their hearts and find naught but a mass of wicked passions and vicious instincts, while if they seek to watch you in their turn, they will not be able to understand your thoughts and actions."

To be brief, the abbé Roche did not return to the château for several days, and even avoided passing its doors. Once he met the countess's father, and on another occasion found himself face to face with the count and his friend Claudius, in the village streets; but he contented himself with exchanging bows, and found means to cut short all conversation. These people terrified him.

At last Sunday came, and from early morning the curé, thinking of the mass he was to perform, felt, in spite of his resolutions, as much agitated as on the day of his visit. He knew that the noble company would attend church; he saw in imagination their amused faces, the count's eye-glass, his father-in-law's white waistcoat, and the important, self-sufficient air of all. Would the ladies appear at mass in a costume like the one they wore the other evening? He shuddered in spite of himself. How would they, accustomed to recline in those immense arm-chairs, which almost resembled beds, endure to sit on the narrow, hard, wooden benches? Were they even clean and well dusted? For the first time in his life he thought of these things.

His poor church was so dilapidated, so forlorn, encumbered with *ex voto* and strange adornments! Appreciating the artless feeling which offered them, he had thought them poetical and touching; would they not appear very comical to these jesting Parisians, who were accustomed to the stately ceremonies of the cities?

This disturbed him more than all the rest; he loved his poor church so much! Pre-occupied by these thoughts, he found his razors horribly dull, and rubbed them upside down on the leathern strap fastened to the handle of the door. "Monsieur le curé, do you know that it is twenty minutes of nine?" asked mère Hilaire, knocking at the door.

"Yes, good mother, I know it. You can come in. Have you seen whether the benches in the church were clean enough?"

The good woman smiled, pleased that she should have thought of the same thing as her curé. "I have just given them a little dusting; they are very nice now; but dear me! they are old, and terribly hard for all these grand people, M. le curé. I said to myself: 'If something could only be put over them'—you will not be angry, M. le curé. People must not be driven away from the house of God, you know. Well! I have a little bit of carpet that is just the thing; I have shaken and brushed it well. I might spread it on the bench, if you think it would be a good plan."

"You have done well, mère Hilaire, but I have also a little mat before my bed, you might spread them both on. It would be better for the ladies."

Abbé Roche stopped short; he was vexed that he should allow himself to be pre-occupied by such trivial cares when about to say mass.

When he entered the vestry, the acolytes were dressed, the choristers ready, and all his parishioners waiting on the square. It was nine o'clock, and yet père Butan dared not stop ringing, that the services might begin, for no one from the château had arrived. Two or three boys, who had played truant, muttered: "I would stop ringing, if I were you," but everybody else said, "Père Butan is right, we must not make the count and countess lose the mass." Fortunately for every one, and especially the curé, who was waiting to begin the service, looking out of the little window of the vestry and thinking that it was very hard to be forced to keep God waiting in this manner, a child ran up, saying that the ladies and gentlemen were coming. The crowd instinctively divided, forming in two ranks, and the aristocratic party entered the little square.

The ladies, dressed *à la* Watteau's shepherdesses, were leaning on long flexible staffs, and seemed to be so exhausted by the little slope they had just ascended, that they could scarcely stand upon their high-heeled boots. They had been obliged to cross on foot the short space intervening between the château and the village, for that portion of the road had not yet been finished and made passable for carriages. But the expedition had been cheerfully performed, if one could judge by their shouts of laughter. When they perceived that the square was full of people, the three ladies, who were walking in front, suddenly stopped. "Ah! countess, see these worthy people taking off their caps," said Mme. de Rougeon, "they are waiting for us."

"Really it is quite a triumphal entry! What honest, respectful faces they have! Look, dear, see all these little children. Oh! I am going to pray for them, it is the least I can do."

"They are pretty little things," said Mlle. de Rougeon, "but they don't wipe their noses often enough."

During this time père Butan was pulling at the rope with all his might, and the poor bell tinkled its best, like some old singer who has lost his voice and has nothing left but a good style.

All heads were bent, and the countess, moving slowly through her respectful vassals, bowed slightly to the right and left, murmuring in an undertone: "Good-morning, my friends—my good friends; good-day, little ones." She enjoyed it thoroughly, and strangely enough, thought of the Bois de Boulogne, where she had often seen a stately head bending in little graceful, sweeping salutes.

The count followed directly behind the ladies, talking very eagerly in a loud tone to M. de Rougeon, without taking the slightest notice of the persons standing by, and gesticulating with his little switch like a man engrossed in some important argument. As to M. Larreau, he was watching his dear little countess with his right eye, and ready to bless the whole population. Two or three closely-shaven servants, stiff, erect, and unapproachable, closed the procession.

The curé had donned his priestly robes long before. Alas! they were shabby, well worn, and much frayed in certain places. It was all in vain that poor mère Hilaire, first washing her hands, wrapped them carefully in a white cloth every Sunday; she could not rejuvenate the old garments. While in the vestry, whose door stood open, Abbé Roche heard the rustling of silken robes, the sound of delicate boots, and the confused murmur of Parisian voices. His ear distinguished all this in spite of the noise made by the sabots and iron-shod shoes striking against the floor, and knocking the benches. He clasped his hands, closed his eyes, strove to abstract his thoughts, murmured fervent prayers, and reproached himself for his want of self-command, as if it had been a crime. At last, as they were now waiting only for him, he made a signal for the acolytes to move forward, and entered the church.

He was obliged to summon up all his courage in order to advance the eight or ten paces which separated him from the altar, so great was the singular emotion he experienced. He had determined not to glance towards the congregation, and kept his resolution. But he dimly saw the kneeling ladies looking around them through their eye-glasses, and smiling at each other, while the gentlemen, with one hand thrust into their vests, whispered and twirled their mustaches. On reaching the steps, he knelt, and in a voice that trembled more than he could have wished, commenced the *Introit*, but soon grew calmer, as his up-raised glance rested upon the crucifix that surmounted the altar; his blood flowed more slowly through his veins, and he forgot all who surrounded him. The wooden Christ was a very shapeless thing, one might almost have supposed that it had been carved by some herdsman's knife, and it was covered with coarse, gaudy paint. Yet before this rude image the poor, solitary priest, destitute of family and friends, deprived of all that was claimed by the secret instincts of his nature, had passed the sweetest hours of his life. He knew every detail of the carving, so grotesque to others, so sacred to him. Each crack, each fracture of the worm-eaten wood, reminded him of some heart throb, a prayer, a tear, or a joy. Thus even those objects least worthy of attention become poetical and dear to the man who has lavished his affection upon them. What do you care for the cut of the garment, the wrinkles on the countenance of the friend that holds out his hand to you, listens to you, and consoles you? His unassuming appearance, on the contrary, invites your confidence, his plain face re-assures you, you love him all the more because strangers do not consider him attractive; his charms are a secret, possessed by you alone. The priest was touched by the thought that the good God of Grand Fort had made Himself poor and miserable, despoiled Himself of His divine splendor, that He might be better understood by His children, and had descended to their level through paternal tenderness. His heart, which was overflowing with repressed feeling, suddenly opened, he dared to speak, to confide everything to the good God who watched over the mountains, and after these unreserved outpourings of his soul, he felt strengthened and purified; he breathed invigorating air, saw society under a loftier aspect, a divine glow animated him; he had a consciousness of being nearer that fire of love of which human affections are but the dying sparks. It was before this defaced fragment of wood that he had comprehended the grandeur and nobleness of his mission, and had accepted his austere life frankly and cheerfully. He then believed his soul to be large enough to contain all humanity; thought himself sufficiently bold and courageous to be the pilot, who watches in spite of fatigue, and forgets wind and rain in the remembrance that the safety of those who sleep depends upon his vigilance and devotion. The sacrifice had appeared to him a triumph, and the suffering a consolation.

When, at the close of the mass, the curé turned to address a few words to the congregation, as he was in the habit of doing every Sunday, the countess was astonished at the expression of his face, the searching tones of his voice, the brightness of his glance, and the simplicity of his gestures.

He was really handsome. "Our curé preaches admirably," murmured Mme. de Rougeon, as they left the church.

"Yes," replied the countess. "I do not understand it; and I have been wondering how he chanced to be cast ashore upon this desolate rock, in this out-of-the-world, almost savage, village."

"He is perhaps undergoing a penance—ecclesiastical discipline—"

"What an idea!"

"It does not follow that he has committed any very great crime. What are considered merely trifling errors in our circle, are regarded in others as unpardonable crimes—some affair of the heart for instance."

"You are right, his face tells the story plainly enough. Ah! poor man!"

"Unfortunate priest!"

"I must leave you a moment. Perhaps we shall find means to learn his story some day. I am going to invite M. le curé to breakfast, I am sure that he will not refuse me."

Abbé Roche in truth could find no pretext for declining Mme. de Manteigney's invitation, and half an hour afterwards found himself installed in the great dining-room of the castle.

IX.

The breakfast was delightful, although much less noisy than usual. The ladies showed the curé the most gracious attentions, and overwhelmed him with little kindnesses. His noble bearing at the altar, his simple, manly carriage, had evidently produced a great effect. The dilapidated church was declared to be delightful, in spite of the opinion of the gentlemen who exchanged smiling glances. They could not look without emotion at the rude pictures, the *ex voto* hanging on the walls; the recollection of the brave mountaineers kneeling bareheaded in the porch, drew tears from their eyes. Even the voices of the choristers, though somewhat harsh and untrained, had a meaning.

"For my part," observed Mme. de Rougeon, "I imagine that that must have been the way that God was worshipped in the catacombs."

"Take a little of the vanilla cream, dear Monsieur le curé," said the countess, "you will not refuse a new parishioner."

And the young wife, holding back with her left hand the numerous trinkets dangling from little golden chains among the laces that adorned her sleeve, offered her neighbor on the right a pretty little heap of perfumed cream in a silver-gilt spoon. Arm, sleeve, hand, spoon, and cream, were all bewitching, somewhat too bewitching, if one may say so without wounding any one, for Abbé Roche, on perceiving the charming little picture, turned away his eyes, and answered gravely: "Thank you, I will not take any."

"Must I tell you I made it myself in order to tempt you? Well! I won't say that, for I did not do it, but the cream is none the less nice. Come, Monsieur le curé, take it to please me."

The curé accepted what was offered with a very perceptible blush. The idea of a serious man blushing so easily! Ah! well, perhaps if you had been in his place you would have changed color too. Mme. de Manteigney had, in truth, gazed at him with an expression well calculated to disturb his mind: not that she was capable of premeditated coquetry—in these delicate matters one must first of all understand one's self; but she had thought her own hand, holding the golden spoon, a very pretty sight, it was an artistic pleasure which all women know.

She had naturally smiled at her hand, rather than the curé, and if it had been unnecessarily sweet, it was merely owing to the unusual delight afforded by the sight of her own charms.

Yet the countess knew that the good abbé might misunderstand her meaning; for she was seized with one of those little fits of coughing which, without disfiguring you, permit you to withdraw a moment from conversation. It is a very difficult thing for a pretty woman to observe all the shades of amiability; they allow themselves to be borne along by the spirit of improvisation, and when the charm of being attractive leads them on, easily lose all discrimination; the slope is so slippery.

Coquetry has this peculiarity, that it is sufficient for itself: it forgets the public, for it can do without it; and a woman who seems bent on our neighbor's destruction, who has brought a whole arsenal into action, has really no other intention than to try her weapons and renew her cannon, so that you will rarely see a woman—I mean a woman who has the reputation of being attractive—distribute to each one the modicum of favor that is his due. With a priest, especially, the just proportion is more difficult to preserve on account of his invulnerability; and the absence of sex, which is morally one of his privileges, gives them a sort of carte blanche. The certainty that nothing will be broken, tempts beginners in the art of shooting to try their skill—they like to fire at a strong black-board, which is too solid to be broken, and yet capable of showing the shots it receives, and bear record of their successes. So, granting what I have just said, is it surprising that the countess, at sight of her plump, taper fingers, should have yielded to the temptation of making her smile as charming as her hand, and afterwards, by a scarcely perceptible manœuvre, have raised the perfumed fingers that held the spoon within two inches of her curé's nose, as he bowed his thanks. The singularity is, under such circumstances, the smile is not all. By some unknown sympathetic influence the eyelids droop coquettishly, the glance softens, the neck bends, and the body sways with unexpected grace, and that is how it happens that, in the best society, a spoonful of vanilla cream may lead to very serious consequences. Fortunately these little accidents are readily pardoned among people who lead a fashionable life.

Abbé Roche pardoned it also, but he was much disturbed. At certain crises strange temptations—why should it not be confessed?—had risen before him; he had caught a glimpse of bewildering, frightful phantoms; he had been tormented, poor man, as one is in some dream or threatening nightmare, but all had been a mere fleeting hallucination, which disappeared in the broad light of day. Confronted with charms whose too evident reality aroused the memory of his former conflicts, he felt the danger to be a thousand times greater than before. He had judged the world as a whole, and from a distance; but he who surveys a battle from a mountain, and comes forth victorious in imagination, would certainly have far less coolness and courage if he descended from his height and mingled with the combatants. It was now with him as it would be with that man; he no longer hovered over the brow of the mountain, but felt that he was entering into the reality of the struggle, and feared that he might lose his self-command in the mêlée. Already the view was becoming less clear: was he not taking the trifling details of a life with which he was unfamiliar for monsters? Was he the sport of a delusion? Why should he have these tremors, whose cause he no longer dared to frankly ask himself? The more he listened, the less he understood the meaning of their words; certain jests which roused a smile were utterly unintelligible to him. The very gestures of his hosts had an incomprehensible peculiarity; the tones of their voices, their mode of constructing sentences, every thing about them was strange to him. If by chance he understood one of their ideas, he found it so different from his own that he would have preferred to have still remained in ignorance.

"Is not my cream delicious, Monsieur le curé?" murmured Mme. de Manteigney, casting an inquiring glance at the priest, for she was saying to herself: "I am going to have some fine sport in finding out what sort of a person this good abbé really is."

"Excellent," he replied, without raising his eyes from his plate; then drew his feet closer together lest his neighbor's dress might brush against them. "Incomprehensible creature," he murmured, "what is she hiding within her soul; from whence come these bewildering charms? Can it be a trial by which God is testing me?"

"Tell me, Monsieur le curé, how do you warm

your church in winter?" asked Mme. de Rougeon, rolling a tiny crumb of bread under the tip of her finger.

"My wife is—what shall I say?—a singular woman. She always fancies herself at the church of the Madeleine or Saint Thomas Aquinas. Do you expect to find all the refinements of our peculiar civilization in this wild region, my dear?"

"Papa is right," interrupted his young daughter, without the slightest ceremony. "This civilization is horrible!"

Abbé Roche looked at Mlle. de Rougeon; he was amazed that at her age she should have so decided an opinion upon such a matter.

"True, my daughter, we are living in a circle which is dele—"

"Yes, papa, deleterious."

"Deleterious, certainly, and which, if I may dare to say so, is the negation of all—of all—"

"Yes, papa, of all principles."

And as the guests all burst into shouts of laughter, except the priest, who looked on in astonishment, she added, pushing back the long earrings which touched her shoulders: "Papa dictates, and I arrange his ideas in words. That is why I think him right; so, to preserve him from the deleterious air of Paris, I shall make him go to bed at five minutes of eight, and give him some tisane. No more balls at the Hôtel de Ville; no more races; no, that is all at an end; no more races! Those are also deleterious circles! No more père Hyacinthe, no more clubs, no skating, no anything; instead, nice hot tisane with honey in moderate quantities; we will read the philosophers among ourselves, and if papa wishes to escape, cling to him and keep him with us."

While the young girl spoke, Abbé Roche looked at her intently. He was not only surprised, but grieved.

"The unhappy child," said he to himself. "What crime can this man, who looks old before his time, have committed, to be thus punished by his daughter's contempt? How he must suffer! What idea do they give others of paternal dignity, filial respect and love? Must one be deprived of family ties in order to appreciate their value?"

"Well!" continued Mlle. de Rougeon, "I have a still more attractive programme."

"More of your nonsense, spoiled child!"

"Oh! it is a very simple matter: we will stay here all the year round. M. de Manteigney shall let us one of his little towers, and we can live in it, far away from the demon of civilization. I will cut off my hair, mamma hers, and papa his, it will only be the work of a moment; we will put on little caps trimmed with a bit of embroidery, and as the church is not heated, order foot-stoves that we can go and sing at matins. M. le curé will be so pleased. Papa can be bass. Ah! that's not a bad idea, is it mamma?"

"Your youth and gayety are some apology for you, my love, but yet—think my child—"

"If mamma is going to begin to preach like papa!—oh! dear."

"My daughter, you are going beyond all—"

"Yes, papa, bounds. I am to be silent because papa wants to talk."

"Yes, I do wish to speak, little rebel! Oh! because I laugh, you think I am jesting. That is the way with our children! Family respect, authority—in short everything; everything — tradition — I laugh, because you are looking at me with your little—your little saucy air, you spoiled child; that is of consequence; I am — I am — the word escapes me—I am right."

"Well! for my part I think you were much more agreeable when you were wrong," observed the count.

"You are not at all amusing with your deleterious age? Where did you learn all that stuff?"

"My dear fellow, the moral is—"

"Well, there he goes again. It is not more than two years since I first noticed this infirmity in poor de Rougeon; he used to be a charming man."

"It is evident that they do not use the word *moral* in its ordinary sense," thought Abbé Roche, who had been very ill at ease during a conversation so utterly incomprehensible to him.

"If that's the way you are going to attack papa, I shall defend him," cried the young girl, with a very pretty show of anger.

"Good Heavens! that child must be crazy," murmured the priest.

Mme. de Manteigney, perceiving that Abbé Roche's manner was becoming more and more constrained, suddenly changed the conversation. "My dear curé, tell us who is that singular looking person who has already been here two or three times. Where does he go, and from whence does he come? Is he a human being? He has a huge beard, half red, half gray, eyes like a rat, and a nose that looks like the beak of some bird of prey; his clothes are all gray, just the color of the rocks. Oh! he is such an ugly man. I will add that he always carries a basket of cheeses. I am afraid of him."

"You undoubtedly mean père Loursière, Madame. Your fears are exaggerated, I think, though in his youth he committed some faults for which he has reason to reproach himself. His life has been an adventurous one; he has been occupied in various pursuits, and travelled in almost every part of the world; but at the present time I do not know that any thing very serious could be alleged against him. He is a shepherd, and watches the flocks which the people of the village and market-town confide to his charge, that they may graze upon the lofty mountain pastures. He lives with his daughter in a lonely hut on the edge of the pine woods."

"What! is the little savage who also comes here occasionally his daughter? The strange creature with the large, deep eyes, muddy complexion, and slow gait!"

"She lost her mother at the time of her birth, poor child."

"Ah! she must have been grown up ever since she was born, the little witch," murmured Claudius.

"I think so too," said the count.

And Mme. de Manteigney, repressing a slight shiver, asked:

"Isn't that ugly man something of a sorcerer himself?"

"There has been such a rumor," said the priest, smiling; "but his principal distinction lies in making very good cheeses, and I do not think he has any other."

"Excuse me, Monsieur le curé, he is a remarkably intelligent man, and has a great deal of information. I have talked with him, and especially in geology—"

"So you understand geology, Monsieur Larreau?" asked Claudius.

"I? not much—a little, just sufficient to amuse myself, and judge of père Loursière's—"

The countess rose, interrupting her father:

"Don't say any more about that hateful family, I beg of you; they frighten me—I dreamed of them all last night."

"Indeed, and I dreamed of the daughter, a singular coincidence."

So saying, M. de Manteigney uttered a little harsh laugh.

"I do not like such jests," said the mistress of the castle, and the curé noticed that she bit her lips.

X.

M. Larreau, who had taken very little part in the conversation during breakfast, but had found time while eating heartily to occasionally half open his famous left eye and watch the company, took the curé's arm as they left the table, and after pulling down his huge white vest, which was always inclined to slip up, drew the priest out upon the lawn.

"Ah!" thought the countess, "my father has taken the curé away from me. He is determined that I shall not have an opportunity to make my enigma talk."

"Don't you smoke, my dear sir?" said the capitalist, in his soft, friendly tone.

"A little, but not at this season of the year."

"Please accept a cigar."

"Thank you, but I only smoke in winter, when we are imprisoned by the snow, and besides, I do not know how to use anything but the short pipes of this region."

"Then, as it does not annoy you, permit me to light my cigar?" And as he touched it to the yellow flame of a wax match, he compressed the tobacco between his short, plump fingers.

"Confess, my dear curé, that this is a charming view; I cannot tell you how deeply I am moved by the magnificent scenery."

"True, Monsieur, our country is very beautiful, but unfortunately it is the will of Providence that the superb landscape you admire should wear a stern face to the poor. The poverty of this population is very great, and their labor extremely severe."

"I understand you; there is much to be done undoubtedly. It gives me pleasure to see that you are not blind to the humanitarian and social importance of—"

"Humanitarian—social—"

"Yes, yes, I have thought just as you do, Monsieur le curé—" and he added aside: "He is timid, we must set him at ease. The prosperity of a country, you know, depends entirely upon an active and regular intercourse."

"Intercourse! but I do not—"

"You will tell me, I know, that these superb mountains are the most difficult of all obstacles to surmount! they are the miserly guardians of their immense wealth until the day when the intelligence of man—of a man—finds means of levelling heights and filling up abysses."

Larreau was no simpleton, talking at random. He knew perfectly well that he should bewilder the priest by this somewhat pompous and confused preamble; but this result was by no means unpleasant to him. He wished, first of all, to make the abbé understand that he was a thinker, a capitalist, on whose elevated views of life he might rely. The curé, with his eyes fixed upon his interlocutor, listened in silence, probably thinking that by degrees he should comprehend his meaning. After the frivolous chatter at the breakfast table, these grave words, and the pleasing manner of the man who uttered them, had an especial charm for him. He was doubtless about to find some one with whom it would be agreeable to converse. Unfortunately the countess suddenly approached, carrying a cup of coffee, which she coquettishly presented to him.

"Very little sugar, if you please."

The lady took up the shining sugar-tongs, and began to look for a small lump in the bowl held by Mme. de Rougeon. She searched and searched—"Is not this piece too small, or how will that do? Wait, wait, we will suit you exactly."

She assumed a thousand pretty attitudes during this occupation; the pearly skin of her wrist, threaded with its blue veins, challenged the attention, and encircling its satin smoothness, gleamed a golden bracelet whose suspended trinkets tingled against the edges of the sugar basin.

Abbé Roche did not understand how so simple an act could furnish an opportunity for the display of so many subtle graces, but he was by no means impatient, and, to tell the truth, might have remained much longer as an observer of the difficulties of sweetening, without complaining.

"And you, dear papa, will you have some coffee?" asked the young wife.

"Thank you, my darling."

"Just think of it, my father cannot be persuaded to give up that horrible white cravat, which, tied in that way, makes him look like a country bailiff. For eight years, Monsieur le curé, I have suffered from the old-fashioned dress in which my father glories. At least, let me re-arrange the knot?"

She approached M. Larreau, whose face brightened till his left eye could scarcely be perceived, and with the artless manner and affected childishness of a boarding-school miss, altered the tie of the cravat, drew down the ends, thrust her slender little fingers into all the corners, retouched and patted her work, half closed her eyes that she might the better judge of its effect, then throwing her arms around her father's neck, kissed him most affectionately. "There is a greatly improved papa, isn't he, Monsieur le curé?" And she turned away.

"Isn't my little countess charming, Monsieur Roche?" said the capitalist, earnestly.

"Certainly," answered the curé, "certainly. Were you telling me that mountains were an obstacle, and that intercourse—humanitarian— I did not exactly catch your idea."

"Well, my dear curé, I have no one else in the world. You do not understand a father's feelings. I love her with my whole heart, the dear little thing.

She does just what she pleases with me. Ah! ah—my little countess! How stylish she is! What do you think of her? She has such an aristocratic appearance!"

Even the tones of his voice changed as he spoke of his daughter, and his face assumed an expression of delight.

Nothing of all this escaped the priest's attention; "Mme. de Manteigney appears to be very fond of you, Monsieur," he replied.

"Oh! you do not know her, you have merely caught a glimpse of her. My daughter is an angel!"

There was a moment's silence, during which M. Larreau looked at the priest with a defiant smile, that seemed almost a challenge.

"I do not doubt it, I do not doubt it."

"You must know that I have always lived for my wife and daughter; family affections are deeply rooted in my heart, Monsieur le curé. I have worked during my life, worked very hard; but may I be hung if I ever spent even two hours without thinking of my dear little daughter. It gives one courage, you see. The day after she was born, as I saw the little cherub moving restlessly among her wrappings, I felt that my life began to have an object, and swore to make my daughter a great lady. I have not managed my affairs badly, as you perceive; besides giving her a title, I have amassed a few crowns for her use. I am very rich, M. le curé; I do not pride myself upon it in the least; but I am very rich."

As he uttered the words, he twisted his cigar carefully between his fingers, which seemed to have grown a fourth longer.

"It must be confessed," he continued, "that she has adapted herself to circumstances wonderfully well, and does not appear to be any more inconvenienced by her countess's coronet than I am by my night-cap. If you could see her at a ball! Between ourselves there is not a duchess in the Faubourg Saint German who is a greater lady than she, and that without the slightest affectation, with perfect ease! How can I help loving her! A father's heart is very tender. And then it is my creation, my work. There, do you see her now? She has just made one of her charming puns. They are all listening, everybody around her is laughing. Ah! good, there they go again. There is more wit in her little finger than in all their brains united. They are perfect starlings: oh! I make no excuses for them. They must have shocked you at breakfast. I have a horror of this empty, noisy loquaciousness in which every one seems to make a point of saying exactly the opposite of what he thinks."

"But why should there be so much dissimulation?"

"What would you have? it is the fashion. Well! Monsieur le curé, she is no more embarrassed when, glittering with jewels, she enters a ball-room, than you see her now. My daughter amazes me. Yes, she amazes me by her style, her aristocratic bearing. And she can be so haughty when she chooses. I have sometimes heard her reprove her head coachman—she was so cutting I could hardly help embracing her on the spot. My son-in-law is not so bad, as far as he goes, but he does not come within a hundred feet of his wife. How do you like the count's appearance?"

"Very well, Monsieur, very well."

"And I don't like it at all. Yet I should wish him to be just as he is. Perhaps I will explain the reason one of these days."

Then suddenly, with an outburst of frankness and cordiality, he exclaimed: "Monsieur le curé, I tell you plainly that I am extremely pleased with you. No, don't be so modest, upon my honor I mean it. If I did not like you, I should say so, for I am as true as gold. Your face expresses integrity, and if you will allow me to say so, a great deal of intelligence."

The priest's smile had a tinge of irony. "What is his object," he thought; "for what motive is he saying all this?"

"And the deuce, my dear curé, it was God who made you so; there is no occasion for blushing. I do not know your origin, but—"

"It is a most humble one."

"Not more humble than mine, certainly—I defy you to surpass that: I am an old spout-maker." The curé made a gesture of surprise.

"Nothing else, and I am not at all ashamed of it, on the contrary. I am rich, it is true; but I have no personal graces, while you, my dear curé, have the bearing of a nobleman. You possess a famous capital in that."

Abbé Roche, vaguely understanding that the words contained something offensive, could not help blushing; perceiving it, the capitalist continued:

"Listen: each man seeks to make a mark in his own career, and dreams of success—it is a matter of necessity that it should be so."

"I think, Monsieur, that you are making sport of me."

"You have everything, I tell you, the bearing, the gestures, the grace, the dignity, everything—I will go farther, and assert that you are not in your rightful place while here."

Larreau stopped before Abbé Roche with the firmness of a prophet, and, thrusting his hands into the arm-pits of his vest, continued: "No false modesty; I know men; people do not attain my position, as you may imagine, unless they understand them thoroughly; well, you are not in your rightful place here, my dear curé, unless this parish, now so insignificant, should acquire—" he made a hem! and smiled—"should chance to acquire an importance which would render it worthy of you. You are ambitious—so much the better! I like that. It is indispensable to careers which are impeded by obstacles."

"But, Monsieur, I—"

"Nobly ambitious, that is what I mean. You feel your value, and you are right."

"Never has my conduct— You judge me without knowing me."

"Pardon me, I know what I am saying. Your glance, your face, everything about you denotes energy, a love for conflict, a contempt of difficulties. You are placed in this out-of-the-way corner for some reason of which I am ignorant, and still young, ardent and intelligent, you desire to make your way in the world and retaliate for the slight. What could be more noble and natural? I have been in your position, and that is why I know your feelings. Consider me as a sincere friend, and let us understand each other."

"You will oblige me by not adding another word," said Abbé Roche, who felt that his anger was gaining the mastery over him.

"You know, my dear friend, that I say what I think, just in this way, frankly and plainly; you must take me as I am."

"After all," said the curé to himself, "this man may be only a fool and monomaniac. What should make him think of insulting me? What wrong have I done him? Besides, perhaps I have misunderstood his meaning."

He controlled himself, and answered coldly, "Monsieur, I presume that I do not exactly comprehend you. All that I ask is that you will wait until you know me better before forming your opinion of me; I think you will then find I am perfectly well suited for my position in this parish."

"Well said, very well said, I repeat. I admire

frankness; you do not wish to leave this region. I only esteem you the more highly for it, since it is a proof of the correctness of your judgment." And, putting his arm unceremoniously within that of the priest, he continued: "Let us speak openly to each other, my dear friend. This country has a splendid future—God has bestowed royal gifts upon it. See how beautiful is the sweep of the vast horizon! Look at yonder mountains, with the silvery light upon their summits, they contain treasures which should be brought forth. These almost abandoned forests only need to be felled; these valleys are as fertile as any in the world; each of the brooks rushing into the plain has a motive power which can and ought to be made profitable. How much wealth there is lying under this virgin soil, only needing the labor of some well-supported man! In what, I ask you, is this earthly paradise inferior to all the cities among the Pyrenees and Alps, to which all Europe resorts to scatter its millions. Bagnères de Luchon, Cauterets, Uriage, Evian, Aix, Vichy?"

"Do not the places you mention possess mineral springs, whose fame—"

"Well, and Monaco, and Baden, and—besides, the mineral springs— Excuse my entering into the details at present. Do not suppose that I purchased the estate of Manteigney at random, I have always put my capital into good investments. In short, trust to me, I have entered upon a grand and beautiful scheme, and I am not the man to draw back on account of obstacles, my dear curé. In accepting this noble mission, devoting the remainder of my days to it, and introducing life, wealth, activity, industry and happiness into this deserted country, I believe that I am acting in accordance with the designs of Providence, and shall deserve the esteem of all worthy men! let us think of all this seriously. Now, what do I ask, what do I hope for from you? Sympathy, nothing more—your official, but sincere concurrence. I ask you to associate your advancement with my work, and aid it by the moral influence which is the result of your position."

"Then you ask something of me? I beg you, Monsieur, explain yourself more clearly."

"Oh! oh! I see that you are like Saint Thomas," said the capitalist, with increasing gentleness and good nature. "You wish the thing to be made perfectly plain. Do not apologize: this caution does not annoy me, my dear friend; business is business."

"So you are proposing some business matter? What is it? I am not at all familiar with such things. Speak to me simply, as you would to a child: I shall not understand you otherwise."

"The word business slipped out unintentionally. The deuce! it is a very ticklish affair," thought Larreau. "I beg you to excuse me, I never meant—it is no question of business, the affair is simply one of sympathy, good-will, active benevolence, my dear curé. It is rather difficult for me, as you can easily comprehend, to enter into all the details of this enterprise just now. Yet listen to me. The population of this country is full of faith and simplicity; it is poetic, has a tendency towards the supernatural: valuable qualities. You have perfect control over them, you know their wants, their desires. During the ten or fifteen years that you have spent here you must have extended your relations far among the mountains; the neighboring curés are your friends; in short, you have an immense moral influence. Now, it is very difficult to undertake anything in a country where one has not first won the confidence of the inhabitants. I wish for their happiness, their welfare, it is true; but they must be made to understand this, and you alone are in a position to explain everything to them. Prejudices are obstinate, habits tenacious; it is for you, my dear curé, who understand how to appeal to their minds, to present the benefits which will result from my work in a favorable light."

The priest concentrated his whole attention, in order to comprehend M. Larreau's words. In the midst of the confusion of his thoughts, he said to himself: "Perhaps, after all, his intentions are good; the poverty is very great, there must be much to be done."

"And then," continued the capitalist, "there ought not to be the least doubt of each other. Nothing can or should be attempted without the aid of religion. If you are anxious about my personal opinions, I can re-assure you, for I am a true Catholic. Progress, in her advance, must be illumed by the torch of faith. These simple words say more than a long speech. Without being what is called a devotee, I am thoroughly sincere in my belief. I practise it—as a man ought in my position; and I really think that Catholicism is the only barrier that can be opposed to the flood of wicked passions, the only barricade that protects the grand principles of social life, respect for authority and wealth."

"The love of God is higher than all that, Monsieur."

"Do I not trust in the love of God—but, pardon me the jest: I have more faith, from a practical point of view, in the fear of the devil. Look you, my dear friend; we do not win murderers by the promise of the cross of the legion of honor, but awe them by the threat of the scaffold; and when we walk at night with money on our persons, in unsafe suburbs, it is better to have a good stick in the hand than a bundle of tracts in the pocket. I speak to you frankly, for you are a man who can understand me."

Abbé Roche felt the blood flushing his brow. It seemed to him as if he had just received a blow in the face, and no longer able to control the indignation which had been too long restrained, he was about to reply as he felt, when Mme. Manteigney suddenly came tripping up.

"Well, gentlemen, have you determined to desert us? Come, we have arranged a game of cricket, and I bet against Monsieur le curé."

"I am very sorry, Madame, but they are expecting me at church, and the vesper bell will soon ring."

"Then I must not delay you; but you know that I am going to pay a visit at your house. You promised to give me a list of the poor people."

When the curé had gone, the young countess took her father's arm.

"You won't wear that ugly white cravat any more, will you, dear papa? It makes you look like your lawyer."

"Yes, countess—yes, my darling, I will give up the white cravat to please you."

"Tell me, father, what do you think of our curé?"

"Oh! my dear child, he is certainly no parvenu."

"You think so, really."

"He is extremely clever, and sees the whole bearings of any matter very clearly. He is also cautious, cold, and circumspect."

"Then he is an incomprehensible man. How did he happen to be the curé of this insignificant village?"

"There are certain occasions, my darling, in which we must recognize the finger of Providence, which prepares events and regulates means of action."

When Abbé Roche reached the end of the terrace, he turned, before proceeding on his way, and saw in the distance the father and daughter, walking side by side, and arm in arm. They looked as if they enjoyed each other's companionship. The young countess's dress, with its floating train, swept over the grass, and the fair hair and white robe made a charming contrast relieved against the green trees. The curé undoubtedly had an instinctive appreciation of colors: for he followed the countess and her father with his eyes until they disappeared behind a clump of trees. Then he continued his walk.

In the court-yard, the head coachman was examining a carriage, from which the horses had been unharnessed, and père Loursière, who had just arrived, accompanied by his daughter, and armed with his basket, was making remarks upon it. The cheese merchant bowed, on perceiving the curé. Abbé Roche, who did not particularly like the man, returned his greeting, passed him quickly, and went towards the door. Père and mère Sappey were still seated side by side before their little mats.

The good woman rose. "Monsieur le curé," said she, "have you spoken to our master and mistress about my husband's red breeches?"

"No, mère Sappey, not yet, but do not be anxious about it, the matter can probably be easily settled. Does père Loursière come here often?"

"Only too often, M. le curé, only too often! We did not see him as you might say once a year, and now he comes with his daughter—"

Abbé Roche left the château, and turned towards the village. The road was bathed in sunlight, and the little brook, which flowed beside it, babbling among the stones, had never been more merry and enticing; but the priest remained blind to all these charms. One by one Larreau's remarks returned to his memory. He thought that he discovered the meaning which had escaped him, and now found the answer he had not been able to frame before. Had not this man asked him to use his priestly authority to aid his speculations—to mingle God's name in commercial enterprises? Was not that what he had meant? He was indignant, and angrily struck with his stick the grass and flowers that bloomed beside the brook; he wished to return at once to the château, explain himself clearly, and undeceive this man, whom he had perhaps encouraged by his silence—to say to him: "I am not what you think;" then he checked himself, and with a revulsion of feeling, accused himself of putting a false interpretation upon the words of the capitalist, who seemed so kind and affable to everybody, so affectionate to the dear little countess, to whom his life was devoted. He had spoken of enterprises, schemes to be accomplished; but he had not mentioned their nature. Perhaps they might be honorable ones. He had expressed himself, it is true, in singular terms, with a double meaning; but was it not natural that he should judge of things as a man of business, a parvenu, a rich man, who could not separate the welfare of a country from its material prosperity?

At every step taken by the priest, the lizards basking on the hot stones by the roadside rushed under the grasses and glided among the shrubs. The air was filled with the cheerful hum of insects, and there was a pleasant fragrance of aromatic plants and shrubs, mingling with the distant odor from the pine trees. Under any other circumstances the good curé, as he walked along, would have been happy, and thankful to God for his pleasant lot. He would have thought of the bowl players, awaiting him after vespers on the smoothly shaven turf of the little enclosure, under the shadow of the lofty chestnut trees, of his cheerful supper afterwards, sitting in the open door-way near his flowers, while before him was the radiant majesty of the sun, sinking behind the icy mountain peaks, and of his quiet slumber, when at peace with others and himself, he went to rest after the day was over.

At that moment he was very far from such calm repose. He was endeavoring, almost obstinately, to excuse the capitalist. He only wished to remember the good words of the conversation. He saw him again, looking happy and cheerful, while his daughter coquettishly arranged his white cravat; and, led on by these memories, heard once more the sound of the bracelets striking against the sugar-bowl, and again saw the white robes sweeping over the lawn. All these recollections rapidly succeeded each other in his mind. He felt as if he had a double personality, and while Abbé Roche, curé of Grand Fort, strove to escape the remembrance of all that he had seen and heard at the château, a second self, who was no priest, but curious about novelties, ardent, free, and bold, sought to understand and recall the phantoms which the curé had just conjured up.

XI.

Abbé Roche, to dispel these preoccupied thoughts, resolved to avoid everything that might interrupt the ordinary course of his quiet life, but, by a singular fatality, which seemed as if it were the result of the malice of some fiend, almost all his sensations and ideas led him by more or less direct paths to the castle of Manteigney, to the motley world which enthroned the countess. She herself returned to his thoughts more frequently than anything else : it was incomprehensible. Did he walk through fields bathed in sunlight, some corner of the landscape recalled the color of the young wife's hair, and if to avoid it he moved on more quickly and looked up towards the sky, the trailing edge of some fleecy cloud borne along by the breeze caught his eye, and in spite of himself, he thought of the lightness of the floating, half-disordered curls that strayed over her shoulders. Everything was a pretext to remind him of her, and one detail recalling another, they grouped around each other with marvellous rapidity, and he soon perceived her whole figure, saw her move, heard her speak. It almost seemed as if every word uttered by her lips had lodged in the poor man's ears and could not be expelled. Suddenly, without apparent cause, these words would begin to reason within him with such a semblance of reality that he stopped short, startled, like a man who has been unexpectedly clapped on the shoulder. It appeared to him as if it were not one of the vague impressions whose remembrance is preserved by the mind, but the continuation of an actual fact. He heard the countess's voice, perceived its musical accents, its soft vibrating tones.

The singularity of the phenomenon to which he was unwillingly forced to yield, irritated him extremely. He was in despair at being compelled to hear, even when he did not listen. He attempted to take himself to task, and entered into a profound analysis of his sensations. What was it after all? A singular quivering of the tympanum, caused by peculiar vibrations in the air, nothing more. If the same sensations were frequently renewed, it was because, by an inexplicable but purely physical fact, the air obstinately continued to vibrate in precisely the same manner. That the result was agreeable to him, instead of being painful, was of very little importance; a skilful physician would have explained it by figures; undoubtedly it was only a scientific detail, which might be readily expressed in a formula. It was very clear that, under any circumstances, moral sympathies had nothing to do with this phenomenon. It was not the attraction of two souls mutually seeking each other. What bond could there be between the countess and himself? He did not know her well! had scarcely seen her. Thus the priest, in seeking to diminish his anxiety, and regain his usual calmness, threw himself, with singular energy, into the depths of the most radical materialism. Yet, if he shook himself free of it, with unconquerable repugnance, it was only to encounter other embarrassments which were equally annoying; for, if the ever-recurring remembrance of the countess was only a physical phenomenon, he must confess himself to be the servant, the slave of his senses, subject to their caprices, a victim of their phantasms. Never before had he been compelled to endure the insubordination and revolt of these vassals, and he felt humiliated by it. His soul must have become very weak and impotent, if it no longer had the power of self-control! He wished to sternly punish his rebellious thoughts, but how? Had he not reason to reproach himself for weaknesses and culpable negligences, which were the first cause of this insubordination?

Abbé Roche did not then know the secret of the uneasiness of which he was a victim. What, indeed, could be the cause of the pre-occupied thoughts which pursued him, irritating and humiliating him, like the buzzing and stinging of a swarm of insects, against which one can make no resistance? It was not that he feared the future: the irrevocable vows that he had pronounced were like a divine and impenetrable shield, beneath whose shelter he could live without any serious injury, and boldly front the world; but as he did not wish to pursue his study of sensations that were unworthy of closer examination, he most earnestly sought for pretexts to absent himself from the château. He called to his aid the memory of Claudius and the Rougeon family, and strove to make his confused recollections of them more distinct. He summoned them from the dark background to which they had been banished by his prejudices, and sought to give more vividness to the outline. He remembered, not without strong effort, their faces, their peculiar manners, their repulsive words; in imagination, he looked into their souls, and, utterly disgusted by the pictures he had drawn, determined to cease all intercourse with these people. He no longer said one word of the countess.

In order to convince himself even more fully, he brought forward fresh arguments: it was to be feared that a prolonged intimacy with the rich and happy of this world might divert his attention from his austere duties, and that amidst this earthly existence, this excessive luxury and comfort, he might permit himself to be drawn into habits which he could not easily shake off. Would it not be said, also, that he accepted the hospitality of the château from effeminacy and indolence, in order to escape from the hardships of his simple mode of life? What would his parishioners say, whose existence it was his duty to share? Such were the reasons he assigned. Besides, he liked to give himself curt orders, to be unhesitatingly obeyed; it was one means of proving his moral energy, which, with secret pride, he opposed to the theoretical submission of his senses. In order to excuse and convince himself, he enumerated in his thoughts all the duties imposed upon him by his ministry, the sick to be visited, the poor, the catechism—but he must have attached great importance to the necessity of ceasing all intercourse with the château, since it led him to such self-deception. Whatever might be the cause, faithful to the resolution he had formed, Abbé Roche strove with all the energy of which he was capable, to occupy his time. He did so well, he combined visits, prayers, meditation and gardening so skilfully that he was at liberty only during the two hours directly after supper, which had always been devoted to his evening walk. It was his time for thinking during a quiet ramble. The sun had set, night began to darken over the country, the women were still spinning at the thresholds of their doors, the men, seated on the stumps of pine trees, which had just been brought from the forest, smoked and talked together, and when the curé passed these worthy people, they exchanged a bow and good-evening. How many times had the priest sat down among them, taking an earnest interest in the thousand details of their monotonous, laborious family life!

Abbé Roche was now less desirous to have these meetings and conversations; he wished to be alone, and avoided the village, which had become noisy and excited. At this hour the inn, formerly so silent, became the rendezvous for the servants belonging to the château, whose Parisian gayety, wild songs, careless self-possession, red breeches, white cravats, and style peculiar to aristocratic-serving men, were beginning to attract the young peasants in the neighborhood. The curé, therefore, left his house by the side door and descended the path which winds along on the outskirts of the village, and turns to the château, or leads to the charming precincts of the deep ravine that serves as an enclosure to the manor grounds, according to whether the right or left hand turning is taken.

This solitary spot, inhabited during the day by the goats, was utterly deserted at nightfall, and Abbé Roche liked to wander there, while the stars gradually appeared in the heavens, and the sounds from the village died away. To judge only by appearances, it might be supposed that our curé was very illogical and inconsistent to walk in this direction. Yet he did so only to conquer his impressible senses more entirely; he wished to render them accustomed to remain at rest in sight of the walls which might recall the memory of the emotions that had disturbed him. He went there with his troubled thoughts, as one would take a dog out walking, whip and leash in hand.

The picturesque ravine, in whose depths the brook of Grand Fort, swollen by springs, became a little brawling torrent, contained one spot where the curé often sat. It was a sort of narrow platform, suspended, so to speak, in space, among crumbling rocks and trunks of trees, half uprooted by the wintry rains and autumnal tempests. When the moon rose there was a splendid view; on the left, a gap in the rocks revealed a portion of the valley, full of white, fleecy, motionless vapors, which resembled the depths of the ocean. Below, and nearly opposite to him, on the other side of the ravine, amid the fantastic forms of the gnarled, twisted chestnut trees, rose the old château, with its lofty towers concealed by sombre ivy, and its pointed roofs, covered with blue glittering slates that reflected the moonlight in long lines of silver. The large glass doors of the picture-gallery and dining-room, illuminated by the lamps and candles burning within, could also be plainly seen. The twinkling gleam of the cigars, moving about among the orange trees on the lawn, could also be perceived, and from time to time the laughter of the smokers, softened by distance and the murmur of the torrent, floated on the air. Often too the shadow of a woman, hooded and wrapped in a large opera-cloak, joined the gentlemen. The curé watched all this quietly, without by any movement expressing the least emotion; but bit his lips sternly, when, in the shadowy outline of the phantom, he recognized the countess.

XII.

On one of these evenings, Abbé Roche had been seated a few moments in the place I have just mentioned, listening to the music of the torrent, and looking at the château, when he suddenly heard a loud rustling in the branches a few yards below him. The cows and goats were all in their barns at that hour of the night; yet it was very strange that any one should come to take a walk in that steep place. He listened, and thought he heard two persons conversing in an undertone. Unfortunately the noise of the water prevented his distinguishing the meaning of the words. The two voices were almost equally sweet and shrill, though one was more drawling than the other. At last, either the speakers had approached nearer, or the abbé had increased his powers of hearing by the intentness with which he listened, for he distinguished the following words:

"Do you know, my little savage, that I almost lost my way in coming here? You are as familiar with every inch of the ravine as if you had browsed here like the goats; but let us stop now. How do you do this evening, my daughter? Dear me, you are in full dress!"

"So that my father asked where I was going in my Sunday clothes?"

"And what did you say to your father? He has a famous beard, that papa of yours!"

"I told him I was going to the castle, to carry some of the cheeses made from the milk of our goats, and the moss the countess had asked me to bring her to place under the fruits. It wasn't true, but he believed it, and said no more."

"You are no simpleton, are you?"

"No, indeed, Monsieur le comte."

"Take off your cap, so that I can look at your hair. How thin your arms are!"

"I am just as thin everywhere."

"But, to make amends, your eyes sparkle brightly, little one. Have people often told you that you had handsome hair?"

"To be sure, Monsieur le comte, of course they have, and it's true: my hair is still longer than this, when it isn't in braids. Shall I undo them?"

"Is all this quantity yours?"

"Whose should it be?"

"You might have bought it, for you like to be admired."

"Bought it? Is it for sale? Oh! if you want

to buy a little of mine, I should be very glad to dispose of it, for I have too much. Is it for sale, truly?"

"Certainly it is, little Velléda. Do you know how pretty you are, my dear, with your big eyes? Turn this way, so that I can look at you. Are you always as pale as you are now?"

"It isn't my fault."

"I am not scolding you, my darling. I like you just as you are: it makes your eyes seem darker, and your eyebrows too. Come and sit down by me.—Well, don't be so uneasy; I only want to kiss you. Are you not willing that the count at the château should give you a kiss?"

"Yes, Monsieur le comte, but if people knew it, they would think lightly of me, and then my father—"

"Your father, your father—he is up there in his hut. We are alone. Are you not cold with that little neck-handkerchief? It is very small, my poor child, and your neck is bare."

"Oh! I am used to the evening mists, and besides—"

"Besides what?"

"It is the most becoming one I have, the others don't suit me."

"I told you that you liked to be admired."

"And I didn't say it was not so."

"Then you are pleased when people say you are pretty, are you not?"

"That depends upon who says so."

"When it happens to be I, do you like it?"

"Yes."

"Then, you love me?"

"Yes."

"Oh Heavens! tell me why?"

"Do not hold me so close."

"It is only to keep you from falling. Tell me why do you love me? Your figure is very supple, little snake—you are like the pine trees, and the wild thyme. Do you believe in ghosts? Don't you hear voices in the darkness? Tell me whether you believe in ghosts, little girl? There, don't be frightened. Why do you love me, little witch. You came here astride of your broomstick, I know you did. Come, I love you because you are a savage, have beautiful hair, walk about barefooted, fear neither rain, wind, nor— And you, now it is your turn."

"Bless me, I don't know—because—because—you are not like other people."

"Oh! she is a flatterer already."

"Is your ring gold? and these buttons too? You have such white hands. If any one else wore a gold ring, it would be ugly; but it looks well on you: and then, when you kiss me, your mustache smells so good."

"Ah! little witch, who taught you to say all that? Faith, I would give a hundred of our dolls for you. Why do you love me?"

"You hurt me, you hold me so tight."

"Once more, why do you love me?"

"You are the count—"

"Well! you are turning your head away from the count— When I tell you to keep quiet, little wild goat?"

It was with great difficulty that Abbé Roche had kept silence during this conversation. He had listened with fixed attention and compressed lips, feeling his anger, as well as disgust and indignation, constantly increasing. Was the last of the de Manteigneys to bring nothing but trouble and wretchedness into the country? While the servants disturbed the village with their noisy songs, was the master to mislead the maidens? Had all these people determined among themselves to utterly demoralize the mountains. The priest remembered the instinctive aversion which he had felt at the first sight of this ill-formed, puny, impertinent little being; then, by a logical sequence of thought, suddenly beheld the woman who had married this baboon, and said to himself:—"She is expecting him now, and is perfectly undisturbed, poor woman!"

She appeared to be all the more pure a victim because the count's crime seemed utterly monstrous. He had a most ardent desire to anticipate divine justice, leap over the few yards that separated him from the speakers, and let the wretch feel the full weight of his stick; then, in spite of his wrath, he thought of the scandal, the sorrow that the poor young wife would feel. However guilty he might be, the count belonged to an illustrious race; he represented the noble family of the lords of Manteigney; and had he, a poor curé, sprung from nobody knew where, however just his indignation might be, the right to punish a culprit protected by long ages of nobility and grandeur? Besides, this was probably only the beginning of their intimacy. The count was thoughtless, but surely incapable of carrying matters farther and injuring a child who trusted him so frankly. His duty as a priest imposed the necessity of acting with prudence and calmness. He would find means of putting an end to the matter; he would speak to the girl, who was not unreasonable—he would do his best.

These thoughts succeeded each other in the curé's brain with wonderful rapidity. Meantime, as he heard no more, and feared to lose his self-control if he remained longer, he pushed aside the branches that surrounded him, and forcing a passage, regained the narrow path by which he had come. As the brushwood rustled under his feet, he heard the count's voice behind him, saying in a suppressed tone:—"Who is there—zounds! who is there?"

Abbé Roche followed the path, not without some difficulty, for as he advanced among the trees, the darkness increased, and the way became more intricate. At last, turning to the left, he found himself in the road that led to the village. He had not advanced thirty paces, when he saw something white, under the shadow of the trees, which chanced to attract his attention. He approached it, and found himself face to face with père Loursière's daughter, pressing closely against the trunk of a chestnut tree, and staring at him with her large, wide open eyes.

At the noise made by the curé, she had left the count, and taking the shortest way, climbing the steep slope like a roe, posted herself on the side of the road, very sure that whoever had interrupted them must pass that way to return to the village, and she might recognize him without being seen. Unfortunately, the curé had excellent eyes.

"What! is that you, Monsieur le curé?"

"Yes, it is I. Where did you come from at this hour?—where did you come from?"

"I came from beyond the path, down below, and I am going directly home—it is late."

They walked on for a moment without uttering a word. Abbé Roche felt that he was too deeply moved, and wished to calm himself before speaking. He had always loved the poor child on account of her delicate health and strange, pallid countenance, which resembled that of the mother who had died in giving her birth.

The priest's voice at first had been stern and severe; he continued in a mild, sad tone:

"You are forgetting God, my child."

"But, Monsieur le curé, I came from the château—on account of the cheeses."

"Do not tell a lie, unhappy girl! I tell you that you are forgetting God, who remembers and sees you. You know what I mean: we will speak of it at some future time. Go home to the father who is waiting for you—this is your way."

And the curé pointed to the path, bordered with

pine trees, that turned in another direction, a few paces beyond.

"But, Monsieur le curé, I was coming from the château."

"Do not tell a lie! Return to your father's house, be quick; you must not be found here at this hour, and I hear some one coming this way. Make haste."

They did indeed hear the footsteps of two men, who were coming from the village. Doubtless the turn in the road had deadened the sound of their steps, and Abbé Roche supposed them to be farther away than they really were, for they appeared almost immediately, arm in arm, staggering from side to side.

"Good-evening, Monsieur le curé," said père Sappey, "a very good-evening to you," and he added, with a singularly embarrassed manner, turning to his companion, who was one of the count's grooms:—"This is my friend, François; he offered to treat me, and now we are going back to the château. But who is that yonder running into the path edged with fir trees, Monsieur le curé!—I don't see double yet—"

"Go home, and go to bed, père Sappey, you need to do so, and your wife is waiting for you."

"But no, I don't see double. That is certainly Marie, Loursière's daughter. Oh! so you no longer say good-evening to people? Where did she come from at this hour, M. le curé? How late young people go to bed now?"

"I came from the castle," cried the young girl, without turning.

"Go home, you are late," said Abbé Roche in a curt tone, "and you, Sappey, had better do the same."

"I am not sleepy, Monsieur le curé," replied the peasant, smiling in the usual manner of happy drunkards. "Isn't that so, François, we're not sleepy."

"Perhaps Monsieur le curé doesn't care to sleep any more than we do," answered the groom, looking in the direction in which the young girl had disappeared.

"The scoundrels!" he murmured, clenching his fists, "the servant is worthy of the master."

And he moved quickly away.

XIII.

Abbé Roche slept but very little that night; he still heard the stupid laughter of the two drunken men. It was the first time that he had encountered such insolence in his parish, and his blood boiled in spite of himself. He also heard M. de Manteigney's shrill voice addressing Loursière's daughter! the scene in the ravine was painted by his imagination with vivid reality. He saw the puny little nobleman clasping the poor young girl in his arms, gazing at her with mocking, bold, insolent looks. And while the priest vainly closed his eyes that he might not see, the emotions conquered in silence once more awoke within him. He thought of the tender affections which still sometimes appeared to him as most enchanting to contemplate, sublime, purified by the union of souls, and the benediction of God. The count seemed still more repulsive to him! his feelings were not worthy the name of love. God would not permit the word to be sullied by being put to such a use. What was it but mere sensuality, in which the heart has no share.

Had vice then a positive charm for certain characters? He remembered the singular books, written in graphic style, in Latin, which had been put before him on leaving the university, and had left no more visible trace on his pure, upright soul than some passing nightmare does upon the mind. Had these books, filled with all the immorality of the human soul, which might have passed for the secret registers of the police in Sodom, any foundation in reality? Were they a faithful mirror in which certain men might recognize themselves? What was there lacking in the life of this infatuated count? He had no toil or suffering. Was not his task the easiest in the world? To be virtuous without effort or difficulty; to walk uprightly in the pleasant path which God made smooth before him, doubtless that it might be more easy for him to guard the sacred virtues of which his birth made him the depository.

The poor curé excused vice among the wretched of the world; but his pure heart could not understand it in this privileged nobleman, who had family ties, could enjoy all legitimate pleasures, and was so richly gifted that, having nothing to desire, he was shielded from the human temptations which corrupt and destroy—in this gentleman who, in return for these benefits, had only to endure the delightful burden of gratitude to God. Must he not be a monster, and what could have been the design of Providence in uniting, with indissoluble bonds, such a being to that poor wife? How she must have suffered—how she must still suffer! Was not her apparent frivolity, her incomprehensible coquetry, the extravagance of her dress, a mere mask, beneath which she strove to conceal the anguish of her heart?

How clearly everything was now explained! The peculiar charm of her person was only that of grief. Instinctively he had formed a correct judgment of her. She sought to divert her thoughts; she was a victim. Had she been a hundred times more coquettish and worldly, the tones of her voice, the dreamy expression of her glance, dimmed by sorrow, were sufficient to reveal her tender, suffering soul. She was not only unhappy, but had also the rare virtue of concealing her grief; doubtless she did not wish the world to despise the man whose name she bore, she desired to save the honor of the de Manteigneys, and feigned these careless manners to avert suspicion. He understood her now. All was explained, even to the caresses lavished upon her father. The poor, deserted, insulted wife, scorned by this misshapen fiend, took refuge in filial love. Who among the brainless fools that surrounded her could sustain her by good counsel, cheer her with a kindly word? "How many martyrs there are in this world whom only God knows!" added the priest, clasping his hands.

As he yielded more and more to the current of these thoughts, a feeling of the most ardent compassion and charity completely overpowered him. He shuddered in spite of himself.

"Why should God have placed me in the path of this suffering soul?" said he to himself; "why should He have permitted me to perceive its agony? why should He have caused me to experience, at the first sight of this unhappy woman, such an extraordinary sympathy that I was terrified by it?"

The priest now dared to confess to himself the deep agitation that he had felt. It no longer seemed to him a mere physical sensation, for which a learned man could have given the formula, it was the emotion of two souls that God wished to bring together.

Abbé Roche opened his window and inhaled the morning air. All around him was pure and fresh. The birds were singing in the gigantic chestnut tree that overhung the porch; the sun was dispelling the lingering mists of night, and making the dew-drops trickling from the petals of the flowers that filled his garden sparkle in its rays. Among the various sounds of the morning might be distinguished the sheep-bells, whose silvery notes rang from the distance. It seemed like a promise—a hope. Poor woman! Was not the thought of her still more sorrowful, amid these tranquil, peaceful scenes?

He was in the midst of these reflections when he perceived Mme. de Manteigney herself, on the other side of the little square, accompanied by two children, who were eagerly devouring a large slice of brown bread. The young wife wore an extremely cool and pretty morning dress. Her head was enveloped in a coquettish little hood, made of a sort of white, woolly lace, through whose meshes a narrow blue ribbon was carelessly twisted, as if to form a frame for her beautiful face, glowing from exposure to the morning air, while her large black eyes, sparkling amidst the white folds, seemed to warm the heart in spite of the intervening distance.

When within a few paces of the house, she looked up, and smiled as she saw Abbé Roche.

" You see, Monsieur le curé, I have made friends on the way, these are two of your parishioners. Don't you want to be my friend ?—tell me, cherry cheeks ? "

So saying, she patted the neck of one of the children, who was silently giggling behind his slice of bread.

" Are you not astonished to see me out walking so early in the morning Monsieur le curé ? "

" It is a quarter of ten, Madame," said Abbé Roche.

" What ! ten o'clock already ! Well, I sent word to Mlle. de Rougeon, who wished to come and visit you with me, and was told that she was not up yet. So I boldly set out all alone."

While she said these words, the priest gazed earnestly into her face, trying to detect in some feature of her countenance the signs of the deep grief to which he believed her a prey.

" Are people admitted to your house, Monsieur le curé ? I have something to say—"

" Good Heavens ! what is the unhappy woman going to confide to me ? " murmured the worthy priest.

" You promised to tell me about your poor people. They shall be mine. Oh ! I wish to do good : I am anxious to perform deeds of charity, I shall go and visit my protégés to-morrow, and carry them a quantity of nice things, in spite of the bad roads. You do not know me; I have a great deal of energy when I undertake anything. Besides, the doctor told me that I needed exercise. Oh! how pretty your house is, my dear curé! How happy you must be here! It is so quiet, simple, and pleasant—and these flowers around the window! This is just what I like, what I have always dreamed of; a little retreat, a hermitage, silence, solitude, and wall flowers. Would you believe that they refused to let me have one poor little pot of wall-flowers on my window at the château? I have such simple tastes, my dear curé, I believe I was born to be a shepherdess. Don't you believe me?"

"Can she confess her sadness more clearly, in spite of her assumed gayety?" thought Abbé Roche, and added, not without involuntary emotion, "What could make you suppose that I do not believe you? Words, I know, are often deceitful: the soul has its secrets. A smile on the lips may at first mislead, but—"

"I was sure," said the countess to herself, "that my curé had some terrible wound in his heart: I must not alarm him about it. By the way, I haven't told you that my white donkey is coming, the donkey that papa gave me to ride. I remember, now, that I did speak to you about it, only I have changed the color of the rosettes, they are to be crimson. What do you think of it?"

"I think that crimson rosettes will be very pretty, Madame."

"Won't it be charming?"

She clapped her hands, and her eyes sparkled as if they were speaking of some very important matter.

The curé's clear understanding of the case was beginning to get cloudy again. It was in vain that he watched her, with the most earnest attention; her gayety was not feigned, or else she was impenetrable.

Was it possible that so young a woman could have strength and skill to dissemble her feelings so perfectly? Perhaps, after all, her unworthy husband had had the infernal art to deceive her concerning his conduct until now; perhaps she was ignorant of the character of this accomplished rake. He now had only a partial belief in the utter wretchedness of the countess, and yet he felt his sympathy increasing as the idea which he fancied had given it birth lost its reality. Must not this poor child be very innocent to be so deceived, and were not her jests, artlessness, and trifling conversation a most convincing proof of her extreme candor?

"You know," she continued, "I should like to take my poor people some bottles of nice Bordeaux wine, tempting porridge, or sometimes a cutlet. All these things will be very difficult to transport, and very heavy to Sophie."

"Who is Sophie?"

"My white donkey—she is already christened." The priest could not help smiling. "You think me very frivolous, don't you? Do not apologize, I read it in your eyes, and am not surprised; but when you know me better you will find that, on the contrary, there is no one more serious. Oh! if you want a frivolous person, one who is really so, you should see Mlle. de Rougeon, with her affected air, her extravagant conversation. She is a person who can be read at the first glance."

"The young girl is undoubtedly a little—"

"A little! Oh! I protest against your, *a little.* My dear curé, say that she is remarkably so. She is unusually, unpardonably so. A little! oh! for instance!—but I have interrupted you; excuse me. She is a little, you said—a little what?"

"A little—what shall I say?"

"Ha! ha! ha! that is capital."

"What is capital?"

"Excellent! excellent! It is exactly so, she is much too—*what shall I say?* She sacrifices everything to *what shall I say.* Take away her *what shall I say*, and what remains—a doll, a pair of nippers."

"Indeed, countess, I—"

"You will be surprised, but I cannot endure her, nor her father either. That man is as irritating as a gutter."

"Oh! oh! that is slander," said Abbé Roche—who in his heart was pleased with her severity—"but why do you say as a gutter," he continued with some little hesitation.

"Oh! so everything must be explained to you!—Well, a gutter when it rains, a gutter that is always dripping, tic toc, tic toc. That is easily understood. M. de Rougeon reminds me of a walking bolster, don't you agree with me? As to his wife—"

"Mme. de Rougeon is very agreeable, she seems so amiable, so—"

"She? she is like a lemon under a peach skin."

"A lemon! you mean that she has a sour disposition?"

"Mme. de Rougeon amiable! If that woman should spit into the Seine, it would turn to lemonade, and her daughter is just like her, that is my opinion. Do you think me spiteful? Confess that you do."

"Rather severe," said the priest, with a slight smile. In fact he did not consider her spiteful. The prattle which a week ago had seemed absurd and incomprehensible, now appeared full of grace and ingenuity. He found a peculiar charm in this piquant irony, exaggerated though it was; there was an attraction in its childish candor; then she accompanied her jests with such pretty gestures, emphasized her words with such bewitching little grimaces! He listened to her with his eyes. How could he censure words that increased her beauty? "You see, my dear curé, I cannot approve—perhaps I am a little too strict, but that is my disposition—I cannot approve of young girls wearing rouge. If you had seen her at the last naval ball, it was enough to make one cry out. And such a dress! A yard of gauze, and a rose bud! It is no use to say that sailors are never surprised at any thing because they travel about so much; I assure you that the little simpleton made quite a sensation. By the way, I can show her to you in her costume."

"Oh! Madame," exclaimed the priest.

"It is only a drawing of the dress, I mean to show you. The illustrated papers all copied it."

"Oh! good Heavens."

"You are amazed, are you not? But I am not exaggerating."

Abbé Roche's face did, in truth, express the utmost astonishment.

"I pray Heaven, dear lady," said he, "that there may be some little exaggeration in your words, for I cannot believe that any young girl, in the midst of a civilized population, would appear in public in the repulsive costume you have just described."

"Ah! repulsive is just the word. She was so thin, her garments were so scanty, she looked so wooden, so *what shall I say!* Ha! ha! ha!"

"But the rouge, I don't understand the rouge; such things seem like the customs of savages! I know that it used to be done; but that is no reason—"

"That is what I always say; it is like savages. To daub one's cheeks with rouge till one looks like a post-man behind time, is absurd. The old bundles may do it, I can understand that."

"What old bundles?"

"Why, yes, I call them old bundles: Mme. de Vautin, the baroness de Fernac, the fat duchess of Blanmon. At that age, coquetry becomes a mad struggle—a matter of life and death."

The priest opened his eyes; he was bewildered, uneasy, charmed, terrified by these fire-works.

"Ah! well, they do as they like; I can pardon them. Dear me! who knows whether, if I were in the place of those old warriors, I might not do the same. Ha! ha! ha! In life, one must weigh the pros and cons of everything; and not do to others what one would not wish others—isn't it so, M. le curé?"

So saying, the countess looked around the apartment through her eye-glass, rose unceremoniously to examine something more closely, and then suddenly sat down again, exclaiming: "Do you know that you have a beautiful crucifix; is it plaster?"

"No, Madame, it is a fine carving on ivory."

"You should say magnificent; it is a work of art. But the velvet and frame ought to be renewed; there is a piece broken. I have been searching, for more than a year, in every corner of Paris to find one like it. Now, my dear curé, to return to what we were saying, do not suppose that I am intolerant, and condemn society from the summit of my little pedestal; it is not so, I am really very indulgent—I, too, have my weaknesses, and am no better than any one else. I am well aware that a woman who goes into society must follow the fashions, and adapt herself to customs. It is the excess, the abuse of these things, that I condemn. Dear me! I have worn rouge myself once or twice for amusement. Now a tinge of black, under the eyes and in the eyebrows, harms no one, and forms a part of one's dress; it is like a sip of Bordeaux when one is tired, it gives expression to the countenance."

"You are very indulgent to—"

"To myself? You are sarcastic, Monsieur le curé."

"What! to yourself!"

"You are jesting, probably; I suppose you saw at once that I pencilled my eyes! Oh! I don't deny it. I put a little brown there in the corner, and on the lashes, too, and then I stump them all around.

What would you have? it is the custom;—but you have undoubtedly noticed it, it's plain enough."

Abbé Roche could not restrain an exclamation of surprise. He stood motionless with astonishment, with fixed eyes and parted lips, and instinctively clasped his hands. It was not indignation that he felt, nor the pious anger of the priest, against the guilty follies of the sinner, but the sorrowful surprise of a man who sees a beautiful dream disappear. The angel had false wings! The touching expression of the glance that agitated him, in which he had fancied he could read the emotions of a pure and delicate soul, was the work of artifice! Was there naught but falsehood and trickery in the world of which he now caught a glimpse for the first time? And yet he clung to the vanished illusion, and said to himself: "She yields to the follies of society, she may perhaps change the expression of her eyes, but her gestures, her voice, with its musical tones, are her own; the charming artlessness of her conversation—"

"You think me a coquette, and it grieves you," said the countess, who had murmured in an undertone: "How strangely the good curé looks at me! He makes me blush under his grave glance. How singular it is. Poor curé! It is really very odd."

She hastily drew off her glove of undressed kid, which was somewhat too large for her, and looking at the rosy, polished nails to conceal the smile that flickered around her lips: "Do you think me a flirt?" she continued, with such satirical humility, such evident impenitence, that she seemed to add: "Confess that I have good reason to be!"

All these subtle meanings escaped the curé, or rather he yielded to their charm without understanding or explaining it.

"I think all such things very wrong," said he at last, with evident effort.

"You are right, M. le curé, strike, oh! strike without fear. I do not resist your blows, but you do not know how hard it is to escape the infection."

"Oh! undoubtedly you would not have done all this of your own free will, of course not. You have too noble a soul, for—This ink, these paints—all this exceeds the bounds of the imagination—"

He was in torture, for even while condemning these miserable artifices, he could not help looking at the face of the young wife, and confessing that the result was extremely pretty.

"You would never have thought of these things if other young women around you—silly, thoughtless—"

"Certainly not. I think I have already told you so: if I followed only my own tastes, my own impulses, I should live—I am not jesting, I should live in a desert, and wear a dress that cost fifteen cents a yard! I have seen lovely ones. I should like to have it fit well, that is all. People think that we are amused because we go a great deal into society; they are wonderfully mistaken, I assure you. Oh, dear! these pleasures are very empty, Monsieur le curé."

"Yes, yes, that is true," cried the priest, with sudden animation.

The countess's remark had cheered his heart, it was a relief to him. She was only thoughtless, carried away by excitement and the example of others.

"What would I not have given," continued Mme. de Manteigney, gazing at the ceiling with a heavy sigh, "what would I not have often given, to remain at home by my fireside, and not put on the uniform of a fashionable woman."

"How could it be otherwise? However powerful may be the whirlpool that attracts it, the soul sometimes desires to reflect, to look within itself, and think of its destiny. Then all these false pleasures become insipid and pitiful."

"That is not all: toilettes are not always successful. At the last moment the waist does not fit, the hair-dressing is a failure, or one's eyes are red on account of a cold in the head, which came on the very morning on leaving the church after mass, etc., etc."

"Those are very trifling annoyances."

"Ah! you can talk at your ease, my dear curé, you who live very quietly under the snow, before a nice little fire, while we are running all over Paris to keep up our acquaintances. You do not understand this business: it is terribly hard, sometimes! 'You know, my dear, that we are to go to Mme. de Blaiserne's to-morrow,' says my husband. 'Oh, dear! we must, we really must, we have not been there this winter.'—'You have not forgotten the prefect's to-night, I hope, my darling.'—'Oh! papa, not the prefect's!'—'You know, my dear, that it is absolutely necessary. If it were not for this question about the gas, you may be sure that I would not tease you; but just as the contract is about to be signed, we can't. Oh! so you are very unwilling. Why, by the time you arrive, every one will be going away, they won't stay to be obliged to mount on the arm-chairs.' Naturally I swallow the prefect."

"What! are your father and the count the first to lead you into these gayeties, poor lady?"

"You do not understand men, my dear curé? Suppose I should tell you that if it had not been for papa and my husband I should never have dyed my hair, never! I wept before I decided to do it. Ah! I wept bitterly. You may think I am jesting, but indeed I should never have determined upon it, if I had been left to myself."

"You dye your hair! What—what do you mean? Why should you dye your hair? Can people really color it? Are you speaking seriously? Poor young wife, poor, hapless young wife! What could be their object?"

"The object! the object!—they thought that it

would be becoming to me, and besides, it is the fashion. Papa said to me: 'My dear child, you must not be odd; as all the ladies dye their hair. Besides, you will be perfectly charming!' And, indeed, it is extremely pretty, but that is not the question. My husband added: 'My dear, you have the prudish notions of a little shop girl. Mme. de Blaiserne has worn golden hair since day before yesterday—it is beautiful. Try it, you will be lovely!' Yet still I wept."

"Ah! good Heavens, and they insisted?"

"Yes, yes, they insisted. It was all in vain that I said to them: Suppose my hair should be burnt by those horrible chemicals!"

"They answered: 'It is impossible.'"

"But you resisted—you did not yield—"

"It must be confessed that I yielded, since my hair is now yellow as corn, and when a child, it was black as a raven's wing."

"What! this hair—"

"It is mine. Ah! I won't exaggerate, the front hair is mine. As to the back, I will say nothing about it; but surely, M. le curé, you must be aware that no woman in the world ever had hair enough to make such a monument as the one which now has the honor to present itself to your gaze."

As she uttered the words, she turned so as to show the back of her head, with a gesture of mingled coquetry and artlessness that was irresistibly charming.

"You think my chignon must be heavy, because it is so large, but it is only puffed--feel it yourself. Nothing could be lighter or more convenient. It is hung on the foot of my bed at night, and found perfectly uninjured in the morning. This is not a mere matter of vanity, I wear it for comfort. Tell me, now, my good M. le curé, honestly, didn't you know that my hair was dyed?"

"I? Heaven forbid!"

"What! didn't you see it at once? It is no difficult matter; false blondes can be detected without spectacles. There is always something peculiar in the color of the hair, something not natural—and it is just that very thing which gives the charm."

Abbé Roche could not help shuddering, and unconsciously cast down his eyes. He felt the depths of mingled truth and sickly sentimentality contained in the last remark, which seemed to have a special application to himself.

"But I am chattering, chattering. Why do you allow me to run on in this way? Let us return to our poor people, for I came here expressly to talk about them. Dear me! how beautiful that crucifix is! To what century does it belong? You do not know? That does not prevent its being magnificent. If I have a passion, it is for relics; oh! how I search for curiosities! I go without eating or drinking while in pursuit of them. You don't wish to dispose of this crucifix, I suppose?"

"No, Madame," replied the curé, "certainly not."

"Excuse me; I did not know that it was a souvenir;" and however curious she might be to hear more, she now assumed an air of the utmost indifference.

"It is a gift that I received long ago, and still cherish, although I never knew the name of the person who sent it to me."

"Oh, indeed! that is very strange."

"It is the very singularity that makes me love the crucifix. I received it in the evening before my ordination, twenty years ago, and have never been separated from it since that time. The memory of a friend is always precious, even when he does not make himself known."

"You are right. Ah! it is a most exquisite carving," and as the priest seemed determined to say nothing more, she added : " Well, good-bye, my dear curé. You know that I love you with all my heart. I confessed it the other day before all the company."

Abbé Roche tried to smile at this jest, but strive as he would, could not succeed. The gay young countess had risen, and was already in the garden, while the sweeping train of her dress still filled the doorway and kept the priest a prisoner.

" So you are not accustomed to receive such declarations as I have just made ? It seems to annoy you ?—Will you allow me to gather a little rose-bud for you ? My husband will not be jealous of my affection. No, the count is not jealous—I may take this rose too, may I not, M. le curé ? "

I do not know what thought passed through her mind, but she blushed, and turning towards the priest, said, laughing in a very peculiar manner, " I love my husband too much."

She had pronounced the last words in a singular tone. They revealed an emotion totally at variance with the rest of the conversation.

" Farewell ! Monsieur le curé."

" Farewell ! Madame."

With her customary ease of manner, she held out her little ungloved hand to the priest, as if it were the most natural thing in the world. Perhaps in a Parisian drawing-room she might have hesitated to extend it to her curé ; but Abbé Roche was to her simply a mountaineer, a plain and simple man, a stranger to the customs of society, ignorant of the thousand details of etiquette. Yet this noble savage had the bearing of a gentleman, and then—and then it amused her. Supposing that the priest had not observed her gesture, she extended her hand still farther, so that he was forced either to accept or refuse it decidedly.

How many varied feelings can pass through a man's brain in one or two seconds ! He wished to appear as if he did not see the motion, and trembled like a child at the trifling familiarity which could have no other meaning than mere civility. At last it seemed to him cowardly to hesitate longer, and he firmly took in his large hand the little rosy, half-closed one that was still outstretched like a mendicant's.

He felt the gentle warmth of the soft, satin-smooth skin pervade his whole frame. He dared not press it, and his own inaction rendered the light clasp of the girlish hand so strangely charming, doubly alluring. At that moment the breakfast-bell at the château was heard in the distance. The countess turned to raise the sweeping folds of her long dress, and hastily crossed the little square. Abbé Roche re-entered his room, closed the door, and watched her through his narrow window-panes.

"Poor woman!" said he. "Does God command me to watch over her, or never to see her again!"

She had disappeared. The curé turned towards the crucifix hanging on the wall, and drawing up a straw chair, knelt before it. His prayer must have been a fervent one, for when he rose, it was with a colorless face, tearful eyes, and trembling hands.

XIV.

Two or three days after the events related in the preceding chapter, the curé of Grand Fort was returning from père Loursière's hut, after a long conversation with his daughter, and had entered the path leading to the village, when he perceived through the trees Claudius standing upon the threshold of a cottage. Undoubtedly the priest, who was walking on with hasty strides, had been heard, for the gallant viscount called gayly:

"Is it you, my dear M. le curé! what a piece of

good-luck to meet you here! You are a great stranger; you never come to the castle now, and are not to be found anywhere. I have just been to your house. Let us go back to the village together, if agreeable to you."

Then turning to the two women with whom he had been talking, he added: "Good-bye, my friends, till we meet again one of these days. You do not regret it, I hope? Don't forget what I told you; all the plates and dishes you find, which have on the bottom a figure, a sketch, no matter what, I will buy of you—I like the oldest best. Does that make you laugh? Well, good-bye! I shall soon come this way again."

And he took the curé's arm without farther ceremony.

"You are surprised, are you not, to see me collecting these old bits of china. I am a lover of antiques, and am gathering the relics of the past; the china of the last century, in particular, is extremely interesting to me. All these things have no real value, and I am perhaps rather foolish; but what does it matter, since it amuses me. Every one takes his pleasure where he—"

"Certainly, Monsieur."

"It is a very innocent mania, isn't it?"

"One that injures no one."

And as Abbé Roche, somewhat embarrassed by the young man's arm, whose light pressure he felt upon his own, looked at the glittering object Claudius held in his hand, the latter remarked: "You do not suspect what this is, I am sure. It's an old silver-gilt cross, which yonder good woman has just given me. Oh! I arranged matters capitally, gave them enough to buy two others, perfectly new, and much more fashionable than this, which is as old as the poles, worn out, defaced, tarnished. I had some difficulty in obtaining it, however. I should not care for it, otherwise, but I have my mania. Ha! ha! ha!"

"And what do you want to do with it? Why did you tempt the woman? On our mountains, these crosses are heir-looms, transmitted from one generation to another. She did wrong to give it up, it was a wicked action."

As he uttered these words, the priest withdrew his arm so decidedly that Claudius dared not take it again.

"Come, Monsieur le curé, be indulgent: all women are a little coquettish, whether they live on the mountains or in the valleys. Now this one wants to be in the fashion. Dear me, isn't that perfectly natural! Tastes and ideas change, traditions fade, and are replaced by others. It is very true that all social transformations have their inconveniences, which are very great when viewed separately, but disappear if considered as a whole."

"I do not understand what connection there is between this woman's cross and social transformations."

"Ah! my dear Monsieur le curé, we are alone together. Don't deny what is undeniable. You belong to an extremely powerful political party, I grant, but—"

"I? I belong to a political party?"

"I do not reproach you; you are defending a great and beautiful cause, I am first to recognize it; only, instead of denying modern progress, and opposing the necessary transformation which ideas and tastes undergo, imitate the sensible and liberal portion of the French clergy, who openly accept these new tendencies and take the lead of the movement in order to control it. Does not this indicate great intelligence? Excuse my speaking to you so frankly, but M. Larreau, who, be it said, has great experience in men, esteems you very highly, and I share his opinion, M. le curé. He has spoken to me about the clearness of your views, the intelligence and breadth of your ideas. In short, you have completely won his heart."

"But I never said more than two or three consecutive words to him."

"One would have been sufficient; a man's intelligence can be determined by a single word. Now, as you so justly remarked, we are in a period of social transformation."

"I said no such thing, quite the contrary."

"We mutually agreed, I meant to say, that society was undergoing a change; but what is there alarming, I ask you, in these ideas of liberty, well-being, free intercourse, equality? The humble in station now desire to gain a footing in the world; ambition, ardor, a thirst for improvement, are spreading, filtering, penetrating. Dare you conscientiously affirm that these things are not beneficial!"

"I should like to believe that things are as you say. It seems to me that all depends upon the means employed to attain this object, which—"

"This object, why, it is the Christian aim! Let us look at these things from a broad stand-point, without any private jealousies or the petty meannesses with which all political parties are infected. What is the actual democratic movement? It is Christianity, which, too long suffocated by the sombre and violent Catholicism of the Middle Ages, and the pompous and aristocratic forms of the succeeding centuries, comes forth from silence and oblivion to unfold its holy wings which will overshadow the world. It is the continuation and completion of Christ's work. I should not speak in this way to every one, but these are my real thoughts. Let privileged classes disappear; let the differences of caste crumble and fall to dust; let all men approach and look into each other's faces without distrust; let constraint and servitude be replaced by the free range of human faculties, and I shall indeed thank Heaven. Riches and noble birth have too long obtained all privileges. Make way for labor and intellect! These few words describe modern progress, and may I be hung if it does not contain the very essence of Christianity!"

"All that you have just said is beautiful, Monsieur, truly beautiful," said the abbé, with sparkling eyes.

"Yes, Monsieur le curé, I repeat it, make way for intelligence and individual capacity!"

"And honesty, you should add."

"Wherefore? Rest assured that sensible people have too good an understanding not to be honest. They would remodel the laws rather than not be in harmony with them."

While engaged in this conversation, they had come in sight of the curé's house, whose green shutters and red roof appeared round a turn in the road.

"My dear M. le curé," said Claudius, "is there any objection to my visiting your church?"

"None whatever, God's house is open to all."

"To my great regret, I have been absent at mass for two successive Sundays, and therefore know nothing of your temple except the outside, which seems to be rather plain."

"The interior is not much more elegant; but the Lord is satisfied with it. You shall judge for yourself."

They crossed the square, and turned towards the porch.

"It would be so easy for you to obtain funds to restore this edifice," said Claudius. "You would be assisted with the greatest alacrity, M. le curé, but," he added, smiling, "if you wish to do anything for your church, you must bestir yourself a little, draw up a petition and obtain subscribers, organize a lottery, devise something. That is what all curés do under similar circumstances."

"I have very little taste for such things. Others undoubtedly have excellent reasons for their actions, but—"

"The count would devote himself to the matter; M. Larreau, too, would make great efforts. Follow my advice, and take advantage of the opportunity!" Abbé Roche turned the key in the lock, and pushed the little worm-eaten door, saying, "Enter, if you please."

Claudius hastily put on his eye-glasses and looked around him. Doubtless the somewhat desolate aspect of the humble church, with the beams of its roof blackened by time, covered with spiders' webs, and strewn with swallows' nests, did not inspire him with very profound reverence; for he continued to speak in the same loud tone:

"You are not rich, Monsieur le curé, not rich, not rich!"

And he looked around, above and below, like an auctioneer taking an inventory, while tapping lightly on the holy-water basin, the ancient benches, and the baptismal font.

On passing a dark corner near the confessional, where all sorts of rubbish, old candlesticks, old ladders, and old ropes used by the slaters in repairing the belfry, were thrown, Claudius suddenly stopped, and standing on tip-toe, drew out a fragment of carved wood, covered with a thick layer of dust and dirt. Removing his glove, he breathed upon it, wiped it, scraped it with his nail, and thus laid bare a little corner, which he examined with the utmost care.

The fragment represented a naked limb, half concealed by flowing drapery. The viscount mounted upon a stool that chanced to be near, and discovered four or five more pieces, rendered absolutely shapeless by the immense quantity of dirt that covered them. After examining the bits, which appeared to fit into each other, and form a perfect whole, he exclaimed: "Phew! my dear Monsieur le curé, your church is certainly by no means wealthy."

"It is very well suited to our wants."

"You have no china, no old dishes! I am always interested in my mania, you know."

Walking up the nave, he passed before the high altar with a careless bow, and began to rummage behind it.

"Why, your vases are absurd, and your candlesticks frightful. Your painted windows—no windows! You don't happen to have any lace, old bits of lace?"

"What do you mean by lace?"

"It would take too long to explain. Have you any curtains—old curtains, or altar cloths?—Your Sunday robe, what is that?"

"Perhaps it would be more becoming to leave the church before talking about such matters."

"You are right; besides, I have seen everything."

Then with the utmost frankness and cordiality, he continued:

"Will you permit me to give your church a little present, M. le curé? A bas-relief, for instance, to make the utter nakedness of the walls striking. I don't see why the Lord's house should not be ornamented, and agreeable to the eyes, and besides, the sight of works of art is a help to moral education. I am going directly back to Paris, and will send you one of the religious carvings which are executed there with so much skill. They are neither too rude nor too elaborate; it will be just the thing, and can be kept in order very easily. All that is required is a dusting with a feather-brush every Sunday morning."

"You are very kind, Monsieur. I thank you, but really I do not know whether I ought—"

"Accept it in the name of your parishioners—you will really afford me great pleasure; besides, if the weight of gratitude— Well, I'll tell you, let us make an exchange, gift for gift. And," he added, laughing good-naturedly, "give me the broken statue I left on the bench—I can propose nothing better."

"I understand the delicacy of your suggestion, Monsieur, and, although I should have no right to dispose of anything that belonged to the church—"

"Oh! I beg a thousand pardons, M. le curé, I only asked for those shapeless fragments to—"

"Take them, then, if they can afford you any pleasure. The rubbish has no sort of value; it should have been thrown away long ago; I do not understand why it still remains here."

"I accept them with thanks. Ha! ha! ha! People will laugh at me, but I can't help it, I always admire such odd trash."

So saying, he put two or three pieces into his pocket, wrapped the others in his handkerchief, and moved towards the door.

"Oh! I was forgetting to take the measure. The best place for the carving would be yonder, opposite to the pulpit, between those two pillars, wouldn't it? The space is rather more than two yards."

"Then you are determined to send it?"

"Why should I deprive myself of a pleasure? Farewell! my dear curé."

"Farewell! Monsieur."

"We ought not to judge people hastily," thought Abbé Roche when he found himself alone. "Yet that is a man of whom I had no pleasant impression."

XV.

In the meantime the capitalist, Larreau, was not idle, but always moving about, busily occupied, dressed in his gray hat and huge white waistcoat, which might be perceived at a long distance. He traversed the mountains on foot, unceremoniously entering all the cottages, caressing the children, smiling at the women, and familiarly tapping the shoulders of the men, who were completely fascinated by his glittering ornaments, affable manners, and immense wealth which the whole country knew he possessed. Besides, M. Larreau had all the qualities necessary to please: he was tall, stout, florid, smiling, well shaven, and at first sight seemed like a father coming to console his children. In the eyes of the peasants, his size and assurance made him appear like a true lord of Manteigney, much to the disadvantage of his son-in-law, whose contemptuous bearing, narrow chest, sloping shoulders, and bow-legs inspired very little regard.

"Well, my friends," the capitalist would say, as he entered without knocking, "are you happy? Do you want any thing? Is that child yours? What a handsome boy! Do you eat meat, do you drink wine?"

"No, Monsieur, not always."

"You do wrong. I wish you to eat meat and drink wine every day; you understand me, I wish you to do it—" And as the mountaineers smiled, he continued: "Come and work in the valley, you will earn two francs a day, and your tools shall be furnished. If you want your first week's wages paid in advance, you have only to say so."

Then with truly paternal interest he would enter into all the particulars of their mode of life, taste their bread, interest himself in the old mountain legends, listen to them with the greatest attention, and when the devil began to play his inevitable part in the tale, say, in the low tone of a man by no means perfectly at ease: "We must not be too hasty in believing all this—it won't do to be too hasty—and yet it is certain that bad spirits can appear—in solitary places, for instance, at twilight, or during the night when the wind blows—" He shuddered slightly to set a good example.—" M. le curé has doubtless explained all this to you?"

"Oh! M. le curé never speaks of ghosts or evil spirits, never."

"Indeed! Well, good-bye, my children. It is strange that Abbé Roche neglects all this, thought M. Larreau; "what a singular curé he is!"

The capitalist's efforts were quickly crowned with success. One after another the reports of his liberality had spread abroad, and the mountaineers arrived every morning in little parties of two and three, carrying over their shoulders, on the end of a short stick, the traditional earthen pipkin, surrounded with bands of tin, which contained their food. What were the important works that had been commenced in the valley? No one could have told, the countess's father having the entire management of them and being by no means communicative. To the curious he always replied: "I am making improvements, I am making improvements." In truth, he was making great improvements.

Besides building a smooth and beautiful road, leading from the valley up to the château, and thence to Grand Fort, he had widened the one to Virez, and commenced a third, which, turning away from the valley about one and a half leagues from Manteigney, wound through the forest. These were important works, but this was not all! he was making immense terraces in the part of the valley nearest to the château. Perhaps he wished to convert the spot into a park. The mountaineers saw M. Larreau spreading rolls of paper upon the grass, while others, strangers in that region, looked through little bottles fixed at the extremity of a sort of broom-stick, supported by three long legs. After gazing into the bottles with the greatest attention, and making incomprehensible gestures with their arms, they seized long chains, and dragged them about everywhere. Here they hollowed the ground, yonder piled up the earth, and farther on cut the rock, and carried the fragments three hundred feet to the right, where narrow trenches, regularly dug, resembled the foundations of some edifice. It would be a difficult matter to enumerate all the singular and contradictory rumors to which these works gave rise. Besides, you would probably prefer to know at once what M. Larreau himself intended. I will tell you, in confidence.

This clever man, as you perhaps may have guessed, wished to create in the valley, close by the château, a fashionable resort for pleasure-seekers, and was preparing the land, so that the buildings could be erected at any moment. The creation of new roads was a necessary consequence of this plan. The means he was to employ to attract wealthy idlers to this delightful spot were of two kinds. He relied upon the splendid stud of horses he intended to bring down, and the race-courses to be laid out! but above all, and this was his secret, on a still more powerful charm, with which the little ditches, so regularly dug, have a certain connection.

On the first arrival, M. Larreau had noticed in a part of the valley just at the foot of the mountains, a certain spot, filled with brambles, where the earth was remarkably moist, and seemed to have a singular color. At first, he attached no special importance to this peculiarity; then, being naturally inquisitive, obstinate and curious, had thought of it again, returned to the place, examined the soil more closely, and fancied he perceived a penetrating, nauseous odor, somewhat difficult to define. The dampness was no great source of surprise; such things are not at all uncommon in mountainous regions, where springs sink into the earth; but the odor, which became more and more perceptible, puzzled him extremely. One day, urged on by some unaccountable impulse, he attempted to clamber down the rugged cliffs that overlooked the spot. Unfortunately, it was a chaos of almost inaccessible rocks, a wilderness of roots and brambles, through which even the goats could not penetrate. Larreau devoted himself to the task with great perseverance, became interested in it, and at last, after toiling for several days, peering into every fissure, lifting the mosses, examining the stones, and searching among the roots, found other damp places of the same color and odor as the former one.

From that moment he was convinced that he had discovered a mineral spring, but kept the secret carefully concealed. He was just the man for great enterprises, and adroitly managed industrial schemes, and began to devote all his energies to the completion of the plan. By means of scraping and digging, he succeeded in collecting a sufficient quantity of the water to enable him to analyze it, having acquired, while in his old trade of a melter of metals, some little chemical knowledge which he thought he might turn to account. He sent for certain books and the necessary articles, and soon, though without a thorough investigation, convinced himself that the spring contained a valuable compound of sulphur, iron, and arsenic. It was necessary to have a perfect analysis, which only a chemist could perform; and also to ascertain the quantity of water in the spring, now buried under the earth. Whatever the result might be, he knew how to restrain his curiosity, not wishing to attempt any excavations until his own experiments were tested by the labor of some Parisian chemist, and as he could not conduct the business by letter, since he desired to keep it a secret as long as possible, waited patiently until he could go to Paris himself.

Nevertheless, this prospect of finding mineral springs instinctively led him to make some slight changes in the work going on in the valley. Not far from the moist spot he ordered foundations to be dug, for, said he to himself, "one of two things is very certain, either my spring is abundant and medicinal, or it is not. In the former case, I will at once put up a building here, that, when the time comes, will be sufficient for the first demands upon it. If the other alternative should prove correct, and I am deceived in my expectations, I can transform the embryo bath-house into a hospital, which will make me highly esteemed throughout the country, or convert it into stables, which will be so much done towards the accommodation of the race-horses." This is the plan that had been floating in the capitalist's brain ever since his arrival at Manteigney.

It chanced one evening that one of the laborers, having forgotten his jacket, went back to the valley to get it, and saw M. Larreau going towards the castle. It was very strange that the countess's father should be out walking by starlight. The workman hid behind a pile of wheelbarrows and waited for him to pass. The capitalist walked on, carrying two large bottles, which must certainly contain some precious liquid, for he clasped them in both arms as carefully as a nurse would hold a new-born infant. The mountaineer, who was terribly frightened, soon took it into his head that the meeting, though perfectly natural, was a very wonderful adventure. M. Larreau walked about after dark, mysteriously, carrying in his arms huge bundles, which must contain treasure: why should a man so enormously rich trouble himself except to go in search of wealth?

The tale circulated over the mountain, and soon acquired a tinge of the supernatural. People wondered in suppressed tones whether this astonishing personage, who had already transformed the château as if by the stroke of a magician's wand, and was throwing the whole valley into confusion without any apparent motive, might not be a sorcerer. Strange as it may seem, the absurd rumor only increased the capitalist's influence, and even attracted fresh workmen, for people said to themselves:—"If it is profitable to be in favor with God, who is not wicked, perhaps it is still better to keep on good terms with the devil, whom everybody knows to be extremely malicious."

To understand the singular medley in the brains of the inhabitants of the mountain, it would be necessary to live for a short time in some secluded corner of that region. The paradise and hell of the Christian, the tales of Perrault, and Pagan traditions, transmitted in some unaccountable manner, form the strange mixture on which they sustain their insatiable love of the marvellous. There are fairies keeping guard in the heart of the mountain over immense treasures of gold, silver and precious stones. How can these simple minds help becoming excited as they think of all this! How can they remain calm and sensible, when in the midst of the dark, mysterious pine forest, full of aromatic odors, where the wind breathes in long sighs, and the roots creak against the naked rocks! Amid the eternal song of the torrents and waterfalls, in which the ear can distinguish all the sounds of nature, they fancy in their most solitary hours that they can hear fairy bells tinkling under their feet, bursts of elfish laughter, and the clinking of gold and silver.

The mountain shepherds are poor, their bread is black, and their garments are worn; this bright dream cheers them. Wealth is not so far away! Who knows? an ingot of gold can soon leap out of the earth if certain people choose, and everybody knows that the elves are capricious. The mountaineer worships the latter class of beings, because he lives in their company, brushes against them every moment, imagines he sees them behind yonder rock, or peering out of the depths of a hollow. To sneer at them is to make them appear. The worthy man loves God, also, and willingly prays to Him; but God is much farther away, up above in the broad expanse of the firmament, and, after sunset, the peasant no longer dares to look at the distant stars for fear the dwarfs who live under the earth might take the opportunity to pull him by the legs. He is not very near the Lord, but the devil and his imps are close at hand.

This is not all; the immense mountains, which resemble a petrified tempest; the long dark fissures with the water oozing into clefts, where the sun never enters; the motionless cataclysm, the silent, eternal nightmare, have a violent, fiendish aspect, that betokens wrath and malediction. Are they not the traces of some punishment? God is not in this infernal chaos. It is the devil who lives here; the devil, chained beneath these rocky masses, conquered, disarmed, but not dead, and for want of something better to do, playing tricks upon poor trembling, terrified human beings. Some mysterious being reigns everywhere, in each hollow, each gloomy cavern. Men shudder lest he should spring out upon them; and, though he is hid, tremble yet more, for there must be some evil meaning in it; if he does not move now, it is only to be the more sure of his hold upon them. Besides, the eyes of the mountaineers, when turned away from these fantastic rocks, see only vast horizons, and flickering, uncertain colors, mingling in inextricable confusion. There is nothing certain, clear, and positive in this wide expanse; the other senses cannot sanction the vague impressions of the eye, and undefined, foolish fancies, which soothe the mind, succeed the exciting visions that have intoxicated it. M. Larreau had instinctively divined all this, and, very naturally, sought to turn it to his own advantage.

It was not without regret that Abbé Roche, who for fifteen years had been struggling against the superstitions of his parishioners, and seeking to win their confidence, saw the capitalist's influence increasing throughout the country. The mountaineers no longer thought of anything but working together on the estates belonging to the château, and, earning high wages with very little trouble, forgot their tiny fields on the steep slope, which were so difficult to dig, so hard to till. Almost all had abandoned their labor in the forest, healthful though it was, and having once gone down to the valley, did not wish to climb the hill-side again. The little village inn had lost its character as a place of refreshment for the mountaineers, a sort of family restaurant, and was now a mere suburban pot-house, never empty, and resounding with noisy songs until far into the night. At the imperious demands of the castle servants, who possessed great influence in the place, the inn-keeper had sent in haste for absinthe, although hitherto ignorant of its very name. It had quickly become fashionable, and père Sappey, whom we met staggering along the road one evening, was one of the first to fall a victim.

Thanks to the increased facility for making money, and the chance of having some in the pocket all the week, the inn was transformed into a gambling house, to the great delight of the count's servants, who being more skilful than the others, easily made very large gains. A taste for drink, as well as play, was developed, and the honest mountaineers, who for years had tilled their fields in the heat of the day, and borne their burdens over the burning paths without anything to quench their thirst, except the pure water of the streams, now declared that they must have wine, beer and brandy to enable them to work, so that it became necessary to put up a refreshment room, built of rough planks, in the valley. None of these changes escaped Abbé Roche's attention, but what was he to do!

"You are in a pretty condition, François," said he

one day as he met one of his parishioners reeling along the road, whistling one of Offenbach's contra-dances. "I have just seen your wife; she is complaining of you; you did not give her your week's wages."

François began to laugh.

"Oh! bless me, Monsieur le curé, things are not now as they used to be: people work and have a good time, they don't wear themselves out digging in the earth to get a handful of buckwheat. We have worked hard enough, goodness knows!"

"Poor fellow, are you any the richer? You no longer attend to your house, your hay is not brought in; how will you feed your cow this winter? And your boys are wandering about like vagabonds!"

"Pooh! there's no trouble about the boys. The count wants them to ride his horses, they will be little jockeys, go to Paris, be lodged and fed like lords, wear gold lace on their hats, and have nothing to do."

"You do not think what you are saying, François. Come, you are not really bad at heart, you love your wife, your children, your home—"

François, with a drunkard's complacency, began to laugh again, and the curé turned sadly away. Twenty times had similar conversations taken place; but whether with Peter or Paul, Abbé Roche could gain nothing but a smile and a bow.

The curé found himself forced to struggle incessantly against the new influences which were gradually overspreading the country. Worst of all, he was especially terrified by the thought that he himself, at certain times, felt their power. One day a cart, drawn by two oxen, stopped before his house. It contained two tolerably large cases, on which were the words: "*A la Reine des cieux, fabrique d'ornements d'église en tout genre*—To M. le curé, of Grand-Fort-le-Haut, by way of Virez, etc."

A little group of curious persons had already assembled around the cases when Abbé Roche arrived. The lids were removed in a twinkling, and amidst the hay and shreds of paper, appeared a huge bas-relief, which elicited a general cry of admiration. It was colored with wonderful art, and represented the "*Flight into Egypt.*" The faces were pink, the enamelled eyes of the figures glittered in the sun's rays, and the Virgin's garments, of an exquisite shade of blue, were adorned with numerous designs in gold and silver. The whole was executed with a skill and patience worthy of the Chinese. Saint Joseph, who was on foot, wore plainer clothing; but to make amends, his beard was imitated with most remarkable perfection. It was really as natural as life. I will say nothing of the ass' foal, which seemed to ask a caress, or of the landscape, whose vast extent touched the soul: on the left were two pink pyramids—the same shade as the faces, unfortunately—and on the right, three little palm-trees of a most peculiar shade of green. The whole was as light as a feather, and provided with two strong rings at the back.

The wheelwright, who had brought his own box of tools to open the cases, proposed to the curé that the precious carving should be put in its place at once, and the worthy man set to work with so much industry that, half an hour later, the colored bas-relief was gleaming in the simple church like a louis d'or amid a quantity of sous. The second box, much smaller than the first, contained a small lamp of gilded copper, undoubtedly intended to be suspended before the "*Flight into Egypt.*"

It might be supposed that Abbé Roche would have been greatly delighted with these works of art, which had already excited so much admiration, but it was not so. The brilliant colors saddened him; they were not suited to the spot where they were placed. The gilding reminded him of the drawing-room at the château. It seemed as if the House of God was profaned by these life-like images, formed to please the eye, and he was offended by the idea that divinity itself was intended to be personified in the pink cartoon of a baby adorned with enamel eyes.

This was not all: the glittering lamp, the dazzling bas-relief made the old church he loved not only with the reverence of the priest, but rather the affection a man feels for the places in which he has had both joy and sufferings, seem still more desolate and dilapidated. He had placed a part of his heart in the ancient sanctuary, and when he entered it, the memory of all the emotions he had experienced rushed forth to meet him, and surrounded him with most delightful recollections. The bas-relief and lamp were intruders which would disturb the charm. The curé's regard for his church had a tinge of filial tenderness, and these decorations made the same impression upon him that would be experienced if a person suddenly saw his old grandmother painted and crowned with flowers. All these thoughts were in his mind, when one of the servants from the château entered the church, and approaching Abbé Roche, told him in a low tone that the countess desired a moment's conversation with Monsieur le curé.

XVI.

It was the first time that the young wife had so urgently requested the curé's presence, and he went to her immediately. Mme. de Manteigney, who was sitting under the trees at one end of the terrace, rose at his approach:

"Pardon me, if I have disturbed you, my dear M. le curé, but I received a letter from our friend Claudius, this morning, in which he tells me that he has sent you a box from Paris."

"It arrived this very day, Madame, and I thank him a thousand times—"

"Ah! bravo! How do you like—sit down a moment—how do you like the lamp? You know that I presented it to the church."

"We are very grateful," murmured the curé in an almost stern tone of voice. The thought that he should have the countess's gift before his eyes every day was painful to him.

"Listen to me, dear M. le curé, do not speak in that severe tone, I implore you. I am in trouble, and wish to talk with you. Indeed you must show me a little friendship, or at least pretend to do so."

"I have never deceived any one, Madame, and I should not begin with you. Speak to me in all candor, and if my counsels can aid you, rest assured that they will be sincere."

In spite of himself he felt a most delightful emotion at the thought that she was about to make him her confidant, perhaps open her whole heart to him, and yet he struggled against the sweet sensation. He dared not look at the young wife, and stood drawing figures on the sand with the end of his cane.

"The better I know you, M. le curé," continued the countess with an expression of countenance quite different from her ordinary one, "the greater is the respect and confidence with which your character inspires me. I tell you things very frankly. I am not in the mood just now to choose my phrases, but the strongest proof of my sincerity is that I appeal to you when in trouble."

"I am listening to you, Madame."

"Well, answer me frankly, who is the little savage that brings goats' cheese here much oftener than she is needed? Her name is Marie, I believe."

The priest started. He suddenly remembered the evening when he had surprised the count in earnest conversation with Loursière's daughter, and answered with an embarrassed manner:

"Good Heavens, Madame, I think I have already told you. She is in very delicate health, and lives with her father on the borders of the forest. As to Loursière, there are some unpleasant things said about him; but we must not believe all the rumors which are in circulation."

"I am not talking about the father, but the daughter," interrupted the countess, looking the priest steadily in the face. "Do you know her?—her conduct, her reputation in the country? Tell me plainly, you see that I am deeply interested in the matter."

"Why, her reputation— Doubtless you have been told—" He dared not go on, fearing that he might inform the countess of something of which she was still ignorant. The latter becoming more and more excited, exclaimed, after a moment's silence, "I am jealous of that girl; there, do you understand now? The count has made her his mistress; is that clear—is that plain enough?"

She had uttered these words very passionately; her face assumed an expression of actual hatred, her nostrils quivered, and her little hands twisted her embroidered handkerchief.

"Calm yourself, Madame, I entreat you. That is a very grave accusation to make; you must not allow your imagination—"

"Oh! none of those common-place phrases, I beg of you; no well turned sentences, no trifling. Should I speak to you on such a subject if I were not sure? And stop, I can read in your eyes that you are as well informed about the matter as I. You cannot tell me a lie; be frank, Monsieur le curé, and answer yes or no. Were you ignorant of what I just told you?"

No one had ever appealed to his truthfulness in vain; he turned towards the countess instantly, but noticing the anxiety expressed in her eyes and the convulsive quivering of her lips, stopped without replying. He was terrified, and felt like a man who, venturing upon a volcano for the first time, feels the soles of his boots become burning hot. He also experienced an emotion of happiness, pleasure, and satisfied pride. The feeling shown by the poor wife ennobled her in his eyes. He had not been mistaken: a passionate woman's heart, capable of enthusiasm, anger and love throbbed in the breast of this little coquettish, prattling, frivolous countess—she possessed soul, mind and feeling.

"Answer me," she said, speaking more rapidly and searching his face with her anxious eyes; "answer. Did you know all this?"

"Yes, I suspected it."

"You understand that the affair cannot continue. It must be ended at once. That is why I wanted to speak to you."

Her expression suddenly changed, her brow contracted, the corners of her mouth drooped, and while two large tears flowed slowly down her cheeks, she continued in a low, soft tone: "You think me very absurd, do you not? Isn't it ridiculous to permit myself to be so deeply moved by the amusements of a gentleman who was trying to kill time? you cannot understand me when I say the affair must end, and yet it is perfectly true. I am no saint, and might commit some folly in my wrath."

"I see plainly that you are suffering, but let us try" (he was almost as much agitated as the countess)—"let us try to reason."

"Reason! that is a pleasant proposition; have you holy water in your veins? People suffer, weep, want to dash themselves out of the window, and you talk about 'reasoning.' Your reasoning is very much like managing a balloon: nothing is more simple if you only have a point of support. The point of support is calmness, absence of all emotion. You do not understand, or don't you wish to understand? Did not you see at once that I am madly, yes, madly, and I am ashamed to say so, madly in love with him? I love him foolishly—degradingly."

"Whom?"

"My husband, of course!"

If Abbé Roche had been stabbed in the back, the sensation would not have been more painful. Yet he murmured, clenching his heavy cane: "It is natural,—it is not at all strange,—wives must love their husbands."

"Yes, but the reason it is so base and wretched is, that I love him because he does not love me."

"Good Heavens! explain yourself."

"Can such things be explained? I am like a gambler who, about three o'clock in the morning, loses his self-control and risks his whole fortune to regain a hundred louis. I want to win—don't you understand? Well, to make myself beloved, I use the means commonly employed by the society in which I move. Suppose I should tell you—you will not be hurt? Suppose I should tell you that I tried to flirt with you to make him jealous? It is shameful, isn't it? I dye my hair as if I were going to a masquerade; I talk slang; I bewilder myself with idiotic prattle, and my greatest anxiety is to make every one believe that all this is perfectly natural to me. I pity myself, when I have time; but I assure you that if it were advisable to tattoo my face with green to-morrow, or put curtain rings through my nose, I would do it at once to attract his attention."

"No, no, it cannot be so," said the priest, wiping away the heavy drops of perspiration that bedewed his forehead. "No, Madame, you are mistaken, you do not know yourself; but God reads the depths of your heart."

"So much the worse for me. He reads sad things."

"Do not say so; preserve your self-respect, if you wish to remain worthy of love. True love never debased any one, on the contrary, it is ennobling and purifying, like everything that comes from God. Are diamonds to be judged by the mire that surrounds them! Purify your affection, free it from the stains that only rest upon the surface. Oh, God! I know that we sometimes despair, believe ourselves accursed, that all around us is blighted, but do not doubt the Lord; pray to Him, cast yourself into His arms. If you know how He calms and consoles our feelings—"

"Then you, too, have been unhappy?"

"Where is the life, however humble, that has not had its storms and tempests? Perhaps all is not as dark and sad as you believe. If you love your husband so devotedly, he must have qualities which unconsciously attract you in spite of his faults."

"If he had, I should not love him so much," she replied in a low tone, covering her face with her hand. And in a voice choked with tears, she added: "Do you know what he did the day after my marriage? He took supper with three grisettes, after losing sixty thousand francs during the evening."

"Good Heavens, but that was infamous!—Pardon me, I only mean that the count is—is—a scoundrel; and was he not reproved, slapped in the face, before them all?"

"Who would have dared to do it, may I ask?"

"I! I swear, before Heaven, I would, had I been present. Patience has its limits, and anger bursts forth when such disgraceful scenes are witnessed. Had you none but cowards near you?"

"The count has fought ten duels, and never received a scratch. He fears no one, I assure you."

"Do you think that I should have been afraid? I would have crushed him with a single blow!" cried the priest, with such passion that the countess cast down her eyes; then suddenly calming himself, he asked: "And you, what did you do?"

"Well! I found that he was a very distinguished nobleman, and could not at once resign the mode of life which he and all belonging to his circle have always led. For the first time I felt a desire to attract him, to triumph over the low-born women he knew, a longing to be loved. And as he had not enough to pay the sixty thousand francs—for my father had been very cautious—I pawned my diamonds, and the debt was discharged before noon."

"Indeed, Madame, and you think that he will be eternally grateful to you for it?"

"Dear, good curé, how I love you! He will never forgive me as long as he lives. I humiliated him, and I ought to have known it. Ah! I had no chance in my first attempt! The count cannot consider me as his equal; in his eye I am nothing but the daughter of a very wealthy and influential shopkeeper, whose riches and power only make his low origin the more distasteful. Urged on by necessity, ensnared in a thousand ways—could he reason calmly—M. de Manteigney, in an hour that he now regrets, bartered his name for a fortune."

"You speak as if it were not a shameful action! I am not a nobleman."

"Yet sometimes you look like one."

"I was picked up in some out-of-the-way corner, forgotten and unknown, and God has done the rest; but I feel wounded by what you say; it is not just. I feel, I am sure, such disgrace is unknown to the French nobility. God would not permit such things to be. The action you mention is exceptional, unique,—yes, unique. It is horrible."

"Horrible! no more so on his part than on mine."

"You are mistaken, you do not judge calmly. Let us say no more about it."

"Yes, but I want to talk of it. The bargain, shameful as it seems to you, because you live far away from the gay world, was honestly made on both sides. I was sure—almost sure—that no one would marry me except for my fortune; my father knew that he was buying a title, only when everything is signed, the gentleman finds himself face to face with a man of business, who is only apparently dazzled, and preserves the superiority of the rich man over the penniless, the protector over the protected. People are so stupid! a gentleman cannot forgive such a thing. I love my father dearly, but, after all, he grew rich by selling spouts."

"Are not all men equal before the Lord?"

As he uttered these words the priest's countenance became illumined with so noble and pure an expression that the young wife hesitated an instant before replying.

"You are above human littleness, M. le curé," she said at last; "but if men are equal before God, you surely know that it is not so in the eyes of society. Have I not seen even at the convent, especially, the daughters of the nobles treated with particular attention, almost reverence, however ugly, poor and stupid they might be! Do I not see wealthy citizens everywhere change their names to make people believe that they are of noble birth? I myself trembled like a leaf when papa said to me, 'Would you like to be a countess?'"

"A noble who sells his name," murmured the priest, "who gambles, and leads a life of dissipation, sinks to the level of the meanest, and then his title does not save him, but degrades him the more."

"All that is very well in theory. Yes, I knew that he was ruined, a gambler, and dissipated; I knew that he had wasted his life in every way, but what of that? His very faults attracted me, they were so different from those of the persons I saw around me. Did not all the gentlemen whom I heard quoted as elegant men lead the same lives as the count? Curiosity becomes excited, the impossible tempts with its charms; we say: 'He will love me all the same!' Economy, prudence, industry, foresight, sobriety, I had heard those words from my very cradle, and have always noticed that the people who practise these precious virtues desire nothing so ardently as to get rid of them, as one takes off a kitchen apron when a visitor arrives. During my whole childhood I saw the hoarding up of sous, and bruised myself against the piles as they grew higher and closer. The idea that some persons threw handfuls of louis d'or into the streets pleased me. Do you suppose that a parvenu could have such carelessness of the morrow, such contempt for money, could preserve such ease of manner when ruined, look fortune in the face and laugh at it? I think such things are noble. They flow in the blood, and are not to be learned or acquired."

Abbé Roche gazed at her earnestly. His brain seemed confused. He felt that the poor wife was bewildered, incorrect in her judgments, and misleading herself; but nevertheless, there was an indescribable audacity, hardihood, and passion in her error, which found an echo in his own memories, and controlled him by its charm. The countess continued:

"I told you that my husband had often fought a duel for some girl of light repute, and that since my marriage. You think perhaps that I was indignant? I suffered because I feared for him and also because it was a proof of his indifference to me, but in my heart I loved him all the more. You are surprised, but it is the truth. I was proud of him. At night, after I had retired, and was left alone, I devoured the papers which related his pranks in ambiguous language that deceived no one. My feelings overpowered me. I wept, laughed and read the article twenty times over. My father would not have exposed his life for a frolic, a jest, a glance, in defiance of all gossip, neither would any of my relatives. The more frivolous the cause, the greater the courage."

Her eyes sparkled as she spoke.

"There is no honor in it," said the priest.

"His is unblemished, I assure you; the count is known everywhere as a gallant man—irreproachable, Monsieur!"

"But he loses your money and your father's at the gaming table. Is that the act of an honorable man?"

"Why should he be economical in using my fortune when he did not value his own? Can he transform himself and suddenly acquire the petty virtues of a shopkeeper, because he has married a manufacturer's daughter? I should have less esteem for him if he had more consideration for us. He scorns us: well, that is frank, plain, honest. I repeat, he has made a bargain—exchanged his name for a fortune. He uses the fortune, and he is right; do not I use his name?"

The young wife paused suddenly, and again began to weep. "I am very wretched," said she.

The curé took her hand, and while in his embarrassment he sought for some consoling word, she continued: "What is good or evil; I can no longer judge of anything? I struggle against my feelings, know not what I say, fear even my thoughts, and seek to escape from myself as a person does whose clothing is on fire. I have tried all means to win his love, and have gained nothing, not a pressure of the hand, not even a kiss." Then, in a lower tone she added: "Every one is more of a wife to him than I! Pardon me, my dear M. le curé, for talking to you so long about my misfortunes; but indeed I need to have some helping hand extended to me, some one to aid me, some one to have a little affection for me. This last scandal must be ended at once—don't you agree with me? All these things were very well at Paris; but here it is impossible. Different scenes require different modes of conduct. The Count de Manteigney in love with a bare-footed gypsy, a ragged goat-keeper—I cannot endure it; my father would not tolerate it, and he must be concilated. We have debts!"

"How, debts! What debts?"

"Yes, I am in debt, and heavily too: I told you that he gambled. What should I have done if I had not borrowed right and left from my seamstress, my dressmaker? It is contemptible: but what could be done? It was better for me to attend to such business."

The conversation continued in this strain for several minutes. Abbé Roche could scarcely restrain his self-command. All that he had just heard was whirling through his brain, and the young wife, who had grown somewhat calmer, but still trembled, continued: "Come, let us think, let us find some means of putting an end to this disgraceful scandal: could not the young girl be sent away?"

"Her father will never consent, Madame, and besides, it would be necessary to find some pretext; but it is not possible that the count can be deeply interested in this child, who probably possesses none of the charms to which he is accustomed."

"That is the very reason; it is the novelty, the singularity, the absurdity that attracts and retains him. The fancy has already lasted some time I know."

"Could you not induce M. de Manteigney to go away for a time, divert his thoughts, and occupy his mind? He will soon forget this adventure."

The countess looked thoughtfully at the priest.

"Yes," said she, "you are right, I must try. He wants to buy some horses, and it is still the gay season at the Pyrenees. We will go to Tarbes, he has a friend in that vicinity; we can go to Luchon, to Cauterets; it is not impossible!—Thank you, M. le curé."

"Then you will go with your husband?"

"Certainly."

"Yes, yes, of course. You are right; it must be so, it must be!"

XVII.

It was with great hesitation that the countess alluded to the trip to Tarbes, in her husband's presence. She said that it would be delightful to go to Paris by way of the Pyrenees, and that it was absolutely necessary to procure some of the little horses so valuable in mountainous regions. In short, she sought for all possible methods of presenting her plan in a favorable light, but, contrary to her expectations, the count was the first to assent, and caught at the proposal to travel so eagerly that the time for their departure was fixed to take place three days after. The sudden resolution was not so very extraordinary. The lord of the manor had been yawning prodigiously for several days. He was overpowered by ennui. His friend Claudius was no longer there, and M. de Rougeon, an unendurable companion and M. Larreau remained; but besides the fact that the son-in-law and father-in-law were of very different characters, the count, now relieved from the anxieties concerning money which had rendered his bachelor life so harassing, no longer thought of anything but the incessant humiliation caused by the mere presence of the capitalist. Must the last scion of the noblest family in the country be the silent vassal of the vulgar rich man, who beneath his apparent good-humor concealed the energy of a keen, inflexible, domineering business man. It was he who gave orders, and planned and directed works whose object he did not even condescend to explain.

M. de Manteigney suffered keenly from all this; but how was he to quarrel with a man to whose generosity he owed his luxury, his style of living, and all the useless splendor so necessary to his comfort? The count wished to dispel all painful thoughts: but he certainly needed to have some agreeable pursuit to aid him in his effort. And then Parisian amusements are not so quickly forgotten. He sighed for the debts, the beloved debts of former days, the bustle, the thousand trivial occupations, and when, reclining in an arm-chair on the lawn before the château, with cigar between his lips, and the paper on his knee, he fixed his eyes upon the distant horizon, he fancied he saw the scenes of a theatre in the mountain peaks glittering in the sun, and his nostrils quivered at the remembrance of the odor of gas and musk which was not without its charm to his Parisian olfactories. Besides, his young wife, attractive as she was, appeared to him to be a mere reflection of her father, and reminded him of his absurd signature. Père Loursière's daughter had amused him for a short time, it is true; but the little barefooted savage soon lost her charm.

In short, M. de Manteigney was terribly bored.

Abbé Roche saw the countess once more as she was leaving the church. "It is all arranged," said she, "we leave to-morrow."

"You see, Madame, that we must never despair; be consoled and take courage."

The following day, about ten o'clock in the morning, he saw two carriages piled with luggage rolling along the valley at full speed towards the Virez road, while the workmen respectfully took off their caps as they passed. The priest had the courage to thank God for the departure which deeply saddened him.

M. Larreau had allowed his children to set out in company with the Rougeon family, and remained alone at the castle, alleging, as a pretext, his need of rest and the necessity of his superintending the works in person. Undoubtedly he took pleasure in finding himself absolute master of this lordly domain, which he considered, not without reason, as a conquest, and the crown of his own life-edifice.

Abbé Roche felt none of these pleasant emotions; everything around him had assumed a sombre hue, the whole country suddenly became a desert. He felt sadly isolated, and sometimes surprised himself in the act of wishing for the return of the merry, frivolous party that he had so carefully avoided only a few days before. He eagerly resumed his excursions to different parts of the mountains; for he was not the man to yield without a struggle to preoccupied thoughts. He wished to take advantage of the last fine weather to visit all the favorite spots he loved so much, and plunged into narrow, rock-walled paths, where tiny rills babbled and chased each other over the stones, sparkling like threads of silver, rapid and untiring, now dashing against some obstacle, dispersing into a thousand drops, and suddenly disappearing to gush forth again more noisy, limpid, and bright than ever. Sometimes these little streams united their waters in a hollow of the rocks, and, resting after their long course, transformed themselves into a pure, transparent mirror, which calmly reflected the sky and trees. Now and then a bird, hopping cautiously along, slowly approached, drank hurriedly, and flew quickly away to the nearest tree, leaving the mirror quivering and wrinkled.

"Everything in the world has its joys, agitations, mutual dependencies, and fears," thought Abbé Roche, "and even that stone, burning in the sun's rays, delights in the caresses of the icy water that surrounds and cools it."

From time to time he saw one of the small houses of reddish firwood half concealed in a grove of walnut trees. The hay was bursting through the garret windows over the balcony, among clothes hung out to dry, baskets of poultry, bunches of herbs, bundles of seeds and strings of onions, swinging in festoons. Here stood a brick oven, with its gaping, black mouth, yonder were piles of faggots, heaped up for winter use; where the hens laid their eggs, ladders, planks, and all the picturesque confusion of articles necessary for domestic life. In the little sun-flecked orchard, under the short, stout trees trained to resist the high winds, long fir trunks hollowed into pipes, moist and dripping, suspended from tree to tree, and supported by stakes, conveyed the water from a neighboring spring into a granite trough, wrinkled and roughly hewn, but carpeted with golden sand that glittered through the crystal wavelets. A cow, with half-shut eyes and swelling flanks, drinks slowly from it, while two merry children, their tangled hair strewn with bits of straw, also sip from their hands on the other side of the trough, and laugh at the good beast, which seems to say: "My children, we will play by and by, when I have finished."

The mother is there, spreading out her washing, and the husband not far off, probably mowing the fragrant grass on the steep slope, for the strange song which accompanies the strokes of his scythe can be distinctly heard. Was he not working in the valley? Perhaps he may be the only one that does not. The priest gazed at the picture with a rapid, wary glance; it no longer afforded him the calm and soothing sensations he had usually experienced. The scene before his eyes, and the thoughts which passed through his brain, appeared only in more violent contrast. "Have I not been imprudent and culpable in advising her to go away? He will be cured for the moment; but she must return to that furnace!" And all that he had imagined about Parisian society returned to his memory.

How was it that these degraded women, who attracted the gaze of the crowd, became famous, and rendered those rich enough to buy their favors famous also! What must be the depravity of a society on which such creatures imposed their laws, their manners, and even their dress? And those suppers, after which aristocratic noblemen lose mountains of gold! must they have recourse to such contemptible meanness the next day to pay the debt contracted the night before? He thought of the Later-Empire and the orgies of Nero. Belshazzar's feast appeared to him, and his imagination becoming excited as his blood warmed, he caught glimpses, amid the riot of bacchanalian scenes, of hundreds of marvellously beautiful courtesans, irresistibly bewitching in satin robes and gleaming jewels, drinking from golden cups, and trampling under foot young men intoxicated with pleasure and accursed passions.

Then he breasted the steep slope more impetuously; the veins of his forehead and neck protruded, a cold perspiration covered his frame, the muscles of his jaws contracted—until the image of the weeping young wife appeared, like a bit of blue sky at the close of a storm. He took refuge in a recollection which seemed almost divine to him. His soul mingled with hers; but the more he felt the charm of this new sensation, the more the ideal vision took palpable, vivid form. It was no longer the sorrow of the poor wife, her grief, her thoughts, that haunted him; but she herself, whose presence he seemed to feel, whose material outlines he saw, the thousand details of her physical loveliness rose before him with overpowering distinctness.

Then he too was accursed, conquered like others, by the lusts of the flesh.

Alas! the poor priest had only one fault; he was a man, and retained the strength of a man's nature in spite of his purity of heart. Exceptional lives do not fall to the lot of every one; it is a delicate thing to mould men after conventional patterns. In the effort to make angels, there is danger of distorting people, and creating monsters, madmen, or idiots but to proceed.

The inhabited region of the mountain suddenly ceased, and with it all luxuriance of vegetation. Nothing remained but stunted bushes, gnarled shrubs, coarse, sparsely scattered blades of grass, and tufts of aromatic plants, with rough, dark leaves, beneath which tiny flowers of singularly attractive color and odor were concealed. At rare intervals a solitary fir tree arose between two rocks, the advanced sentinel of the forest. At this height one breathed a purer air, and beneath the burning rays of the sun felt refreshed by the invigorating breeze that blew over the icy mountain peaks. The whole landscape was revealed—paths, cottages, thickets, orchards, and even the little houses of Grand Fort lining the yellow highway; the château of Manteigney, and the narrow valley extending to the foot of the nearest mountains whose misty outlines mingled with the clouds.

It was a beautiful spectacle, and the curé, listening to the distant sounds that reached his ears, said to himself: "Man has a short arm and a vast soul; he is the son of God and the earth. Beyond the narrow circle commanded by the physical organs, beyond these human passions and feverish desires, the spirit, purified from earthly stains, springs toward the limitless horizons which succeed each other until God is reached."

For the moment he believed that he had entered one of these horizons; the immensity of space exalted him, he felt grief and delusion gradually fading—lost in his enthusiasm as a drop of muddy water is absorbed in the depths of a crystal lake. He grew taller, stronger; a feeling of nobility and pride overmastered him; he became his former self, and the miserable agitation of his troubled senses, the anxieties which had so lately disturbed him, now appeared unworthy of his thoughts. Had he not a divine mission? Was he grown so weak and cowardly that the least trembling of the man's nature within him should overcome the priest! Should he hesitate to go to her aid because she was a woman, and beautiful? Of what consequence was her sex? Ought he to know that she had one?

He continued his walk towards the forest. It was dark and cool; the paths, at first distinct upon the soft, black soil among the heather and wild strawberry plants, soon disappeared amidst naked roots, intertwined like osiers in a basket. Everything was moist and dripping, even the air was full of dampness. The mosses that covered the rocks and trunks glittered and quivered like a tuft of wild thyme bathed in the morning dew, and long green sprays hung from the lips of the gnarled, twisted branches, like the beard of some sea god. A luxuriant vegetation encumbered the earth, clung to the trees, penetrated everywhere; even in the clefts of the old dead pines, rotting on the ground, hundreds of little plants shot forth with the eagerness of heirs anxious to enjoy their wealth.

It might have been supposed that nature, restricted in space, had here poured forth her exuberant fruitfulness. One was compelled to force a passage through the dense foliage, and cling to some root, when the foot slipped. Overflowing, vivid life seemed to envelop one; there were millions of little confused sounds and indistinct murmurs in the motionless air; not a human being was present, but a whole world of existences! They were heard, divined. All luxuriance mutually attracts. Whole populations were in motion in this wilderness of plants, herbs, and mosses. The plants, herbs, and mosses themselves breathed, lived—perhaps loved. Under what ardent kiss had the earth laughed so joyously, under what divine caress had all this life burst forth? As man looks more closely and concentrates his attention, the clods of earth become animated and peopled, the grains of sand have their architecture, their caverns, their horizons, nothings acquire importance, and the feelings are agitated by finding under a tuft of moss the limitless immensity that we dreamed of seeking only in the heavens.

Such were the dreams of the priest. How many times had he seated himself at this great banquet of life! He drank, he revelled in this pure spring of poesy, forgetting the narrow bounds of his humble existence, his struggles, his weaknesses. His chest expanded; he opened his heart and arms to the invisible and fruitful mistress whom God permitted him to love. He unconsciously enjoyed her as a poet and an artist, feasted on her with his eyes, his ears, the keenest of his senses. Then drawing from his pocket a large piece of brown bread, and sitting on a rock with his feet almost in the water, he breakfasted, enjoying the luxury of existence.

On finding himself once more surrounded by these memories, Abbé Roche felt as if he had been born again. "I am stronger than I believed," he thought; "these temptations are only illusions. Why should I waste my strength in struggling against myself, in grinding to powder the instincts within me? Why should God have deprived me of all human joys; why should He, at my very birth, have severed the bonds that unites men to each other? Why should He have condemned me to solitude, even in my childhood, if not to make me, thanks to these trials, superior to ordinary weaknesses? The sacrifice that exhausts and ruins the weak, purifies and reanimates the strong.

The priest has all humanity for his relatives, his heart is open to all, without distinction of caste, fortune, or name. In defiance of his personal sympathies, or antipathies, he should give his time, his care, and his prayers to all."

The repugnance that he had experienced towards the count now seemed a reprehensible feeling. He had avoided these people; but was disgust for their vices his only motive? Had there not been pride on his part, and, not understanding their words, manners, and behavior, had he not held aloof through fear of ridicule? He accused and condemned himself, saying: "I will be more humble in future." Joyfully did he accept the humility which ennobled him in his own eyes, and before God. "My duty is to go to them, persuade, convince, and lead them into the right path in spite of themselves." And he delighted in the thought that he was nearer God, between humanity and Providence, far from temptations, nearer his reward.

XVIII.

The autumn was far advanced, the branches of the trees were beginning to be distinctly outlined against the gray sky, and heaps of yellow leaves encumbered the beds of the brooks. In the morning, the fires lighted by the workmen to warm their soup gleamed here and there in the valley, as if through a mist of gauze. The air had become more sonorous, as if one were in an unfurnished room, and the bells on the flocks coming down from the mountain to take up their winter quarters in the village were heard in the distance. Although it rained frequently, and the roads were very bad, M. Larreau was always out of doors. Abbé Roche avoided meeting him as much as possible, but one day the capitalist accosted the curé so resolutely that he was obliged to enter into conversation. "Are you going this way, my dear curé? So am I; let us walk on together, if agreeable to you."

The curé, who was not skilled in making evasive answers, slightly bent his head in token of assent.

"Do you know that Manteigney and Grand-Fort-le-Haut are making a noise in the world, my dear M. le curé? One of the papers I received this morning—Where in the world is that paper?"

While speaking he looked over a number of newspapers and pamphlets he held in his hand.

"I have just been reading an article that, upon my honor, was a most charming one, very witty and highly colored although somewhat indiscreet, in which this country is particularly described: primitive customs, legends of the other world, geographical conformation, etc., nothing was omitted. To believe the author of the little essay, we are living in a veritable earthly paradise, somewhat haunted by evil spirits, it is true, but that only serves to make it the more striking and original. There is the paper, M. le curé, you can read it at home. You see it has a very pretty engraving of the château, and here is your church in the vignette. It is a very correct likeness. On second thoughts, take all the papers, I have not opened half of them; but my time is fully occupied—this is pay-day."

Abbé Roche was stupefied with astonishment. Why should people trouble themselves about Grand Fort? What interest could it have for Parisian readers? He instinctively divined that this publicity boded no good, and it made him sad to see his old church reproduced on paper.

"Who could have written this article?" he asked anxiously.

"Oh! I'm sure I don't know, unless you are the author, M. le curé."

"I?"

"I was jesting. The truth is, I strongly suspect that indiscreet Claudius, who prides himself upon his literary talents, and really does not write badly. Besides, this little piece is sprightly, witty, and humorous like him, it is exactly his style—a charming manner his!" Then, suddenly changing the conversation, he exclaimed: "Well, M. le curé, winter will soon be here; the mornings are uncomfortably cool already. Luckily wood is not dear in this region. Have you seen the works?"

"From a distance, Monsieur, as I passed."

"I believe, between ourselves, that the whole country is very much puzzled about them; it seems so to me. It is strange how the simplest things assume a fantastic character among these mountains; everything appears supernatural, even the adornments a simple private citizen adds to his dwelling. Your parishioners are people of imagination, my dear curé, and are willing to be guided by it. Try to make them prosperous, to secure their welfare by simple means: they will energetically refuse to accept. Use a little shrewdness in the matter, show progress to them under a glittering haze, besprinkled with the marvellous, and they will rush towards it, you cannot hold them back. Well! it is the eternal history of humanity. After all, of what importance are the means, if the result is good? Once more, what do we desire? The prosperity of this country, which has not yet received the benefits of civilization, and contains buried wealth of incalculable extent— I am a rich man, I do not conceal— But what is the matter with you?"

"I am somewhat pressed for time, and I think I am expected at home."

"Wait a few minutes, we do not often have an opportunity to exchange our ideas. Besides, this is a very important matter. I believe I have already told you that you are no ordinary man, your intelligence is remarkable, and—I beg pardon, remarkable. I am only a capitalist, to be sure; but I have my value. In our time, all social crises are money crises. Revolutions have never been anything but questions of property; the fate of empires depends upon the price of cutlets; question history. The moral uneasiness of the masses rests solely upon a legitimate desire for general material prosperity. Now I ask you what is this prosperity if not the constant and skilful employment of capital, the prudent utilization of resources?"

"Good heavens, Monsieur! but are not morality, virtue, happiness, those three words which mean but one thing, above and beyond the mere material prosperity of which you speak so enthusiastically?"

"Stop there, my dear friend, you have rightly understood me. The improvement of the morals of mankind! That is the supreme object towards which the efforts of all moralists should tend, that is all men of action; for they are the only true moralists. Well! do you not feel that the improvement of the masses is based entirely upon the satisfaction of that thirst for material prosperity, whose first word is: as-so-ci-a-tion? What a noble word that is! Men are mutually bound to help each other, and become powerless when solitary; but let one bring his capital, another his intelligence, activity, and knowledge of men; let a third add to this the moral sanction which is inherent in his person, his profession, his character, oh! then, these three men might move the world! That is association. Come, let us speak frankly: what urges me to dream of the happiness and moral improvement of this country? You will not do me the injustice to believe that it is a narrow feeling of self-interest? Thank God, my fortune is made, entirely made, I ask only quiet and repose; my hair is gray, my daughter's fate settled."

Abbé Roche started; the word *settled* was painful to him, he felt that it was only too true.

"What urges me on is the desire to make a residue of intelligence and the powerful resources at my control useful to a new, artless, and interesting population."

M. Larreau paused a moment, half opened his left eye, and stroking his chin, said carelessly, "Have you ever visited the uplands of la Salette, my dear friend? What an admirable thing is that noble enterprise? what marvellous results have been obtained in a few years! Ah! M. le curé, you are right to say: 'Faith moves mountains!' there is now an immense amount of property there. It is a treasure—sprung from the earth, one can use no better expression."

"You were speaking just now of this region," observed the priest, "and you remarked—"

"As a Catholic, I must confess that the miracle of la Salette is one of the dogmas that inspire me with more respect and—"

"The miracle of la Salette is not an article of faith, and the word dogma has nothing to do with us," interrupted the priest hastily.

"You don't give me time to explain myself. Wait; I am not one of those people who mistake one thing for another, pray believe me. I am a good Catholic, I have faith, implicit faith, it is the true, the only religion, that is what I think; but if any one should say to me point blank, M. Larreau, do you believe in the apparition of the virgin at la Salette? then, my dear friend, that would be quite another matter; I should feel wounded. I am frank, as I have already told you; I should feel my private convictions wounded by such a question; and answer honorably and nobly as you have done, I should reply: 'What does it matter to you? The miracle of la Salette is not an article of faith!' But while bowing before the liberty of conscience, which is the very basis of—between ourselves, it is well to confess it—it is the basis—there is no getting over the difficulty; there, M. le curé, there is the basis. The only thing that prevents the wonderful success of this enterprise."

The countenance of the priest had assumed an anxious expression, his eyebrows were contracted, his glance fixed; he crossed his arms on his breast, saying in a firm tone: "Monsieur, I will not allow any one to use that word before me in speaking of a miracle which the church approves. There has been no enterprise. God would not have permitted his name to be used for a miserable speculation."

"And who says anything to the contrary? What a devil of a man you are! Pardon the expression, my dear friend. I was going on to say that God would not have tolerated that. I merely wish to arrive at this point, that there is something miraculous in the success of this belief which is no article of faith, I admit, but has resulted in the prosperity and wealth of the country. And yet the plateau of la Salette is barren, arid, destitute of charm, and has neither bathing establishments, casino, stud, nor race courses; what would it be if it possessed all these things. There has never been any important apparition in this country? I am surprised, it is just the place for one. These forest-covered, mysterious gorges, these torrents, these roads, walled in by gloomy cliffs, these barren heaths—the mere thought of them makes me shudder. For my part, I assure you that I would not watch cattle for eight successive days in such places—I am nervous, I should have visions, though I should not complain of that, since it would make the fortune of the country."

Abbé Roche for some time had been under the influence of angry feelings which he heroically controlled. He now stopped suddenly, and facing the capitalist, said: "Monsieur, are you depending upon my aid to assist you in performing a miracle in these mountains?"

Larreau darted a strange glance at the brave curé from his left eye, which suddenly opened wide, and instantly burst into a laugh.

"Ha! ha! ha! are you joking? Ha! ha! for what do you take me, tell me in good faith. If that were so, I should have a saint at my side. I spoke to you of la Salette as I should talk of anything else. Dear me, how you have made me laugh! What! I talk carelessly, in all simplicity, and you put an interpretation upon my words! From any one else the remark you have just made would have annoyed me greatly—wounded my feelings. Do not believe that I wish to hurt yours. On the contrary"—and suddenly recovering his usual self-possession—"I am delighted with this conversation, my dear M. le curé, it gives me another proof of the nobility and frankness of your disposition. I like this pride, this ticklish susceptibility which takes offence at the mere idea of a proposition, and sincerely admire these rare qualities, even when they cost the sharp answers you just gave me and which I might have expected. If I have a regret," added the capitalist with a very cunning and somewhat patronizing smile, "it is that the bishop did not hear our long conversation; it would surely have confirmed him in the opinion I know he has of you, and of which mine is merely the echo, and convinced him, my dear M. le curé, that your position is far below your merits."

"So it was a trial," thought Abbé Roche, unconsciously rustling the papers he held in his hand.

"Hypocrite!" muttered Larreau between his teeth. "No matter, he is influential—very influential."

XIX.

When Abbé Roche had returned home, he sat down before his white wooden table, laid his band in his Saint-Augustine—he was very economical of his bands—and began to reflect. What was he to believe and what discredit in the singular words of M. Larreau? What was his motive; why had he made such an exhibition of pompous maxims, whose precise meaning had escaped him? What was the object of his contradictions, his theories about association? All that confusion of empty words—but were they empty? Did they not perhaps convey an intelligible meaning to a man accustomed to the subtleties of city language?

The curé, weary of trying to penetrate the obscurity, opened one of the papers which he had placed upon the table when he entered, and first of all selected the article mentioned by the countess's father. It was a sort of supplement, entitled: *A singular walk.* The piece was written in a pretentious, sparkling, extravagant style, and contained all manner of absurdities.

The country was described in such vivid colors that it might have been taken for one of the wildest regions of Australia, and yet while reading it, one seemed to receive the odor of paste and colored pictures peculiar to toy-shops. The customs of the inhabitants were at least five centuries behind the times; they possessed the candor of the Golden Age, were innocence itself; their dancing on the grass was performed to the sound of a peculiar instrument that dated as far back as the fifteenth century.

The fantastic description of the landscape formed an excellent background for the outline of the château, which was sketched in glowing colors: sombre towers frowning over the abyss, dark, sonorous vaults, long galleries, battlements, drawbridges, etc. It was reality itself, but skilfully arranged, transformed into a frightful but charming nightmare, so that amid these surroundings, the rich, luxurious furniture of the castle, Parisian mode of living, excursions on donkeys, breakfasts in the depths of virgin forests, champagne cooling in icy torrents, even the family concerts in the evening, the coffee served upon the terrace in silver cups engraved with coats of arms, in full view of a most beautiful landscape, formed a delightful contrast well adapted to excite the reader's imagination. At the close of the article, the author, as if by chance, carelessly mentioned the name of this fairy castle, then struggled with wittily-expressed scruples, and at last determined not to efface a proper name so well known to the fashionable world that it was unnecessary to make a mystery of it.

The last lines aroused the indignation of the priest. They were not true. Why should the author affect scruples that certainly had no reality, since he might have removed them by a stroke of the pen? There must be some hidden motive; but what were these designs? The good curé was not sufficiently familiar with the customs of certain papers to perceive the true object of the article: a very skilful catchword, all the more so that it was concealed, and presented in the form that would be most certain to impress it upon the minds of all who read the sketch. He was ignorant of the thirst for publicity then making every throat dry, curious samples of which were presented in different parts of the same paper: everywhere were personal anecdotes, confidences, revelations, indiscretions, but Abbé Roche, somewhat disgusted, and not understanding what possible interest any one could take in the publication of such scandals, laid the sheet aside. He was about to unfold another from the pile, when his attention was attracted by a little piece of paper without signature or address, which seemed to have fallen out of some letter. He mechanically read the following words:

"After all, I soon consoled myself for the breaking of one of the bottles; the other was quite sufficient. Made under the circumstances I have just related, the analysis was perfectly satisfactory. We were right, as you shall see; this is the result—a splendid one:

Sulphate of Chalk	0,170
Chloride of Sodium	0,024
Bicarbonate of Chalk	0,036
" Magnesia	0,036
Silica	0,008
Oxide of Iron	indications
Arseniate	traces
Total	0,305

"If you are not satisfied, you are certainly hard to please."

The priest had read these lines with the utmost good faith, never dreaming that he was encroaching upon private matters, but he now felt a tinge of regret, and carefully put the bit of paper under the cover of one of the pamphlets. He had understood none of this scientific information. It was no great source of surprise that M. Larreau, in his former business of melting metals, should have acquired some little chemical knowledge: but he would never have supposed that his love of science would induce him to maintain such a correspondence.

However, it was a matter of very little consequence.

He tore the wrapper from a second paper. It was a journal of art, from which he learned that a certain landscape, inscribed with a famous name, though one unknown to him, was a work whose brilliant and tempered shades, dark yet radiant, opened new horizons to art. He read that there were "independent lines and sympathetic and progressive half-tints in the clouds; that the vibrating mingling of tones revealed the storms of a noble soul struggling with the philosophical aspirations of the last century, and vigorously supported by the analysis of æsthetical traditions, successively and eternally palpitating in the breath of the persistent individuality of him who—" Abbé Roche bent his head over his clasped hands. How small he felt in the presence of this immensity! Of how many things he was utterly ignorant! Yet he turned the pages more rapidly, and discovered a portion of the magazine, where short items of news were separated from each other by asterisks. Naturally he stopped, expecting to find lighter reading. The following words met his eye:

"The museum of Cluny has just added to its rich collection a wooden statuette of the greatest interest. It is one of the finest and purest specimens of the wood-carvings of the fifteenth century, and we do not believe that any work of that period exists more elegant in design and perfect in execution. The figure, amply draped, represents Saint John. He is standing, and measures about twenty inches. Although we are not in a position, after a cursory examination, to assert authoritatively a fact of so much importance, everything leads us to the belief that the statuette is not of French origin. The letter F, plainly visible on the left hand side of the pedestal, and certain peculiarities about the drapery, induce us to think that the work should be attributed to Francesco, son of Domenico di Valdambrino, who flourished at Sienna in 1409. How did this precious carving find its way to one of the poorest churches in France? We cannot explain it.

"It now remains for us to congratulate and thank Viscount Claudius, to whom the honor of the discovery of the treasure is due. It was only in compliance with the entreaties of the administration that this skilful connoisseur, whose learning and correct taste are well known, consented to relinquish this unique relic. We consider this act of self-denial in favor of the public worthy of all praise; and we are happy to mention it, all the more so, as we are permitted to reveal a fact greatly to the honor of the donor—all the more so, we say, because the generous connoisseur surrendered it for the same price that he paid, which was, we are informed, five thousand francs, an insignificant sum, when it is considered that this curiosity is one of the finest in the museum of Cluny, rich as it is in antiquities of every description."

Abbé Roche read the strange article just quoted twice over, then suddenly dashed the magazine down, exclaiming: "But that is perfectly infamous! The man is a scoundrel! He has robbed us!—he is a liar!"

To see the priest striding from one end of his room to the other, with flushed face and clenched hands, it was easy to perceive that this holy Hercules had a very passionate temper, notwithstanding his usual gentleness of demeanor.

His forebodings had not deceived him; fashionable society was composed only of knaves, and some unaccountable chain of reasoning led him to think of the countess, living in that infected air. He would tear her from such surroundings. He would quarrel with them all—tell them of this deed—spit in the scoundrel's face. His poor Saint John! a friend had been snatched away. A bold liar had entered the church and profaned it, his dear old church, which was so pure, so full of God's presence!—Could he keep the gilded bas-relief that perpetually reminded him of the rascal's crime? He went to the church at once, without delay, listening only to the promptings of his anger, intending to take down the accursed sculpture, break it into a thousand fragments, and leave no trace remaining; but when he saw suspended before it the lamp which had been presented by the countess, his anger gradually cooled, and he thought he would merely send back the *Flight into Egypt*. The box was still in the vestry. Where did this Viscount Claudius live? The priest did not know, and he would not ask the address from M. Larreau, who alone could give it.

Besides, if he sent the case back, would it not be supposed that he took this course in order to claim his share of the five thousand francs? Was it not his duty to bear all this with dignity, to despise and forget the shameful transaction? And if he quarrelled with the count's friends, with the count himself, the doors of the château would be closed against him—he would lose all influence there, and then how was he to aid and succor the poor wife who had no friends save himself.

XX.

A few days after the events just related, M. Larreau set out for Paris. The winter, in his opinion, had become unbearable, and the cold was indeed terribly severe in the lofty château, perched upon its lonely pedestal of rocks. At four o'clock in the afternoon the whole valley became filled with a dense icy fog that rose to the foot of the castle walls. Nothing was to be seen in the dull, gray, hueless sky, except an occasional bird of prey, flying swiftly away from the glaciers. At night, the sound of the creaking doors and windows reverberated through the long corridors, and startled one from slumber. However anxious the capitalist might be to continue the work of improving Manteigney, he could bear no more, and wrapping himself in his fur overcoat, hastily started for Paris, leaving the field clear to the severities of the climate.

The snow fell in heavy flakes, covering the whole

country with its thick shroud, so that the poor village, attacked on all sides, resembled a ship shut in by icebergs. No sound was heard save the lugubrious croaking of the ravens, circling above the cottages, or alighting in flocks upon the towers of the château. There were no songs amidst the foliage, no rustlings among the grass. The frozen brooks had ceased their music, all was sad, cold, and dull. When the wind blew, long plaintive moans, that sounded like the groans of souls in agony, echoed from the forest. The snow, dislodged from the trees, whirled along by the tempest, penetrated through all the chinks of the dwellings, filled up the chimneys, accumulated in heaps before the doors, and blocked up the entrance to the cellars. It was necessary to stop up all the crevices of the windows, the poor people were besieged, and they hung up their garments, and collected all their rags to keep out the icy wind that whistled under the doors. What a furious battle raged in the forest, whose depths could no longer be entered! How many ancient pines were shattered, whose gray skeletons the following summer would find extended upon the moss!

When the pleasant weather returned, people emerged from their houses, removing the snow from the thresholds. Every face was wan and violet-hued, every nose red, all eyes moist. The men, wrapped in their large brown coats with little double capes, and the women concealed in their black cloaks and folded hoods, walked quickly along on their way to the stables, from whence sounded the voices of the cows and goats, apparently in friendly conversation. The children were the only ones who enjoyed the fine weather; they might be seen, with their heads hidden under their red caps, tumbling about in the snow, or pushing their sleds before them with shouts of laughter.

As soon as evening began to approach, the village

was again deserted, all the inhabitants retreated to their homes, and assembled in groups around the hearth before a huge fire of pine logs, whose odorous flames licked the smoky walls and the black bottom of the kettle. Then, while the children screamed, and the women twirled their spindles, the old mountaineers filled their short pipes by the light of the rosin, and told long stories, strangely vivid tales, full of marvellous incidents and mysterious struggles between light and shade, good-luck and misfortune. There was the never-ending fable of the mountain opening its sides and admitting the favored wood-cutter to immense caverns heaped with treasure. The cold, the wind, the gloom was forgotten as they listened. There was the legend of the shepherd overtaken by the snow-storm, whom the good fairy received with his flock in a suddenly enlarged cleft of the rock, and in imagination they followed him as he walked on and on so long that when he emerged from the dark gallery, he found himself in a meadow surrounded by the best of pasture land, under the rays of a June sun. And the curés of former times, who cured all kinds of diseases! And the wood-cutter, possessed by an evil spirit—the devil in person, perhaps—who by a chance blow of his axe had split the mountain and divided its summit into two portions!

What a long-lived tradition is that of the rock cleft by a hero! We meet with it in the Alps, find it in the Pyrenees at Roland's beach, and in many other places. Before these immutable, eternal masses, at whose base generations spring up and die without leaving any trace behind, it seems as if man wished to console himself for his powerlessness and weakness by these singular fictions. Man has a ceaseless longing to make an exchange with the nature that surrounds him. He gives her his time, his labor, and his strength; he penetrates her depths, changes her aspect, imprints his human seal upon her.

She penetrates him also, feeds him, affords him the means of living. There is no conflict between them, but a perpetual exchange. He cultivates the earth, she supports him; he watches, searches, studies, caresses. She pleases his senses, consoles him, cheers him, adorns herself for him, dons bright colors, and, to complete the charm, fills the air with sweet odors and harmonious sounds. Such is the common law; but when a sterner nature, more impenetrable to man, refuses his advances, and, sufficient for herself, allows him neither to tame, caress, nor understand her, exists wholly without relation to him, man renews by his imagination the bonds that the stepmother has broken, and consoles himself for being crushed by ruling over her in his dreams.

Abbé Roche no longer thought of these old legends; he now had very different visions. While the wind howled and blew in gusts down the chimney, his whole life passed in review before him. No, he never had his share of tenderness, his share of all the good things of the heart, which, after all, are not superfluous.

He had deluded himself by considering his misfortunes as privileges; he had sometimes believed that he was walking at the head of his flock, leading the way, and animating them by his own example; he had prided himself upon it! but was he not in reality a poor man, who was deprived of everything! For a long time he had borne the rude winters of the mountains without complaint, nay, even with joyous courage; he had never experienced so deep a feeling of sadness and isolation. Although his mode of life was essentially the same, and he made the greatest exertions not to change it in the smallest particular, it seemed to him as if the whole world were upside down. The wind no longer had the same voice, nor the snow the same hue; the cold was more piercing, his very heart shivered. He sat motionless for whole hours, gazing into the fire as one might look into a magic mirror that transformed thoughts into images.

He saw the countess, looking as coquettish as on the day of their first meeting; she had dried her tears, forgotten her sorrows. Fêted, adorned, joyous, radiantly beautiful, and—décolletée, she moved on through the throng, which parted, gazing at her loveliness. He experienced so keen an emotion that he trembled, and felt ashamed. Then the picture changed, and he saw Claudius selling the statuette to the Cluny museum. The nobleman smiled, showing his white teeth, and said: "Gentlemen, I present it to you." He stretched out his hand, the gold was counted out, and poor Saint John, cleansed, brilliant, and unrecognizable, was installed in his new abode. Soon after Mme. de Manteigney, leaning on her husband's arm talking with Claudius, and surrounded by all her friends, came to admire the statuette, and everybody burst into shouts of laughter at the story of the poor, simple curé, who had given up this masterpiece as one casts aside an old cracked kettle.

"I am mad," said Abbé Roche, rising suddenly; "I must have an attack of fever! Why should these people trouble themselves about me? How could the poor wife win the affection of her husband—what influence could she obtain over a nature so perverse? No, no, she is still unhappy, still suffering, alas!" The thought was a solace to him. "No one around her can understand her. In whom could she have confidence, to whom could she open her heart? She has only one sincere, disinterested friend—to her I am not a man."

He clasped his hands over his brow, saying: "What is to be done, oh! God, what is to be done to save her?" And he soon forgot himself in her, as a physician might do who, watching his patient with too much care, no longer thought of the sickness.

Then to recall himself to his duty, his position as

a friend and spiritual father, he talked aloud, as if she had been present—became excited by the sound of his words, the warmth of his own emotion—discovered consoling thoughts and salutary counsel, and, lest he should have forgotten all this when she returned, took notes in his large handwriting on a sheet of paper. He was relieved—she would listen to him—and waves of indulgence for her surged in his heart.

"We must avoid too severe judgments," he wrote. "Before condemning any one, let us remember the society in which he has lived."

He said *we*. He joined himself to her; made her cause his own, and she accepted the community of interests, since she did not reply. As he wrote the *we*, he heard the rustling of her dress, and inhaled the perfume that always surrounded her. She was there, looking at him with her tearful eyes, and saying: "You are indulgent, my dear curé, like a man who is shielded from the weaknesses of the world."

And he was glad that by accusing him of too great indulgence, she aided him to mislead himself, for in the depths of his heart, he felt a profound contempt, which at times resembled hatred, for the miserable libertine. "You have employed the usual weapons to win him; now use other means, my child—show yourself disarmed before him. Compel his affection by the modesty and simplicity of your manners; surprise him, fix his attention by the gentleness of your virtues, let him find in you what he meets nowhere else, a Christian sister, an angel who protects, calms, and cheers him. Unless he is the devil himself, how can he help being touched? That you may the more surely win his love, renounce all immoderate luxury of dress, the foolish allurements of useless coquetry; no longer transform your physical nature by deceitful artifices, lay aside your jewels and adornments; no longer hide yourself under silk and gold like a Pagan idol; show yourself as you are."

He then entered into the most minute particulars, explaining his idea with increasing emotion, seeing her, if I may so express it, transformed before his eyes, approaching nearer to him, becoming the supernatural being of whom he constantly dreamed, instead of the woman he could not forget; he yielded to the irritating charm of this angelic disguise. "Do not seek, poor young wife, to win his love too soon;" —his hand trembled—" by devotion and sacrifice purify your affection, that God may bless it. And if in this noble effort you at first meet with cruel obstacles, do not yield to despair, which is a common weakness, do not content yourself with mere courage, but boldly examine your own sufferings, and you will soon find in them the stern but deep joy of the Christian victim, who looks sorrow in the face without turning pale. Who told you that others have not suffered as much as you, that somewhere there are not souls as wretched as yours, which, having no right to complain, await their deliverance in silence?"

His writing became more rapid, less legible. "Raise your heart above your griefs and the fetters of humanity, my child, my sister; ascend in thought to those divine heights where, under the eye of God, beings who understand each other can love for ever without a blush; where all barriers crumble; where the vows of men are annulled; where affection, free from all carnal stains, beams— Grant, grant that my soul may mingle with yours!"

Suddenly he stopped, dashed his clenched hand upon the table, and crushing the paper on which he had just written, threw it into the fire. "How I love her!" said he. And raising his eyes towards the crucifix suspended over the chimney-piece, he added: "Dost Thou not permit me, oh, God! to love her *thus?*"

It was the crucifix that she had noticed, in regard to which she had said one day, with her little off-hand manner: "My dear curé, do you wish to dispose of it?" Thus, while looking at the image of the Saviour, he heard the words, as if repeated by some distant echo, saw again the gesture she had made with her little ungloved hand, the movement of her fingers, and even her pink convex nails, in whose corners the gloves had left a little of their white powder; but these memories inspired his heart with so pure an affection that even before the divine image he did not blush for his emotion.

From whence came this Christ, that he now gazed at through his tears, his life-long friend and confidant? He was thinking— How many other mysteries might still be contained in his own existence?

"Are you sick, M. le curé?" said mère Hilaire, touching Abbé Roche on the shoulder.

She had spoken in a low, confidential tone. The words had been upon her lips for several days, but she had not dared to utter them.

The priest, who had supposed himself to be alone, turned suddenly, and perceiving the loving face of his old friend rose, took her head between his hands, and kissed her on the forehead.

"My poor child, my poor child! are you then so very unhappy, tell me? What is the matter? You neither eat nor sleep! Ah! I see very plainly that— I say nothing, because I am only your servant, but I have eyes. If you would only tell me: 'Mère Hilaire, that is what troubles me,' perhaps I might help you. He must be in some great trouble to embrace me in that way," she added, speaking to herself and wiping her eyes with a corner of her apron.

"No, it is nothing; it will soon be over, my friend."

But she could not believe him, for while saying: "It is nothing," he had taken her hand and pressed it more and more warmly. After a moment's pause, he looked earnestly into her face and asked: "Do you know who gave me this crucifix? Tell me the truth."

Mère Hilaire recoiled a pace or two, as if terrified.

"I know nothing about it, M. le curé. Why do you ask me that? It is the first time that you have spoken of it for more than twenty years. Is that the cause of your grief? But I cannot, for I know nothing about it."

"Yet I always thought that you had something to do with the gift."

"I? oh! I assure you that I did not give it to you, my child. I was so poor at that time."

"No doubt, but you might have been told to send it to me at the seminary, for instance—"

She became suddenly agitated. "How do you know that?" she exclaimed, "how do you know that?"

"I have never had any positive proof of it; but as the box containing the Christ was sent me from Virez, and I do not know any one in the city or suburbs except yourself, I thought at once—"

"Dear me! that is true. And why didn't you ever speak to me about it before?"

"Why did you not mention it yourself?"

"Well; then you want to know everything that I do about it, my child? I would have told you willingly, although it is very little; but I thought that you might perhaps be troubled about it, and I had been compelled to promise to say nothing."

"By whom?"

"The person who brought the crucifix. It is true that I sent it to you myself, because I was requested to do so, and besides, the old gentleman did not know your address."

"And was that the first time that you ever saw him?"

"Why do you ask all these questions, my child?—It is so long ago! I don't remember much about it."

"Tell me, I beg of you."

"Well! yes, I had seen him several times, because he was the person who brought me the money—" Is it not hard to be obliged to tell him these things! "He brought me the money for you—that is, for a child that had been entrusted to my care, that is all."

The priest's eyes brightened strangely.

"And you never knew the name of this old gentleman, as you call him. Did he seem to be interested in—the child that had been entrusted to you?"

"Oh! he didn't even look at you, poor little innocent that you were, and I loved you all the more on that account. He came to bring the money because he had received orders to do so, and then quietly mounted his horse again. One day, in my anger, I told the whole story to M. Vilain, who was the curé of Virez; but M. Vilain, though a very amiable man, silenced me at once, telling me that I must say nothing about it for the sake of the child. Bless me! when a curé tells you such things of course you keep quiet, and I almost shut my eyes when the other old man came."

"And was this person the one who gave you the crucifix?"

"He gave it to me—no; he was commissioned to send it to you by another person who had just died and left it to you."

"And you never knew who that person was?"

"Never, my poor child. Yet I have understood that it was a lady, but that is all. You see it wasn't worth while to question me, it is useless. God sees all things, M. le curé, and what he does is well done."

"You are right, mère Hilaire, you are right, we will say no more about it."

XXI.

When Noah at last saw the sacred dove bearing the consoling olive-branch, he could not have experienced a sweeter emotion than that of the curé of Grand Fort when he saw the plains growing green once more under the first smile of Spring. The snow had disappeared, the grass sprang up luxuriantly, the swollen streams filled the land with their music—people felt invigorated, and inhaled the air with expanded lungs.

News of the count and his family soon arrived; they had sent word to have the château prepared for their reception, and the intelligence created great excitement in the village, for life at Grand-Fort-le-Haut seemed now to be wholly dependent upon Manteigney. The innkeeper laid in a stock of hitherto unheard-of liquors, and the grocer suddenly decided to have his shop painted bright red.

One fine morning the count's steward arrived, followed in a few hours by the baggage, and two days after the lords of the manor made an almost triumphal entry. Abbé Roche dared not go and meet them like the majority of his parishioners, but he took a position from which he could see the carriage pass. His heart throbbed joyously,—he was no longer master of himself. She was there — she had returned. All his ugly dreams flew swiftly away, and he felt so happy that he did not even think of Larreau and the count who accompanied the countess. The following morning he did not resist his wishes, but went up to pay a visit to the château. He was received with the utmost cordiality. M. Larreau, who was as active as ever, overwhelmed him with questions. Had the winter been very severe? Had the poor people needed bread, or the cattle forage? The countess seemed perfectly happy, and the griefs of last autumn had doubtless vanished entirely.

"My dear curé," said she, "how glad I am to see you again! It seems as if we had known each other for ten years. And you have not been frozen? Come, move your arms. All winter long I have been asking myself the question: Is Abbé Roche frozen or not?"

She made all these extravagant speeches with such sprightliness and grace that it was impossible to help smiling. The curé was then informed that the count would remain only a few days at Manteigney, as it was his intention to set out very soon for Tarbes, to superintend the forwarding of several horses that he had purchased there.

In fact, a very short time after his arrival M. de Manteigney resumed his journey, and the countess was left alone with her father. One morning, just after breakfast, she was walking on the lawn, seeking for the early violets hidden in the grass, when some one informed her that père Loursière had asked to see her. As he had insisted upon it, even when told that M. Larreau was not at home and he had better return, Mme. de Manteigney gave orders that he should be admitted. At the first glance the young wife perceived that the visit of this disagreeable personage had some important object. He advanced slowly, bowing humbly, with his hat in his hand, and did not carry his inseparable basket, which gave him a peculiar appearance.

"I am very sorry to disturb the countess," he murmured with a troubled expression, "and indeed I would not have come if I had not been compelled—one might say compelled."

"What do you want of me, père Loursière? Go on, I am listening." To the great surprise of the countess, he looked cautiously around as if to convince himself that there were no curious ears within hearing, and then approaching nearer, said: "Did you have a pleasant journey, Madame?— As true as the sun is shining upon us, I meant to speak to the count; but I am told that he is away—I am very sorry for it, for I shall grieve your kind heart, Madame." And he uttered two portentous sighs, one after the other.

"Well! a truce to your regret, père Loursière, tell me at once what troubles you."

"It gives me pain to say it on account of the respect I feel for the château; but necessity—and then duty. Dear me, we cannot desert our children—it is natural to have a father's feelings."

The young wife suddenly recollected her husband's intimacy with the little cheese merchant, and her face crimsoned. Nothing escaped the old rascal; he cast down his eyes, and continued in a still more dolorous tone:

"In spite of one's respect for— In short, there are some things too hard to be permitted to pass without explanation — especially when people are poor, honest, have no reason to reproach themselves, and have always lived without giving cause for scandal—by the blessing of God." His manner became more bold and assured as the countess's agitation increased. "What would you have! People are accustomed to be obeyed, to meet with no resistance. It is natural, when they are rich and of noble birth. Oh! yes, of noble birth! then people think that everything belongs to them, cattle and men, plains, forests, mountains, everything—everything—even the young girls of the country."

"Speak more plainly, and be brief. Whom do you reproach, whom do you accuse?" Unfortunately the young wife's voice trembled and did not harmonize with the firmness of her words. The other clasped his hands, and his eyes glistened.

"Oh! good heavens! I accuse the count! Madame knows very well that I should not dare— Is not the count master here? He is young, and likes to amuse himself. There is no harm in that; the mountains are not gay, and we are far from the city; then he meets a young girl who is by no means ugly. Of course the count did not mean any harm; the injury was done afterwards. But I see that Madame is tired; I did not intend to speak to her; I will come back again some other time, when I can see her father, who is a very honorable man. Madame has only just breakfasted, and poor people's troubles, so soon after eating, spoil the digestion."

"You will go on to the end of your story, although you seem to delight in making it as confused as possible. Has the count betrayed your daughter? Is that what you mean?"

"If you knew that, Madame, you must also be aware of the poor child's situation."

The countess started, and as she unconsciously made a gesture expressive of the disgust with which the man's manner inspired her, he continued eagerly:

"Oh! I see that you don't believe me, but fortunately the whole country can prove that the child has always borne a good character, and never until the count's arrival—I thought at first that it would be my death blow! Oh, God! it is hard that a father should be so afflicted at my time of life!" He was almost weeping. "Oh, yes! the whole country will say that she has been deceived. How was she to oppose a count? She was young, weak, and knew nothing of the world. Ah! all will admit that she loved God."

"I believe what you tell me; there is no need of calling the whole country to prove it."

"That is just what I thought," he replied in a milder tone, "that is what I thought; so I said to myself: 'No doubt the countess would prefer to have me come and tell her of this accident, before it is talked over in the valley and at Vircz. Stories are not long in going the rounds of the valley; I never suspected anything, because she kept the secret so bravely."

"Well! what do you ask of me?"

She felt that she was turning pale; in addition to her grief in being reminded of the faithlessness of the count, whom she loved in spite of herself, she felt deeply humiliated on finding herself confronted with this man and forced to accept his conditions. She looked Loursière steadily in the face, and, convinced that she had divined his motive, said:

"You want money, do you not?"

"Good heavens! am I not already miserable enough? Yet they wish to humble me still more! Madame knows that such sorrows cannot be paid for — A young girl's reputation, a poor man's happiness!" Here he drew the sleeve of his jacket across his eyes. "But this is not all: when you can barely earn your bread by the hardest toil, how is another mouth to be fed? And then I am old! perhaps you have not noticed that my hands are beginning to tremble, and my hair is already gray. I had expected my daughter to marry, and that my son-in-law would come and live with us— Alas! the son-in-law is far away! Who will marry the poor girl now?"

"How much do you want, tell me at once?"

The peasant's face changed suddenly, and his eyes, until then so sad and tearful, assumed an expression of peculiar cunning.

"For us poor mountaineers," said he, "a note of— Ah! it is not much! a note of—five thousand francs would enable us to live; it is something to depend upon, to keep us from starving."

Loursière had his reasons for asking neither more nor less; he claimed a sum that the countess might obtain from her own private purse without being obliged to apply to her husband or M. Larreau, who would probably have sent the afflicted father away with a note for five hundred francs in his hand. He had relied upon the young wife's emotion, terror, and ignorance of the laws. Proofs were almost imposisible to furnish, and the young cheese merchant had not been famed for her prudery. Loursière therefore resolved not to make too much disturbance about the accident, as he called it, not wishing to get into any difficulty with M. Larreau, as he foresaw the importance of keeping on good terms with him in the hope of reaping some advantage.

"You want five thousand francs? Very well, I will see what is to be done; you can go."

He raised his little gray eyes, and stroking his red beard said: "If Madame thinks that I have time to wait, she is mistaken."

"Do not forget to whom you are speaking, and go away."

"Oh! that's the way that the unfortunate are treated. We are ruined, our daughters are betrayed, and people even refuse to pay the expenses! Fortunately there is a God who sees all, and there is some justice in this world."

"Have I told you that I would not pay for your silence? I must have time to reflect before giving what you ask, that is all."

"Reflect! It seems to me that the count didn't take much time to reflect when he betrayed my poor little girl, who has to bear her misfortune all alone. Who is the one to suffer, the count or my daughter? And suppose she should die like her poor mother, would Madame still wish to reflect? And what is to become of me during these meditations, with no one to carry my cheeses, or bring me soup when I go to the mountain pastures? To whom am I doing a service by coming quietly in this way to arrange the affair pleasantly, when anybody else in my place would have demanded justice with loud outcries?"

Mme. de Manteigney felt that her patience was becoming exhausted.

"Don't say another word," said she, "you will be the gainer," and suddenly turned her back upon him.

Loursière, not daring to follow her, slowly put his hat on and went back by the way he came. The truth is, that although the countess was irritated by the words of this wily personage, she was still more terrified at thought of public scandal. She had been on the point of giving him the money he demanded at once, and putting an end to the affair, but was ashamed to yield to such threats; besides, there was nothing to prove that he spoke the truth. Was it not a mere menace of Loursière's? Why had he chosen a time when she was alone in the castle? Why not wait until the count's return, instead of addressing himself to her? If on the other hand he had spoken the truth, and the poor child, who was after all only partly to blame, was really ill, suppose her father, enraged at not obtaining what he desired, should carry his threats into execution?

It seemed to her that the wisest course would be to go and ascertain the truth. She could take the money, and if Loursière had not deceived her, would buy his silence as he demanded. His hut was not more than a league distant. Although the roads were bad, she would pretend that she wished to take a walk and execute her project without attracting any one's attention.

After forming this resolution she grew somewhat calmer, and in her heart even felt an emotion of joy in imposing this sacrifice upon herself through love for her husband, in defending him, aiding him, and conquering his dislike. But there was one thing that aroused her anxiety. It was absolutely necessary to have a guide, for she did not know the way; she had seen the rugged paths that led to his abode too often to dare to venture into them alone, and the bare idea of going to this monster's lair unprotected, made her shudder from head to foot.

She was thinking of this the following morning when a ragged child was brought in who asked to see her without delay. As soon as the little savage was left alone with the countess, he awkwardly pulled off his dirty cap, drew out a folded bit of paper perfectly disgusting to the sight, and, without saying a word, handed it to Madame de Manteigney, who opened it instantly with the tips of her fingers.

The note contained these few words:

"Answer me at once. There is no time to wait; it will be too late to-morrow."

"Who gave you this paper, little one?" asked the countess, advancing so hastily that the terrified child retreated two or three paces, "who gave it to you?"

"It was—it was Loursière, who told me to carry it to the lady of Manteigney."

"Very well, I will answer."

Doubt was no longer possible, she must form some resolution, Loursière had told the truth about his daughter. Mme. de Manteigney reflected a moment, and then went hastily to the curé's dwelling. Her face had doubtless retained some trace of her emotion, for the priest exclaimed as she entered:

"Good heavens! what brings you here? what is the matter now, poor wife?"

"I have a service to ask which no one but you can render; will you promise to do it? Let me sit down, I have walked so fast."

"What do you wish, Madame? I am listening, and if what you ask is possible, be assured—"

"Oh! do not speak so, I implore you. I am anxious, wretched, you can see that plainly. It will cost me terribly dear to carry out the plan I have formed, and if you do not encourage me by a little kindness, I shall not dare to venture farther—I can rely upon no one but you, my friend. You must—you must accompany me this evening, I am obliged to take a walk up among the pine trees."

"With your father?" asked the priest anxiously.

"No, indeed! If I could let any one but you into the secret of this visit, should I come in search of you, make demands upon your time, your kindness, your—charity?"

"Why not make the visit in broad daylight? It would be much better."

"Why, why? Because I don't want to meet any one on the way; it must not be known."

"Good heavens! but—"

"I am going to see Loursière's daughter; there, are you satisfied?"

"Loursière's daughter—!"

There was a world of meaning in the simple words. The countess rose, and continued in a lower tone, which revealed the approach of tears:

"Pardon me; I see that I am mistaken, I have been imprudent, I deceived myself, let us say no more about it. Tell me of some peasant, some steady, discreet man, who can guide me, and I will leave you. I had thought that after giving you proofs of the most perfect confidence, I could rely upon your regard, and did not even think that I might compromise you; you are doubtless afraid—"

"I will go, I will guide you wherever you desire. Compromise me! I afraid!" He drew himself up suddenly: "Afraid of whom, afraid of what, except of not doing my duty?"

"I should have explained everything to you, but I wished to have your promise first; it would have done me so much good. This is the rest of the story; nothing is more simple; unfortunately—"

"I do not wish you to explain, since my questions have made you suspect me. I do not desire it, at least not now. I trust you, do not deprive me of the pleasure of serving you blindly."

"How good and noble you are, and how I love you for it!"

"Enough, enough! When do you wish to start?"

"This evening, as soon as it is dark. It will take about two hours to go and return, will it not?"

"Two hours of very rapid walking; but you cannot take two hundred steps on those paths, piled with sharp, rough stones. You must have a donkey, then we might go by a circuitous way, and meet no one."

"I trust the matter entirely to you. Isn't it difficult to obtain a donkey?"

"I will do my best." After a moment's reflection, he continued:—"This evening, at eight o'clock, you will take the path that leads from the castle bridge."

"Just at that hour all the servants are at dinner, and I can dismiss my maid."

"You will walk along the path for about a hundred paces."

"I shall be afraid, alone at night—"

"Do not be anxious, I will wait for you; then we can take the right hand, turning into the old road by the saw-mill, which is very easy, and on reaching the woods, where we shall be obliged to follow the bed of the stream, and walk over the stones, we will find a donkey to carry you."

"Are you sure to find one there."

"Do not be uneasy, I will fasten it myself just at the edge of the woods. The place is very lonely, and I shall not be observed. I will neglect nothing. If I have done wrong in taking this course, God, who reads all hearts, will doubtless forgive me for it."

"Why should you wish God to pardon you? Are you not the best and most self-sacrificing of men? Eight o'clock, you told me. Eight o'clock," she added in a low tone—" how late it is; suppose he should think I did not mean to answer ? "

" What did you say ? "

" Nothing. This evening, at eight o'clock—the path leading from the bridge ? Oh, I know it. Thank you, M. le curé, thank you, with all my heart ! "

She pronounced the words *thank you* with such an expression of gratitude that Abbé Roche, much agitated, could find no words to reply.

" Why should she thank me so earnestly ? " said he to himself.

" It ought to appear a very simple matter, and she cannot guess what it costs me to render her this service." He had indeed struggled violently with himself. He was terrified at the thought of being alone with her at night, in solitary places; but he feared still more that she might consider him a selfish being, capable of bargaining over his services and recoiling before a difficulty.

XXII.

" Is it you, Monsieur le curé ? "

Eight o'clock had struck long before; the darkness was intense, and the wind, sighing through the trees, made a noise that drowned the voice. Yet she could not speak louder, poor woman ! She was trembling from head to foot, stopped at every step, thinking that she discerned the dark outline of the priest, and repeated more and more timidly : " Monsieur le curé—answer, is it you ? "

Had she not mistaken the path. It seemed as if she had been walking for a century, and she was beginning to yield to her terror, when something black moved in the darkness about ten paces before her, and she heard the words :

" Come, Madame, do not be afraid; I am here."

"At last!" she murmured. "I have kept you waiting, but indeed it was not my fault. I did not wish to start until the servants had gone to dinner, and then I could not open the little door that leads to the lawn. I am trembling now. I was so frightened while walking along that horrible road! Oh! now, I feel safe once more. Let us hasten on; it is very late, and I am expected, at least, I hope I am still expected."

Abbé Roche, standing at some little distance, replied, "Yes, yes, let us walk on as fast as possible, Madame! We are near the cottages, and might meet some one, we must be quick."

"I am coming as fast as I can, my dear curé, I am coming as fast as I can; but I can't see very distinctly, the road is rough, and I am a little frightened."

She instinctively approached nearer him, although he as instinctively recoiled. "Take courage, Madame, we shall soon reach the woods. Would you like my cane to help you?"

"Thank you, yes. Dear me, how heavy it is!"

Abbé Roche suddenly felt his cassock pulled, and turning, saw the countess standing motionless, with her head bent forward, pointing at something. "What is that, look, there, there?" she murmured, drawing so near the curé that her silken robes brushed against him.

"Do not be afraid, it is only the trunk of a chestnut tree."

"A chestnut tree—are you sure? Oh! dear, it is frightful, it seems as if it were staring at us. Let us turn to the left, won't you?"

"Certainly, Madame; calm yourself, it is nothing but a chestnut tree."

"I believe you; but no matter, let us turn to the left."

The young wife had not relinquished her hold

upon the priest's cassock. In spite of her efforts to appear calm, she drew nearer and nearer to her companion, walking close upon his heels, and often, when a stone made her stumble, even clinging to his arm as a drowning man clutches a branch.

Abbé Roche's brain was in a whirl; yet he could not say: "Release me, Madame." He could have endured the delightful but dangerous companionship in broad daylight, under the brilliant rays of the sun, but in this darkness, which, wrapping them both in the same veil, produced a strange feeling of mutual confidence, they spoke in low, mysterious whispers; the dread of discovery drew them together, and the priest, to dispel the agitation which was destroying his self-control, murmured all the prayers that he could recollect with the energy of a martyr. At last they reached a spot where the paths crossed. "We can light the lantern now," said he, "let us stop a moment."

"Oh! how glad I am! I was almost frightened to death!"

Abbé Roche drew from his pocket a small dark lantern which he was in the habit of using when he went out in the evening, lighted the candle, and then partially closed the two doors, leaving only a narrow ray of light to shine upon the path.

The country became more and more lonely, and they began to distinguish the sound of the great waterfall; while on either side rocks protruded from the ground amidst the grass and shrubs. "Do you see the wood yonder, Madame?"

"No, I can distinguish nothing but a black mass."

"That is the very spot, and the fatiguing part of your journey is now over. I fastened the donkey there, and the remainder of the road is easy."

"Well, it is quite time. I don't think I could have walked ten paces farther. I feel as if I should be more composed when I am once on the donkey's back, and then I will tell you why we are going to visit the horrible man who lives up yonder."

On reaching the edge of the little wood, the abbé stopped, and giving the lantern to the countess, said: "Wait for me a moment, Madame, while I go for your donkey. He is close at hand, don't you hear him stamping?"

"I shall never be able to stay here alone."

"I entreat you to do so. You see I must climb this slope, you could not ascend it, and we should only lose time."

"Then come back as soon as you can."

She wrapped herself resignedly in the gray opera-cloak she had donned for the evening journey. Cough occasionally, to encourage me, M. le curé, so that I can at least know you are there."

When he had moved away three paces, he wiped the perspiration from his brow. For the first time in his life he felt the delightful emotion a man experiences in protecting a woman. Now that he was at some little distance from the charming danger, he regained his self-control, struggled less vehemently with his emotion, and while parting the branches to enter the thicket, said to himself:

"She depends wholly upon me, she is impatiently expecting me." He remembered all the timid, anxious little phrases that she had just whispered, bending towards him. He thought of the happiness of a man to whom God entrusts the fate of such a creature, shrinking yet earnest, courageous though timid, only asking to be directed, beloved, cheered, and in return gives herself wholly—

A little discreet *hem* warned him to hasten. He coughed in reply, and soon emerged from the thicket, leading the donkey by the bridle.

It was a very quiet animal, furnished with the huge pack-saddles on which the peasant women sit with their baskets, their milk, and sometimes their children. "I took what I could find," said he in a low tone.

As he spoke, he arranged his heavy cloak, doubled four times upon the saddle, fastening it with the girths. "All is ready, will you mount?"

He saw very plainly that it was a difficult matter, but what more could he say or do?

The poor lady tried her best; clasping the saddle firmly with both little hands, and summoning all her strength, she endeavored to spring up. Alas! the effort was vain. She tried two or three times, biting her lips with anger, and murmuring words drowned by the roar of the wind. "I can't do it, I assure you I can't, my dear curé," she said at last. "Oh, dear! oh, dear! and how fast the time is passing. Please lift me, I am not heavy, and you can do it in an instant."

He had thought of it, still thought of it, but dared not. A few moments' reflection would have been necessary to enable him to decide upon such a course. The difficulty was not in the action itself, but in performing it calmly, without losing his self-control. In Abbé Roche's state of mind it required absolute heroism to accomplish such a result. "I assure you I am not heavy," she continued. "No one will see you, M. le curé, there is no harm in it. It must be done at last. All things are fair in war!—and it is so late!"

Abbé Roche was suddenly endowed with singular courage. His hesitation and fear vanished, and taking the young wife in his arms, while she laid her head on his shoulder, he lifted her from the ground like a child; but when he held her pressed against his breast, heard her satin cloak rustle under his grasp, and felt the warm, sweet breath of the countess, who was leaning on him, the poor man lost his self-command, the world of reality disappeared. He held her, clasped her in his arms, lost all consciousness of aught else, surrendered every other thought so utterly that, when he had placed her in the saddle, no longer realizing what he was doing, and still carried away by his feelings, he covered her hands with kisses, sobbing like a child.

Mme. de Manteigney pushed him back, and involuntarily uttered two little cries, a pardonable imprudence, certainly. Yet there must have been a very singular echo near by, for a third exclamation, almost exactly like her own, at once replied.

Abbé Roche felt like a man who, while burning with fever, is plunged into an icy bath without the slightest warning. The countess hastily opened the lantern she still held in her hand, threw the rays towards the spot whence the sound proceeded, and to her extreme terror saw among the bushes, about fifteen paces distant, two shining eyes fixed upon her. Were they those of a wolf or some other wild animal? She was not long in uncertainty. The child, who had been crouching among the brambles gazing at her, rose slowly, with every outward sign of the most extreme terror, and advanced a pace or two, repeatedly making the sign of the cross.

She tried to speak, but was too much agitated to utter a word. Besides, the thought occurred to her that her voice might be recognized; and as the child still advanced, she ordered him back with a hasty gesture, and suddenly closed the lantern. All this had taken place in much less time than I have related it. Doubtless the countess's gesture was instantly obeyed, for the little mountaineer was heard running wildly, at full speed, down the steep path that passes the ruins of the old saw-mill, and leads into the valley.

The young wife and Abbé Roche stood motionless with horror. Both listened earnestly, and the wind having died away, they heard in the profound silence of the night the noise of the stones rattling loudly down, and the dogs barking in the distance. Mme. de Manteigney, who, in the moment of danger, had summoned all her energies, lost her strength when assured that the child had disappeared, and began to tremble like a leaf. The priest, too, was greatly agitated. In his own eyes he had committed a sin. It was shameful. And he had been surprised, recognized. Was it not an act of divine justice? Suppose the whole village had been there! He would have deserved the disgrace of such a punishment. In a single instant he had sullied thirty years of a pure and honorable life. He dared not even ask God's pardon.

"Chastise the unworthy priest, O Lord! Crush him in Thine anger," said he to himself, and he was deeply in earnest; "chastise the proud fool, who thought to aid with his counsels, to save the wanderers of this world, when far more guilty than they." Yet he trembled at the thought of meeting the countess's eyes, hung his head, and sought for fitting words to humiliate himself before this angel, who was a thousand times more pure, since he had insulted her. The poor wife's indignation and scorn, restrained for an instant by their very depth, would soon burst forth in withering language. He accepted all before it was uttered; but contrary to his expectations, he felt a light touch on his shoulder and heard a faint, trembling voice, whispering in his ear: "I implore you to take me back to the castle, my dear curé, quick, quick, or I shall die of fear—"

Not a word of the guilty kiss, the insulting embrace. The truth was, the countess had, for the moment, forgotten it in her fright. "Let's make haste," she continued, "I am frozen, my teeth are chattering, I cannot stay here an instant longer." The priest touched the donkey with his heavy cane, and they rapidly descended the path. "Oh! dear, oh! dear," murmured the countess, "that terrible Loursière, what will he think, what will he do, if I don't go? Bring a complaint, rouse the whole country, he is capable of anything! Go to him, this evening, this very instant, I implore you, go to him, save the count's honor and mine also—you understand the rest. No one must know of the affair, and that horrible man threatens to tell everything if he does not receive the five thousand francs from me this evening. You see, it is absolutely necessary for you to go; I could not, I should fall down by the way. You will not refuse me, tell me? Say that you do not refuse me?"

Abbé Roche clasped his hands, while tears flowed from his eyes, tears of gratitude and admiration. He would gladly have thrown himself at the feet of this noble woman, who feigned that she did not remember the deadly outrage, the infamous treachery of which she had been the victim, but still condescended to entreat, when the most imperious commands would have been too indulgent. "I will go, Madame, I will go," he murmured.

He regretted from the depths of his heart that he could not have given his life to make amends for his sin.

Meantime the donkey, urged rapidly down the sloping path, moved quickly on, and the countess soon found herself before the little door opening on the lawn by which she had left the château. She took the key, put it in the lock, and turning towards the priest, exclaimed: "You will save us, will you not? Go quickly, M. le curé. Here are the five notes—go at once."

The Abbé fastened the donkey to the nearest branch, put on his cloak, and clenching his heavy cane in his hand, rushed—the word is a correct one—towards père Loursière's dwelling. It would not have been prudent to stop him on the way. The man, but lately so humble, walking with drooping head beside the young wife, before whom he would willingly have knelt, now advanced boldly, with dilated nostrils.

The energy of his movements, the night wind blowing in his face, aroused new emotions within him.

It was no longer horror of his sin that occupied his thoughts, but the memory of that one moment's intoxication which made him shiver. Again he clasped her in his arms, to his heart, only far more violently, with almost suffocating strength. His blood boiled, his limbs became stronger and more pliant, his brain clearer. For one instant he had lived and loved, he had absorbed the poison of a single arrow, and experienced a strange joy as he felt the terrible yet delicious venom flowing through his veins, and invading his whole frame. He remembered that he was most wretched, gnashed his teeth, would have liked to fall prostrate in the dust, and yet he was triumphant: he seemed to hear a celestial harmony, in the midst of which an awful voice cried: "Thou art accursed!" Heaven and hell were both half open to receive him, and he held out his arms to embrace the world and fasten himself to it.

While all these thoughts were whirling through his brain he was climbing among the rocks and brambles, taking the shortest way; he moved with a sort of frenzy, like a soldier in the vanguard that is rushing to the assault. His pace was so rapid that, three-quarters of an hour later, he found himself before the hut occupied by Loursière, and stopped to wipe the perspiration from his brow.

A reddish light shone from under the door, and as he approached, he heard groans from within, that recalled him to reality. He knocked; père Loursière, armed with a candle end, opened the door. "Ah! is it you, M. le curè," said the peasant, raising his huge fur cap, "come in, you are late! The poor little thing is very ill, M. le curé, very ill."

"Yes, I know it; but before I enter, while we are alone, I have something to give you from a person—"

"Oh! the kind lady!"

"Do not utter her name, it is unnecessary. I am to give you this little packet. I will say nothing now about what I think of your conduct, your shameful threats; God sees all things, père Loursière."

"Oh! the dear lady, oh! the dear soul! Threats? *I*, threats? Can she believe that I intended to threaten her! Threats of what, my dear M. le curé? What can a poor man like me do? Proofs must be had before we can threaten! A misfortune has fallen upon us, that is all we can say, and the kind lady wishes to help us bear it. I was very sure that she would not abandon us."

While speaking, he opened the packet (rather awkwardly, on account of the candle that was in his way) and counted the bank-notes.

"This is not all," said the curé, advancing a pace or two.

"Ah! you would like a receipt? The affair is not pleasant to talk about, and naturally—"

"I was not commissioned to ask for any. I wish to see your daughter, that is all."

"It is much better so for every one. Come in, M. le curé," and his voice suddenly changed its tone: "Alas! poor child! she appears to be about to enter the other world. When I look at her, it seems as if I saw her dead mother again. It is very hard for me, M. le curé, at my age—"

The miserable hut had a sinister aspect, and the air was heavy and dense. From the ceiling, formed of broad, roughly jointed boards, hung bits of straw and hay, handfuls of dried herbs, strings of onions, and numbers of other things that could scarcely be distinguished in the obscurity. The floor was black and dirty, and on an old chest, one of whose feet was replaced by the fragments of a broken pot, were piled the tin boxes, with rows of holes, in which the cheeses were made. There was an indistinguishable heap of rags, baskets, branches, and even whole trunks of fir trees in the room, and at the back of this den, near a worm-eaten staircase leading to the garret, the poor girl lay motionless, stretched on a miserable pallet, amidst shapeless, colorless rags.

As the curé approached, a tall thin man, no other than the village doctor, rose, lifted his cap, and advanced to meet the priest, saying:

"Good-evening, Monsieur le curé, you see it is all over with the poor child, which is no great matter of surprise to me; her mother died in the same way. I had expected it! When girls have the evil spirit in them, you know, M. le curé— There are half a dozen in the village just like her."

"You are sure that there is no hope?"

"Oh, perfectly. I was called too late; the child is a very fine one. Just look at this boy."

The physician drew aside some rags, and the priest beheld a tiny, restless little mortal, lying on a mattress close beside its dying mother. One would almost have thought that life was passing from one to the other, and the poor girl's last sigh would become the first cry of the new-born infant.

Abbé Roche approached the expiring girl. She was already unconscious, and her face had assumed a yellow hue that resembled waxen tapers. The sunken nostrils scarcely quivered, her cheeks were hollow, her cold hands lay motionless on the bed, and when she opened her large black eyes, they had the peculiar expression of the dying, who seem to be searching their own hearts.

The priest bent over her: "Do you know me, my child, do you hear me?"

Thinking that, notwithstanding her silence, she might perhaps understand his question without being able to reply, he spoke to her of pardon, of the goodness of God, who reads all hearts. "Repent, my child, think that the hour is approaching, when—"

"She does not hear you, my dear M. le curé," said

the doctor approaching him; "do you not see that she is dead?"

Then turning towards père Loursière, who had removed his huge cap and was looking at the corpse with his little eyes full of tears, he added: "Come, take courage, old man! this death was inevitable; you should have watched. You must bear this. I am going home and will send you one of the sisters from the hospital; you can't stay here alone. And now, what are we to do with this child?"

The curé, who had been kneeling in prayer, rose hastily: "He must first be made a Christian, doctor."

And père Loursière, having brought the water, the priest baptized the child. His hand trembled, for the recollection of his own sin returned to him, and he asked himself whether God would accept the consecration.

"This is certainly a sad thing, my dear M. le curé," observed the doctor, before taking his departure; "but what can be done about it? Such things have occurred ever since the world was made. The child remains and is likely to live, so the most pressing necessity is to return to him. These poor little creatures, fallen from nobody knows where, have been known to make their way in the world and find a place for themselves. Don't you know of some nurse in Grand-Fort-le-Haut, M. le curé?"

"No, I do not; but one must be found;" then recollecting himself, he exclaimed: "Marianne has not yet weaned her little girl."

"Do you think she would take this child?"

"She must. I will attend to the matter, doctor, I will attend to the matter."

Half an hour after the events just related the priest left the hut, holding his little lantern in one hand, and with the other carrying a tolerably large bundle under his cloak. It was the baby, half buried in its mother's clothing, which had been wrapped around it. Abbé Roche, with his tall, athletic figure and broad shoulders, was a comical yet touching sight. He walked with the excessive care of a man who carries a glass filled to the brim—watchful, awkward, bending half double, and seeming almost bowed down by the weight of his light burden. "Suppose he should take cold, he thought, suppose he should be too warm? The little thing's life hangs by a thread!"

He experienced an emotion never before imagined, while thinking that the fate of the little creature was entirely in his hands, that he might suffocate it by a slight pressure, or crush it by making a false step. He had a feeling of almost paternal tenderness for the tiny nursling, and took pleasure in holding it on his arm and making every effort to shelter it; he would willingly have caressed it! Was it not a reminder of his own past? He, too, had doubtless been carried secretly away by night, concealed under some stranger's cloak. Was he not paying a debt by taking care of the poor deserted child? Once the infant moved in its hiding-place and began to cry. The priest was greatly troubled. How should he soothe it, how ascertain the cause? He was afraid to uncover the child, the night air was so cold, and scarcely dared to touch the little man, his fingers seemed so huge and clumsy. Fortunately, he remembered what he had seen the mothers of Grand Fort do under similar circumstances; and while moving the little one up and down as gently as possible, he endeavored to recollect some simple song; but not recalling any, began to intone the vesper service, as if it were the most natural thing in the world. The effect was almost magical, and quiet being restored, Abbé Roche continued his walk, but on reaching Marianne's house found that he was exhausted with fatigue. Never in his life had he performed a harder task.

It was some time before his knock was answered; but at last a window opened, and a head appeared.

"Why, good gracious, there must be the deuce to pay when people come knocking at one's doors in this fashion! What do you want? What time is it?"

"Let me in, good mother," replied the priest; "it is three o'clock in the morning."

On recognizing the curé's voice, the good woman lighted a candle and opened the door at once.

"My good Marianne," said the priest entering, "here is another child that God sends you!" He drew aside the cloak, and revealed the infant's little hand hanging below its folds.

"If you will not take him, he must go to the other world for food and drink."

"Poor little innocent! let me give him something immediately," and she threw into the fire-place a handful of dry twigs, that blazed up instantly.

Meantime, Marianne's husband was dressing himself behind the bed-curtains.

"What! you have brought us a foster-child, haven't you, M. le curé? Of course I should not want to turn the little thing away; but there is a great deal to be done—a great deal to be done," repeated the wood-cutter.

Marianne removed the infant's coverings, revealing his large head and tiny, active, vigorous limbs, and turned him to the right and left, saying: "He is a handsome fellow: aren't you a beauty, my lad?" Then hastily wrapping him up again, and encircling him with her left arm with the wonderful skill that is one of the instinctive gifts of maternity, she went towards a large chest, and took out some blankets and infants' clothing. "Come, husband, warm these things. You see, M. le curé, there is a great deal to be done. I have four already! if I had not, I wouldn't say anything, but—"

The wood-cutter had both skill and experience in

these matters, for he took the clothes in his huge, bony hands without the least hesitation, and stooped over the fire to blow upon the flame.

"After all," continued the good woman, "he is a handsome boy, and welcome. Is he a child from the hospital, M. le curé?"

"Yes, he has neither father nor mother. You will be paid, of course."

"Yes, that's all right," murmured the husband, still blowing the fire.

"And well paid," added the priest, "I promise you that."

"Ah! it's a fine boy, and my wife knows how to take care of children as well as anybody. It is strange that the fire don't kindle."

"Well! and the caps, where are the babies' caps?"

"Can't you go and look for them, and keep quiet, you everlasting chatter-box? It's very hard luck, isn't it, M. le curé, to have a husband that is always talking? When he don't chatter, he sings; when he doesn't sing he talks, and whether one likes it or not, makes very little difference. Oh, good gracious! there is the other little monkey waking up. Go and see what it wants, husband."

"It wants—it wants something to drink."

"It wants—it wants— What on earth do you mean by your *it wants, it wants?*"

"Bless me! of course it wants—"

"It wants what?"

"It wants something to drink, I tell you."

"Well! after all my asking, must you put on mittens to say: It wants to nurse? Isn't it natural for a child to nurse, M. le curé? But it shall do no such thing, there now. Give it some sugar and water; it sha'n't nurse. It must be weaned at once."

While speaking, Marianne had dressed the newborn infant in a twinkling, and was now dandling it in her arms.

"Well, my friends, you have kind hearts," said the curé, "and now good-night, I must go home and rest."

He approached the baby and gently embraced it, then turned towards the door, saying: "Good-bye, until to-morrow."

The wood-cutter accompanied the curé, grinning until his little round eyes were almost lost amidst his deep wrinkles. At last, shrugging his huge shoulders, accustomed to carry heavy logs of wood, he murmured: "She scolds me a little before people, but I love her for all that, M. le curé."

"What is he saying now?"

"I said that I loved you for all that."

"It is strange that you should say such ridiculous things! I love you just the same, too."

XXIII.

Day was just dawning as Abbé Roche returned home. He threw himself on his bed, hoping to obtain a little quiet and repose; but scarcely had he closed his eyes when he was assailed by a tumultuous throng of visions. The château was in flames. The old church bell rang violently, and all the villagers, suddenly roused from slumber, ran to seize their fire buckets. He rushed into the midst of the conflagration, and perceived the countess, half dressed, with dishevelled hair, wringing her hands and calling to him for aid. "I forgive you, my friend," she cried; "save me, save me!"

He leaped over every obstacle, reached her side, and raised her in his arms. She clung to him with all her strength, exclaiming: "You are my preserver, I love you."

At these words he seemed to be endowed with threefold power, and bore her through the midst of the flames. The ceilings and roofs were falling. People shouted: "Come here, go there." He could not move. He saw her lose all consciousness—and the thought of dying with her in the midst of the tumult excited such keen emotions that he suddenly awoke. On emerging from the clamor, and finding himself in his silent little chamber, dimly visible in the bluish light of early morning, he clasped his hands, crying: "My God, my God, grant me peace once more!"

Then his head drooped again, his eyes closed, and he saw her once more walking beside him, but it was on the edge of a precipice. They talked in whispers, for they were pursued. Suddenly the young wife drew him towards her, and clasped in each other's arms, they sprang into the abyss. It was one of those interminable falls which sometimes occur in dreams, and afford time to die most blissfully. As he took her hand and raised it to his lips, the doctor said:

"You see that she is dead; take the child and fly." Then he entered a vast cathedral, which was suddenly filled with light, crowded, and echoing with music, as if for the ordination of some priest. He felt the child move under his cloak, and although he strove to lose himself in the throng, was pushed into the front ranks. All eyes were fixed upon him with an expression of contempt and repugnance. He saw the bishop advance to meet him, and as the prelate approached, recognized under his mitre the livid features of the Count de Manteigney, who publicly slapped him in the face. The crowd rushed upon him, drove him from the temple, and he found himself in an immense desert, holding in his arms the new-born infant, and bathing it with his tears.

The *Angelus* roused the curé of Grand Fort from these haunting nightmares. He opened his windows to admit the fresh morning air, and remembering that the bell-ringer would be awaiting him in the vestry, went there as usual. On leaving the church, his mind was somewhat calmer, and he discovered that he was very hungry. Cutting off a large piece of bread, he began to eat it eagerly; but when about to pour out some wine, stopped, replaced the bottle, and drank a large glass of water. Was he imposing a penance upon himself, and did he wish to begin, by this little sacrifice, a life of reparation?—Who can tell? He took his breviary and went towards Marianne's cottage, intending afterwards to visit père Loursière. While Abbé Roche was ascending the mountain, a very singular rumor began to spread through the village. Already on the square before the church, and at the doors of the houses, groups of people were eagerly talking. They related the following tale:

The preceding night, a little shepherd named Pierre Ribat, scarcely more than a child, while returning home rather late, had perceived on the mountain, near a grove of trees, at the spot called the White Cross, on account of two rocks placed one above another, a sort of light, a tremulous light, something like a Will-o'-the-Wisp. The child, greatly surprised by this unexpected sight, had also noticed a strong smell of incense in the air, and although much terrified, crouched among the grasses and crawled towards the light, which at times disappeared and then re-appeared. On arriving within a certain distance, he heard a confused murmur of voices, and hiding behind a little bush, gazed at the scene as steadily as he could. The light flickered like a star that was about to return to the skies. Suddenly a cry arose, a frightful cry, such as he had never heard before, a cry that seemed to proceed from the rocks. The child was so frightened that he felt his hair stand on end, and he could not help uttering a shriek, when the light was instantly transformed into a dazzling flood of rays, in the midst of which he saw with his own eyes the Holy Virgin mounted on an ass, and Saint Joseph walking behind, so that any one would have supposed the colored statues in the church of Grand Fort had suddenly appeared in a burst of sunlight. The Child Jesus was probably concealed under his mother's cloak on account of the night air, so the shepherd did not see him; but he was almost sure that he had heard him. Unfortunately the splendor of the heavenly light was so great that his dazzled eyes could not distinguish the details of the picture very clearly. Be that as it might, Pierre Ribat plainly understood that the Virgin did not wish to be approached, for she raised her arm, and ordered him by a gesture of the hand to go at once towards the old saw-mill; then everything disappeared. The little shepherd lost all self-command on finding himself alone in the darkness, and began to run at full speed over the stones and through the brambles, leaping over rocks and hedges and climbing the steep slopes; the dogs, hearing the uproar, sprang out of the sheep-folds, and rushed after him. Half mad with terror, he reached the plain, cut by the stones, torn by the thorns, and, still pursued by the dogs, stopped behind the new building, which barred any further progress, and failing on his knees, recited five *Paters* and five *Aves.*

Such was the strange tale which, after going the rounds of the village, reached the ears of M. Larreau about ten o'clock in the morning by means of his valet. This man unfortunately was tinged with free thinking, so that he had somewhat perverted the meaning and changed the words.

"And you say," observed the spout-maker, who had at first smiled but now appeared to be lost in meditation,—"you say the child stopped behind the house I have built in the valley?"

"Yes, Monsieur, that is where the Holy Virgin commanded him to go,—at least, so he says."

M. Larreau stroked his chin thinking: "The abbé is certainly extremely courageous. I should never have suspected that while looking so demure he was, in fact, a master of strategy; if he don't carry matters too far!" He was strongly tempted to laugh, but restrained himself in the valet's presence, and continued to murmur: "This is a very serious affair, very serious—I shall go there at once."

"You will find the whole village in an uproar; everybody is out of doors. What a country of savages!"

"What are you talking about? Do me the favor to keep your remarks to yourself, and hand me my boots."

The village was becoming more and more excited; the inn of the Sapin-Vert was constantly filled with noisy, inquisitive, ever-changing customers, among whom the two coachmen from the castle harangued the throng with the authority of persons who have seen a great deal of the world, and made the discussion still more vehement by their critical remarks. As the door of the church had chanced to remain open, a number of women, desirous to ask Heaven about the great event, were kneeling in the porch, praying fervently in an undertone, so that the voices sounded like the hum of a bee-hive. Among them was the little shepherd, bewildered, terrified, yet proud of the increasing importance given him by the story of his adventure.

At last M. Larreau appeared, walking along, bestowing smiling glances with his right eye, and watching the scene from the left. Saint Louis, standing beneath the oak, must have had just such a noble, simple, paternal bearing. The capitalist was held in high esteem at Grand Fort; the good women buzzing in the porch rose at his approach, and père Baravoux, mayor of the village, and one of the fattest men ever seen, was among the first to greet the new arrival.

"Well! père Baravoux, well!" said M. Larreau, "well—?"

"As you say, Monsieur," replied the other with the utmost gravity of demeanor, "it is astonishing!"

"I did not say it was astonishing; I said nothing at all; do not put words into my mouth that I never uttered." The crowd began to gather around the two wisest heads in the country. "Have you questioned the child, my dear Baravoux—has M. le curé seen him? What does M. le curé think of it? Why, where *is* M. le curé?"

"He is not at home, he has been sought for in every direction, and no one has been able to find him."

"May God bless him!" muttered the capitalist between his teeth; "when people do such things, they ought to remain at their posts. He did not give me the least warning—he—oh! he's a devil of a man! After all, perhaps it is a part of his plan."

"Not finding M. le curé," continued the mayor, "I asked the child a few questions myself, and even wrote down the answers in legal form."

"I was very sure, père Baravoux, that you would not spare trouble under such circumstances."

At that moment the by-standers gave way with respectful consideration, and the little shepherd approached, accompanied by his mother, who led him by the hand. Her face was as red as fire. He was dirty, ragged, in tatters; but his glance had the confidence imparted by success.

"Good-morning, my lad. Well! what is the matter with you?"

Before the child had half opened his mouth, the peasant woman smiled and courtesied. "This is my son, I am his mother," said she.

"Oh! oh! so much the better; I congratulate you."

"And he has always been an honest lad, and feared God, we can truly say that he never caused us any sorrow."

"Indeed, that is well; he looks wide awake. Take your fingers out of your nose, my lad."

"He is so excited, poor child! Take your fingers out at once, you rogue, when the gentleman speaks to you."

"Continue your examination of the boy, my dear Baravoux, don't let me interrupt you in the duties of your office; you are the first magistrate in the country."

M. Larreau had pronounced these words with the most vivacious carelessness, smiling good-naturedly as he looked around the circle; and the men smiled too, not wishing to appear more credulous than their master.

Baravoux, excessively flattered by the important part assigned him, coughed, bowed, and modestly continued in the following words:

"Before the father of the countess, the mayor of Grand Fort."

"Oh! ask him the questions as simply as possible; it won't do to frighten the lad, and besides, this is not an official examination, it is a matter that principally concerns M. le curé."

Baravoux, nodding assent, replied: "Well, little one, tell your story."

And the shepherd, who had been relating his adventure ever since daybreak, began again for the twentieth time, in a very weary voice, the story that we already know. When he reached the point where the Virgin made the famous gesture, M. Larreau hitherto smiling and skeptical, became extremely grave, and the whole assembly, whose eyes had been fixed upon him, redoubled their attention. Père Baravoux, perceiving that the gesture must be of the greatest importance, became more precise in his questions: "Do you distinctly recollect," said he, "in what direction the lady—the Holy Virgin, I mean, for every thing leads us to believe—does it not, Monsieur—"

"It is a very serious matter," murmured the speculator.

One might have heard a pin drop. "Do you remember in what direction the Virgin extended her arm?"

"Why, yes, of course I do, because I instantly ran where she told me to go as fast as I could, and it was directly towards the new building, where I stopped, because the wall prevented my going any farther."

All looked at each other in silence.

"Dear me, my children," said the rich man, tapping lightly on the lid of his snuff-box, "I am no more credulous than other people. If we believe all we have heard, you understand clearly that—" Every head was bowed in token of assent. "For my part, when I was told of the apparition this morning, I shrugged my shoulders, I won't deny it, I shrugged my shoulders; but after hearing the story of this child, who has always been, his mother assures us, perfectly truthful, and blameless—"

"That is the exact truth; I said so, and I say it still; you don't see such a child every day, and he deserves to be well rewarded."

The mayor stopped the good woman by a motion of his hand: "Hush, mère Ribat, let the gentleman speak, and try and keep your proper place."

"I confess, then, my children, that in the presence of these facts— It is impossible to deny it, the matter is a very serious one."

"I think so too, I think so too," panted Baravoux respectfully.

"We must not be too credulous, of course; but on the other hand, we ought not to deny everything positively."

"Like Pagans!"

"Like Pagans. The mayor, who has hitherto acted so discreetly, is perfectly right: like Pagans. I am sorry that M. le curé is not here to enlighten us; let us wait for him, my friends, let us wait for him."

And M. Larreau, unceremoniously putting his arm within that of the municipal officer, began to walk up and down the square. "You know, my dear friend," said he, "that whenever a supernatural event presents itself, there are always a multitude of people ready to say: 'God has nothing to do with it.' I, on the contrary, make this reflection. Why should Heaven be unaware of what happens? You are an upright and intelligent man, père Baravoux, am I right or wrong?"

"Perfectly right, Monsieur; that is the exact truth."

"For instance, there is the miracle of the grotto of Lourdes. Do you know about the miracle of the grotto of Lourdes?"

"Yes, Monsieur, I read it in a little pamphlet a peddler, who was trading in cotton stockings, sold me last year on his journey through the country."

"Well! every one exclaimed: 'It is no miracle, no, it is no miracle.' Yet it proved to be one. What was in the grotto before the fountain gushed forth? A little dampness, that is all, a very common thing among mountains; nothing is more common than to meet with a little dampness. Without seeking farther, just here, within two hundred yards of the new building, towards the rock, there is a very wet spot. There is nothing extraordinary about it, nobody was surprised that the grotto of Lourdes should be damp; but all at once (Baravoux listened with the greatest attention), all at once, by the information of a child, enlightened by some revelation—"

"Yes, Monsieur."

"They gently removed a little of the damp soil in the grotto, and—"

"Yes, Monsieur."

"The fountain gushed forth."

"Yes, Monsieur."

"Now I ask you, my dear friend, as a man of sense and judgment, was that a miracle or not?"

The mayor made no reply, so great was his preoccupation. His eyes were fixed on vacancy, and he breathed heavily like a tavern-keeper coming up from a wine cellar.

M. Larreau thrust his hands into his pockets, and casting a scrutinizing glance at the mayor, added: "I repeat that this is a very serious matter; I deeply regret that the curé is not here. In any case, you have examined the child as carefully as possible, and I congratulate you. Farewell, my dear friend, I am going to breakfast."

Scarcely had M. Larreau departed when the mayor, turning with the solemnity of a three-decker about to tack, said to four or five peasants who were standing near: "My lads, go and get your pickaxes and shovels, and follow me. I have an idea."

When the men had brought their tools, they set out in silence, followed by a crowd of people, and preceded by the mayor in person, who seemed to be suddenly inspired.

XXIV.

By the merest accident the countess, who according to her maid's report had spent a restless night, remained in her own room, sending an apology to her father for not coming down. M. Larreau, therefore, breakfasted alone. After finishing his meal, he went into his study, and had already been busily occupied for some time, when his valet, the free-thinker we have mentioned, entered, and with a very tolerable display of indifference, informed him that the mayor requested his presence in the valley. "Very well, I will go at once," said the spout maker; and making a slight concession to his servant's opinions, added, with a weary expression: "What do they want of me now?"

"If you do not need my services for an hour or two, I should like to ask Monsieur's permission—"

"You can go wherever you like."

"Permission," he continued with a smile, "to visit the place where the miracle was performed."

"Miracle! What miracle? Who is talking about miracles? Go wherever you choose, but speak more respectfully of sacred things."

"If you believe in these things, Monsieur, I believe in them too. People in your employ are too well off to—"

"You must not shock any one's feelings, that is what I mean—"

"The rascal is as transparent as amber!—"

Half an hour after, perceiving M. Larreau strolling slowly along like a man walking for pleasure, père Baravoux came to meet him, and exclaimed in an agitated, panting voice, pointing to the large hole that had been dug: "A spring! Monsieur, a spring in the sand—red—that I have discovered!"

"A spring, my dear friend; is it possible? The deuce"—and quickly regaining his usual imperturbability, which for an instant had deserted him, he added, loud enough to be heard by all the by-standers: "Well! to tell the truth, I am not so very much surprised; I have always had an idea there might be a spring there."

He sought with his eyes the invisible curé, the only man whose position enabled him to publicly support the weight of this miraculous event, and not perceiving him, wished to lessen the supernatural character of the discovery. "Really, I am not surprised that there should be a spring in this spot."

The mayor seemed to be very much annoyed by the capitalist's remark. "Monsieur," said he sharply, "you did not tell me so this morning; and with all due respect to you, I beg leave to observe, that if you had suspected it, you would probably have at once pursued the course that I did."

Baravoux must have been deeply wounded when he dared to speak to the countess's father in such a manner. He continued with equal excitement, while his whole person shook like a mass of jelly: "It was after the examin—"

"The examination, père Baravoux?"

"It was just after you went home to breakfast that the inspiration flashed upon me to come here, as true as the sun is shining upon us, and if it had not been for that inspiration—well! they—they would not have found the spring."

M. Larreau was about to make a soothing reply, when the mother of the little shepherd, still leading her son by the hand, pushed through the crowd, and planting herself before the mayor, exclaimed: "Well! then, if that is true, what did my boy do?" She did not attempt to conceal her indignation. "So he wasn't the one to run where he was told to go? He wasn't the one who pointed out the place, and said: 'It was there, nowhere else,' and told the whole story, from the very beginning down to the smallest particular."

Baravoux, who had flushed scarlet, replied: "I do not pretend—"

"Oh! indeed, but as true as there is a God above us, the mayor did pretend—yes, he did pretend—I am only a poor woman, but I speak the truth. It is because we are not rich; if my husband was alive, people would not dare to rob the child of his reward; the mayor doesn't need it, and he is very hard upon poor people." Then turning towards the crowd with increasing excitement, she added: "Tell me at once, was it my son who saw the Holy Virgin that night?"

"Of course it was, of course it was," murmured all the women, deep-touched by the appeal.

"I wish them to answer me, too," cried Baravoux: "who found the spring?"

"You, it was certainly you," said all the men who were present.

"Well, then! since I had the inspiration, I shall remain here, because it is my work—"

"And that devil of a curé does not come," thought M. Larreau; "he ought to bless them—speak to them. Where does he hide himself? Good heavens! where does he hide himself?"

"The mayor can stay here if he chooses," replied mère Ribat, with a menacing glance, "but my son and I will go to the White Cross, and if it should prove necessary, ask the Virgin to return."

She walked rapidly away, dragging by the hand the little shepherd, who was almost exhausted with fatigue.

The hole that had been dug by the mayor's orders gradually filled with water, and the number of curious people, eager to view the spectacle, increased every moment. They tasted the reddish, muddy liquid, whose odor, however, was by no means attractive, bathed their faces with it, and made the sign of the cross. Meantime, as the number of the inquisitive still increased and the earth became softened by their footsteps, those nearest the hole began to be inconvenienced, slipped, jostled each other, and scolded loudly. Baravoux, whose anger was only partially appeased, told the workmen to disperse the throng, and gave orders that a strong palisade of stakes should be erected.

As for M. Larreau, we need scarcely say that he had taken advantage of mère Ribat's departure to return to the château. He found that the success of the miracle was rather too rapid, and was particularly vexed by the prolonged absence of the curé. What would be the result of all this? He had wished to have a slight tinge of the mavellous, to insure the success of the affair, but nothing more. How was he to suppose that the worthy cure, apparently so calm, so little moved by impulse, would of his own accord, without informing any one, have organized such a colossal piece of jugglery?

"He did not believe in the real efficacy of the water, and therefore relied solely upon the power of his apparition," he thought to himself. "It is a very bold stroke—the boldness of an ambitious man who thoroughly understands the human heart. Have not all who endeavor to establish anything, even to the general advantage, been forced sooner or later to risk everything to gain their object? Under any circumstances I am very well satisfied to have no part in this foolery. I should have dissuaded him from it, if he had had the good sense and politeness to consult me. How the deuce did he manage to carry out all this? It is bold, extremely bold, but very clever. In Paris, or any other great intellectual centre, one would be apt to get caught in playing such a game. Who knows? but no! Bah! the firmest, most unchangeable quality in man is faith—blind faith. It was bestowed by Heaven to aid him in submitting to be governed; just as the horse's mouth was formed to permit the rider the use of the bridle. Thus the history of humanity can be told in just these words: You are horse or rider according to the degree of intelligence. The animal bears its burden and grows weary, it is true; but the position of master has drawbacks also: besides being fatigued, he runs the risk of being thrown to the ground sooner or later. Everything is equally balanced; God is good, Providence is just. Perhaps, after all, my curé is only a demure starling. I will write to Claudius."

XXV.

While Baravoux was enclosing his discovery in a strong palisade, and the capitalist engaged in writing to his friend Claudius, Abbé Roche was slowly returning towards his home. He had prayed for hours beside the body of Loursière's daughter, then walked on to Virez, and now retraced his steps over the same road he had taken the night before, somewhat calmer in mind, and thinking more coolly of all that had occurred, when, on approaching the spot where he had committed what he still continued to call his sin, he thought he heard the confused murmur of a number of people talking together. The place was usually but very little frequented—what could be the cause of this gathering?

The curé hastened on with an anxiously throbbing heart, dimly foreseeing that the disturbance had some connection with the events that had transpired the evening before. At a turn in the road, he stopped in amazement on perceiving ten or twelve persons kneeling before the White Cross. All rose at the priest's approach, and there was the most perfect silence.

"What are you doing there—why are you kneeling before that stone?" asked the curé.

Mère Ribat, who had just arrived, advanced—rushed, one might almost say—towards Abbé Roche, and, rendered half wild by all she had said and done since morning, scarcely took time to breathe, and thus addressed him: "Monsieur le curé, it was my boy that saw the Holy Virgin that night, close by this stone, with Saint Joseph and the ass, saving your reverence, who discovered the spring."

The curé was evidently agitated, and looked at the good woman with an expression which, under any other circumstances, would have made her tremble.

She continued with increasing excitement: "Yes, yes, it was he that discovered the spring and not the mayor, as people will tell you to get us into trouble. It was my boy; he—he himself, and the Virgin said to him: 'I wish it to be you, and nobody else. You will go there.' And he went with great difficulty, on account of the dogs, and the spring has been found; and if it cures all the diseases in the world, my boy will deserve the reward that is always given to children who perform miracles."

"Hush! mad woman," cried the priest, who could no longer contain himself.

"No, Monsieur le curé, I won't hush, my boy's welfare depends upon it, and I will keep on to the last, for there are unjust people who think they can hear the Virgin's voice better than we, because they have two pairs of oxen, and we have none; but that makes no difference; God performs His work by whom He wills, and the mayor has nothing to do with the miracle—no, nothing at all. I will be torn into four pieces before I will say he has. You must put my boy's name in your report, M. le curé, because he did everything, and because we are poor and honest, and work hard, and always go to confession; and he ran till his feet bled, while the mayor couldn't run, saw nothing, heard nothing, and was fast asleep at that hour."

"Hush!" cried the priest again, but this time in such a tone of wrath and menace that all drew back several paces. "Be silent, and let all here return to their work. Do you hear me?"

They knew the curé too well to dare to make any reply, but murmured in an undertone: "No, no, that isn't right, Baravoux did nothing. The good God knows everything, and the Virgin too." They still retreated as the priest advanced; but terrified as they had been by the manner of their pastor, were still more alarmed by his irreverence upon the spot where the apparition had been seen.

Yet he must know best about it, and there must be some reason why he did not raise his hat before the White Cross, but turned his back upon it as if it had been any other stone, and could not endure to have prayers offered there. Who knows, after all, whether this miracle was really performed by the will of God, and not one of those made by the devil to mislead human beings and maintain his power.

Abbé Roche, on perceiving the perplexed expression of the poor peasants, who at the worst had only been guilty of an excess of zeal and simplicity, suddenly realized how imprudent and unjust he had been. Was he not, after all, the first cause of this unfortunate event? Strange that he should be angry with them on account of his own fault! Was he not aggravating the evil, instead of soothing it? Was it not unworthy of him to fall into a passion, and threaten those whose indulgence and forgiveness he ought to implore? He was doubtless on the point of speaking to them gently and soothingly, when M. Larreau's valet emerged from the grove of trees in which the donkey had been fastened the night before. The free-thinker had desired, as we know, to bring the forces of modern criticism to bear upon the examination of the place. His search had probably been successful, for he had a most cheerful expression, and, carelessly beating the air with a switch, whistled a hunting song. On perceiving the curé, he made a rapid motion as if to conceal something within his vest. Then approaching with the most imperturbable self-possession, he bowed before the White Cross, and turned towards the curé, whom he also greeted respectfully, though an almost imperceptible smile, whose shyness increased its impertinence, played around his thin lips.

"It was here that the miracle took place, was it not, M. le curé?" he inquired.

The priest, who felt the insult veiled beneath the apparent natural question, replied in a tremulous voice: "Go along at once."

"The road is open to every one, M. le curé, by day—as well as by night," and turning carelessly on his heel, he passed on.

Abbé Roche soon found himself alone before the accursed stone, listening to the footsteps of his parishioners returning to the village. His face suddenly flushed as he remembered the mocking expression of the lackey. It seemed impossible to bear his shame; he was tempted to rush after the knave, compel him to speak, and punish him instantly.

"Why should he have smiled in that way," said he to himself, "if he had not been aware of the whole adventure down to the smallest particular. And then, what did he hide under his vest as he left the wood; for he had concealed something—doubtless some overwhelming proof. What could it be?"

He became alarmed, and as he grew more and more agitated, his natural disposition gaining the mastery, he felt the necessity of forming some decided resolution. He wished to confess everything honestly, and publicly make a frank and full acknowledgment. He would be sentenced, disgraced, but what did that matter? His duty was to receive the well-merited punishment, rather than allow a stain to rest upon religion by his cowardly silence, and a falsehood become an article of faith.

If he had been alone, he would have taken this course; but it was not only himself. Had he a right to compromise the countess, to drag her into such a scandal? Could he reveal a secret that had been entrusted to him, but was not his own; and make the count's crime public, when his wife so nobly, with such a Christian spirit, endeavored to conceal it?

Other thoughts crowded upon him: it was impossible that the little shepherd could have helped seeing the countess when he clasped her in his arms; he must also have seen him covering the young wife's hands with kisses. Doubtless the child had said nothing of all this through shame and fear; but if questioned, he would confess the truth. Those particulars had become the principal, almost the only, event of that frightful night. He estimated its importance by the depths of his remorse, and could not imagine how it could have passed unnoticed.

He soon resumed his walk. At every step that he advanced towards the village, he feared that some new revelation might start up before him. The enclosures he passed seemed more solitary than usual; he had never found the cottages so deserted as today. He saw through the trees, in the distance, two women ascending the path, one of whom was carrying a large bottle with unusual care, and, for some unaccountable reason, he imagined that it bore some relation to the great event; so, forgetting his desire to escape from all knowledge of the affair, he climbed the slope, and concealed himself behind a low hedge on the side of the road, for it seemed as if he could not help blushing if he met the women face to face. As they passed him, one said to the other: "If this water cures people, it must be good for cattle, too."

"Yes, but we must first find out whether it *does* cure people," replied the other.

When they were out of sight, Abbé Roche resumed his walk. He intended to make a circuit, in order to reach his dwelling unobserved; but had not reckoned on the obstinacy of Mayor Baravoux, who, learning from the people driven away form the White Cross that the curé was in that direction, had determined, in spite of his obesity, to go and meet the priest.

"Ah! there you are at last, M. le curé," cried the

worthy man as he perceived the priest; "everybody has been looking for you since early morning. Where were you? Good heavens! where were you at such a time?"

"I was with père Loursière, whose daughter has just died."

"But she don't belong to the parish, M. le curé, and everybody was looking for you all that time."

"I am sorry. What do you wish to tell me?"

"You have been informed, I suppose, M. le curé, of this event, whose results cannot yet be calculated?"

"I am in haste," said the priest.

"No more so that I, M. le curé; I am in a great hurry to tell you about things as they really happened. I have always been an honest man; well! I assure you that I was the one who found the spring. All at once a thought entered my mind; I felt hot and cold by turns, and said, almost without knowing it: 'My lads, take your pickaxes and shovels, and follow me.' Every one should have his due. Is it not so, M. le curé? If I said I saw the Virgin on her ass that night with Saint Joseph, I should tell a lie. Mère Ribat's little boy saw that, and in one point of view, it was fortunate: they are not rich, and it will, as usual, exempt the child from military service. I do not wish to lay claim to having any share in the miracle, not the least, M. le curé."

Abbé Roche, anxious and agitated as he was, felt disarmed by the extreme simplicity of the worthy man, and striving to retain his calmness, said: "And how dare you, père Baravoux, speak of a thing that you have not seen, and make all this uproar, because a child tells some incomprehensible story? How dare you mingle with this foolish prattle the purest of all names, that of the mother of God?"

"Yes, that is true, M. le curé, perhaps there is nothing so very remarkable about the miracle; I have said so myself a great many times to-day. In the first place the child is very artful."

"He may have been frightened, and taken some very natural occurrence for a marvellous event—"

"Oh! bless me, he is a coward—as great a coward as his mother is a chatterbox. Besides, some people see double at night. Now, you know, M. le curé, there is always room for doubt in all the wonderful things that take place at night. So far as the boy is concerned, as a man, I wish him well; but as mayor, I say nothing. Besides, it is all the same to me. The really important thing is to have had an inspiration from God, in broad daylight before everybody, and said: 'My lads, take your pickaxes and shovels,' and to have found a spring that will cure all kinds of diseases. That is the real miracle, and I was the person who performed it." He was becoming more and more excited. "Yes, that is truth, that is justice; and if they seek to rob me of my due, well!—I will go to law—I will go to law as true as this is a cane; and I will gain my cause, or there is no justice in God, no truth in anything."

"You do not know what you are talking about," interrupted the priest in a curt, imperious tone, that astonished the mayor.

At that moment they reached the square before the church, where they were immediately surrounded, and père Baravoux, however anxious he might be to answer the curé's incomprehensible outburst, was forced to content himself with muttering between his teeth a stream of sentences that nobody understood.

Mère Ribat had probably already related what had taken place at the White Cross, for the people who were present approached the curé whispering and staring, but did not venture to speak to him. Besides, the expression of his countenance was by no means encouraging; he was extremely pale, and walked straight on without looking at any one. Having crossed the square under the fire of all these curious eyes, he advanced towards the porch, pushed open the door, and entered the church. He had not expected to meet any one there at that hour; he hoped to avoid all conversation, at least for the time, and enter his house by way of the vestry, whose door opened into his little garden.

Great was his surprise to perceive in the centre of the church a group of men and women, kneeling, not before the altar, but in front of that glittering "Flight into Egypt" which the parish owed to Claudius's generosity. A bouquet, freshly gathered and placed in a vase, had been set below the bas-relief, and several bits of candle were burning near.

Unfortunately Abbé Roche was not a man for concessions and prudent temporizing. On meeting again, even in the House of the Lord, the pretended miracle that for the last two hours had been rising before him like a phantom at every turn, it seemed to him as if all these nasal prayers were so many insults hurled in his face, whose recoil might even reach the countess. Walking directly up to the bouquet, he tore it from the vase, dashed it against the wall, overturned the candles with his foot, and turning to the amazed worshippers said with tolerable calmness: "Leave this place!" but it was easy to perceive, by the sound of his voice, that at the lowest murmur, the slightest gesture, there would have been a furious burst of anger.

He folded his arms, and looking steadily at the crowd, waited until every one had gone; then turned towards the door, locked it carefully, and put the key in his pocket. He heard outside the dull buzzing of excited and indignant voices. When he had reached his room, he murmured: "O Lord! if I have done wrong, punish me, or teach me what I ought to do, for if this should continue I shall soon go mad!"

Indeed, he could not remain in this situation for any length of time; he must put an end to it in some way.

He held the most extreme views respecting his duties, his honor as a priest; and the thought of permitting a falsehood to receive public credence through his weakness, seemed to him a disgrace that it was impossible to endure. Again the plan of making a frank confession recurred to his mind; but before doing so, he must speak to the countess. He was about leaving his room to go to the château by a roundabout way, when he heard a loud knocking at the door.

XXVI.

"Open the door, open the door, my dear curé; it is I, M. Larreau."

The priest obeyed. "Ah! there you are at last! God bless you! Where have you been hiding? But what is the matter? You are as white as a pocket-handkerchief. Are you ill? That would be the climax of our trouble."

"I am perfectly well, thank you. What do you want of me?"

"Ah! you can boast of having puzzled me confoundedly. I have sent to your house ten times, but always found you absent."

"I regret it."

"I have no doubt of it, but confess that I had far more reason for regret than you. After all that had taken place, you must understand that my position was peculiarly embarrassing."

"Yet I do not comprehend you, Monsieur, and most assuredly do not see why my absence should have occasioned you the slightest embarrassment. Besides, my absence, at which some one else has also expressed surprise, was extremely natural. I went to visit Loursière, whose daughter had died during the night. I was about going to tell the news to Mme. de Manteigney, who is interested in her."

"Oh! that would be quite useless. My daughter can see no one to-day, she is ill. I only saw her for an instant, and she had scarcely strength to say three words. What! is the little savage dead? I was just going to speak to her father. You are surprised that your absence should have been a source of embarrassment. That is very flattering to me; but listen, my dear friend, I am not accustomed to these things, and this miracle, so suddenly performed, the whole country in a tumult—rather too much of an excitement, I confess. Don't you think the affair is going on a little too fast?"

He said these words with the utmost ease and gayety.

"Speak more plainly, I beg of you. I am aware that the village has been much excited this morning by the story of a child, in consequence of which, I am told, a spring has been discovered—nothing very extraordinary in this country. That is all I know, and I regret it, deeply regret it."

"This curé is cool enough, certainly," thought M. Larreau; "it would be droll if I should be obliged to console him." And smiling at the idea, in spite of himself, he continued: "What's to be done, my dear curé, let us reason together. Let us talk as friends. It is true that the credulity of the masses is a source of regret, when intriguing men turn it to their own advantage, with the shamelessness, I might almost call it, that is the result of a blind egotism; but on the contrary, when this credulity, this simplicity—it has its poesy and grandeur, too, when we take a lofty view of things—when this simplicity leads a population towards intelligent, devoted, disinterested men —disinterested in human measures, be it understood —towards men who will be able to secure their happiness and prosperity, oh! then, Providence—I speak seriously— Providence sometimes employs strange means to attain its ends: it is not for us to criticize the opportunity. We speak of providential men; but are not all intelligent men somewhat so? Above all individual and fleeting missions, there is the irresistible march of Progress, that is, of intelligence, wealth, improvement, moral activity, the increase of commerce, greater facilities for business—in short the advance of nations in morality. I have my religion, too, my dear curé, my dogmas, my principles. I have the faith natural to a successful man, whose whole career has been an argument in favor of Progress. Ah! I speak to you in all frankness, for it is but right that you should understand me perfectly. My mission has been to hasten the development of public wealth, or in other words, to increase the power of capital by concentration. Force and speed are really one and the same thing. Where there is no quickness, there is no strength! There is no power without concentration! A cloud of steam is nothing: concentrate it in a solid receiver and you have a locomotive. It is the same thing in morals and politics. Now, in our times, the providential instrument which serves to concentrate everything—is the capitalist. Scattered riches, accumulating in his hands, become powerful and fruitful. Once more, my dear curé, let us look at things as a whole, and from an elevated point of view."

Abbé Roche, erect and motionless, with contracted eyebrows, and hands clenched on the back of a chair, stood listening, and gazing at the rich man so intently that the latter was, for an instant, thrown off his guard.

"In short," said he, after coughing several times,

"I do not intend, I do not wish to reproach you, my good friend; I had not expected so striking a scene, I confess; if we had understood each other better, we might have hit upon something more simple and less compromising; but after all—when the wine is poured out, as the saying goes, we must drink it."

At that moment, M. Larreau was interrupted by the noise of a chair suddenly breaking. Whether the curé had leaned too heavily upon one whose back he was grasping, or whether his hands had suddenly contracted with unusual violence, the chair was crushed to pieces.

"Apropos of chairs and miracles, you don't manage either with a light hand, my dear friend," observed the countess's father gayly.

If Abbé Roche, instead of being partly in the shadow, had been standing where his face was more distinctly visible, it is probable that our providential capitalist would have kept his last remark to himself. The countenance of the priest, hitherto so pale, was now flushed, and quivered convulsively; the veins in his forehead and neck were swollen, and his irregular, panting breath seemed like that of a man who had been running violently.

"Go on," said he in a stifled tone; "go on, go on, I want to know all. Go on, do not trouble yourself about me."

"You seem to be agitated, my dear curé, and you are wrong. Besides, it is not necessary to exaggerate the consequences of that story; true, it might become compromising in the hands of awkward people; but it is not with us. I only regret a little excess of zeal. It would have been sufficient to have instantly placed the spring, found no matter how, by chance, in an almost providential manner, under the protection of the Virgin. I said *almost;* that would have been sufficient. Masses of thanksgiving, endowments for commemoration masses,—consecration of a hospital by the bishop, erection of a church dedicated to Our Lady of Manteigney, would have been a six months' affair—of stone and cast iron,—it would be solid, and could be finished quickly; it would only be necessary to send the proportions. The building would be erected, of course, by means of a subscription throughout France. An excellent thing for religion, an excellent affair for my springs too. Subscribers' names upon slabs of black or white marble, according to the amount of the sum paid, pilgrimage of art, etc. We should not be refused a relic, if we asked for it politely. I have a great many acquaintances. Once establish the springs of Manteigney, particularly beneficial for irritation of the larynx; build a house for the reception of convalescents, cottages specially for clergymen, a model casino, and a railway line; issue a Catholic medical pamphlet praising the therapeutic wonders of the spring, which had been almost providentially found, I repeat *almost;* oh! that would have been sufficient, the public would have done the rest. Researches into the history of the country, controversies, discussions, excavations—"

"Yes, yes, I am beginning to understand," murmured the priest.

"Of course! And thus, without the slightest difficulty or theatrical display, we should have accomplished our little stratagem. We shall attain the same result, I hope, by the present arrangement, which is perhaps bolder and more rapid, but less sure; and, under any circumstances, gives the enterprise a different character—a totally different character."

M. Larreau hesitated a moment, tapped his snuff box, winked his left eye, and continued:

"Let us speak frankly. In business matters we must play with our cards on the table. You did not expect, by entering upon the affair so energetically, to obtain a share in the profits of the enterprise? It is not at all probable that your actions were influenced by such an idea, is it, my dear curé?"

"It must be confessed, Monsieur, that you are a very frank scoundrel!" said Abbé Roche.

Violent as his efforts had been to control himself and hear the spout-maker, who was at last unveiling his true character, to the end, he could bear no more. He continued: "I now understand the service you have been asking at my hands; to aid your speculation by sacrilege and perjury; to write the name of God upon your prospectus with my own hand; hang my priestly garments at the door of your shop; sell my conscience, wallow in the mud of your spring. Then in my place, you would have been capable of doing all this!"

And as the wrathful Hercules approached, the millionaire turned pale.

"Are you jesting, my dear friend?" he stammered; "what is the matter, what have I said? Wait a moment, I have not explained myself correctly. A priest's robe is sacred to me, I assure you."

Abbé Roche had turned away, and with his arms folded across his breast, was thinking: "The first time he saw me, he said to himself: 'That is the very man I want!' So I look like a scoundrel? For more than a year he has considered me no better than himself, studied my character, sounded me, and I did not understand!"

Larreau, reassured by the apparent calmness of the priest, recovered his self-command, thrust his hands into his pockets, and advancing in his turn, exclaimed: "But, my dear fellow, you adopt a very singular manner towards me, and I think it extremely presuming. Perhaps you do not know that you are addressing a man whom every one respects; who—to whom even the ministers are deferential, and who could crush you under foot if he chose."

"Try it, scoundrel!" replied Abbé Roche, drawing himself up to the full height of his tall figure. He looked so noble, so proud in this outburst of indignation, his eyes had such an expression of profound contempt, that the capitalist, spite of his relations to the ministers, was intimidated.

"After all," said he, "let us cut the matter short, and not get angry with each other. I perhaps gave you to understand, in previous conversations, that there was in this country, on the estates of Manteigney, a spring of mineral water, hitherto unknown, which I intended to make useful. I have perhaps also informed you that your aid, your sympathy, your moral influence would be of great assistance to me. That is true; but are you sure of having correctly understood what I told you? People don't act on the strength of mere words. You have, so far as I know, no paper signed with my name requesting you even in the most ambiguous terms to perform upon the highway the masquerade displayed that night. You thought it would be more advantageous to you to act without my advice and approbation,—and you crown your master-piece by speaking insolently to me! You think I am compromised; you think you can hold me,—but, my dear friend, you don't know even the first move of this game: you are a child, Monsieur l'abbé."

"Very childish and very foolish, certainly, since I did not see at once that you were the greatest scoundrel that ever lived."

"No more such speeches, or you will find that they may have a disagreeable result. Devil take it! I like your simplicity. Do you pretend to say that you had nothing to do with the apparition which was seen that night? Is that what you mean? Oh! I ask nothing better. Explain yourself—exculpate yourself. Prove that you were in bed at that hour and neither invented nor planned the jest. I am listening; come, come, I am all ears."

"Have you really the audacity to question me? And in whose name, by what right? Why are you here? Do you not perceive that I can scarcely control myself, that I should consider it the greatest possible disgrace to vindicate myself to you; that people only explain their actions in presence of a judge whom they can respect; that your voice irritates me, that my anger is increasing"—he slowly approached as he uttered the words, and unfolded his arms—"and that instead of answering you, I intend to slap you in the face?"

"Fool," cried M. Larreau, hastily opening the door, "you shall pay for this!"

And he disappeared.

XXVII.

On the following morning, at a very early hour, the countess, much more closely wrapped than usual, hastened towards the priest's dwelling. Her bearing no longer possessed the ease, the charming carelessness that formerly characterized it! She was anxious, restless, and trembled at the thought of meeting any one as she hurried rapidly on. It really seemed to her as if the little shepherd, surrounded by all the villagers, was waiting at every turn in the road to exclaim, as soon as she appeared: "There is the lady I saw near the White Cross." Who knows whether the truth was not already suspected? At the simplest question, she should surely lose all self-command, and reply in spite of herself: "Yes, it was I."

She had remained shut up in her own room during the whole of the preceding day, looking out of her window at the throngs of curious peasants hastening to the valley, questioning her maid, trying to laugh at the girl's stories, and when she stopped, racking her brain to find a pretext for asking anew. Soon she feared that her prolonged stay in her private apartments might arouse suspicions among the servants in the château, and therefore went down in the evening to the drawing-room, where she found her father, who, still under the influence of ill-concealed wrath, had spoken in very threatening terms of Abbé Roche. Perceiving that this state of affairs must be ended as quickly as possible, she set out for the priest's abode. When the curé opened the door, she entered hastily, sank into a chair, threw back her hood, and clasping her hands, exclaimed:

"Good Heavens! my dear curé, what have you done—what have you said to my father?"

If there was any one to whom the priest desired to explain his conduct, it was certainly the countess; but just as he was about to open his lips and relieve his heart, he remembered that it was unworthy of him to accuse a father to his own daughter, and said quietly: "Certain words spoken by M. Larreau wounded me deeply, and I resented them somewhat vehemently. That is all."

"That is all, that is all! And you think that perfectly natural? Then you do not know that my father is the best of men, the most kind hearted and scrupulous." (Abbé Roche could not restrain a gesture of surprise.) "Yes, yes, the most scrupulous and honorable. Well! my father has the faults natural to his temperament; he is sensitive, and never pardons an insult. He is very angry, and is going to search and inquire into everything; he wishes to discover the truth, and he will, for papa always succeeds in everything he undertakes."

"Oh! Heaven," cried the priest, "let him ascertain! I wish it, I prefer the truth, whatever its consequences may be, to the shameful position in which I am now."

"If all is kept secret, there will be no shame for you to bear."

"If I only had cause to blush when alone, it would be too much. And the anguish of seeing a lie become a religious belief—do you count that as nothing? Am I not a priest, a Christian, Madame? No, no, there must be an end to all this!"

"You are an egotist, you think only of yourself. Do you forget that the scandal will recoil upon the count and myself? How will you explain our nocturnal excursion? You will tell the truth, I wish you to do so, but who will believe you? Besides, have you a right to dispose of a secret that I entrusted to your loyalty? Will you also say, the more completely to vindicate yourself that the count betrayed Loursière's daughter? Will you relate in public the confidences I have given you? You will be compelled to do so; when people tell the truth, they must tell the whole truth. By so doing, you will perhaps act the part of a good priest; but I doubt whether such would be the conduct of an honorable man. How is it possible that you did not understand all this? Why did you not conciliate my father? I would have confessed the truth by degrees, everything would have become quiet, and the adventure been forgotten ere long—while now, my father, vexed and irritated, thanks to you, asserts that he must discover this mystery; that his honor is concerned in it; he says he does not wish to take the responsibility of these fooleries, and will doubtless immediately ask the bishop to make a serious investigation. Oh! how wretched I am!"

She covered her eyes with her hand, and continued, in a very gentle tone: "You are harsh, M. le curé, harsh towards others. You perhaps mistake for virtue what is only austerity. And suppose I, too, wished to confess the whole truth? Suppose I questioned my memory, do you not think I might find causes of resentment against people who consider themselves beyond reproach? You place a high value upon your dignity as a priest, your honor as a man; do you think, Monsieur, that I have neither dignity nor honor as a woman, and that I have no right to be indignant when insulted? A few words from my father, somewhat hastily spoken, perhaps, have urged you to violence—which has been extreme, if I can judge from the resentment it excited. Why should not I too be enraged, when forced to submit not only to impulsive words, but unheard-of acts—yes, Monsieur, unheard of, especially coming from you? Yet I, who am no saint, who do not consider myself above human weaknesses,—I, whose duty is not, after all, to give an example of the virtues, I am silent, and wish to forget. It is strange that you have not courage to keep silence as well as I."

While the countess spoke, Abbé Roche, amazed and motionless, did not utter a single word, and yet many thoughts had passed through his mind. He was like a culprit listening to a sentence from which there could be no appeal; but even while he felt sorrow at hearing himself thus condemned, he shared the emotions of his judge, followed each thought depicted upon the young wife's face, and gradually forgetting himself in her, shared her impressions. He was at the bar of the accused and on the bench of the judge at one and the same time. "Yes," thought he, "Abbé Roche is a proud fool, and we are too indulgent to him."

He forgot Larreau and his insults to think only of his own conduct. He had acted the part of a violent, brutal, and unjust man. That was evident, for she said so. He accepted his sentence with embarrassment, even took an undue share of blame, and found a strange joy in reproaching himself for indulging in anger. He believed that he was convinced by the countess's reasoning, when only charmed and dazzled by her presence; and thought he saw more clearly, because he no longer looked with his own eyes.

His predominant emotion was the irritating, perhaps guilty, but delightful thought that he could not drive away: the countess and himself were henceforward bound together by the same interests, the same fears, the same hopes. Chance had formed ties between them which they could not sunder.

Angelic creature! She still deigned to come to his dwelling, reproached him for his shameful conduct with a gentleness of which he was unworthy, and, to utterly overwhelm him, granted him forgetfulness of it — almost forgiveness. He would have liked to throw himself at the feet of his judge, kiss her very footprints, and say to her: "I belong to you, my life is yours," for it was in silent shame, patiently endured, that he now saw nobleness and courage.

"Command, Madame," said he in deep agitation, "command, I will do whatever you wish. I have offended you—forgive me."

"Promise me to say nothing, that is all I ask. Let me be the one to act,—I will soothe my father. You promise neither to approve nor condemn anything—for a few days? You see this is the only way to put an end to the whole affair, and that there is no other course to adopt in the interest of all parties. Does not God judge of our intentions? You will say nothing, you assure me?"

She had pronounced the last words with a voice so sweet, a smile so alluring; she had appealed to his generosity with so much confidence, that he murmured almost with tears: "I will be silent, I promise you. I will be silent."

"The silence may be somewhat hard to bear for one of your temperament; but make this little sacrifice, my dear curé, make it for my sake, I implore you. It is no act of weakness that is asked of you; there is nothing disgraceful in permitting a fire of straw to die out of itself, and abstaining from blowing upon it through excess of zeal;"—then, with a most confidential manner, she added: "You have been very anxious about this affair, very much annoyed, have you not? I can read it in your face."

"Yes, yes, I assure you I have." He felt soothed, enchanted by the sweetness of the voice he loved so well.

"And I too! If you knew in what a state I have been! I thought of you, and said to myself: 'If he only does not allow anything that could compromise us to escape; if he does not attach any importance to these rumors, does not believe himself under obligations to deny this absurd apparition, and thus complicate the affair instead of simplifying it!' When I was told yesterday that you had driven all the people who were praying out of the church, I was terrified."

"It is true, I did wrong; I was excited, beside myself." He was ashamed of the violence whose mere recital had alarmed her.

"You are right, we must keep calm, we must on every account. Even in the interests of religion, it is the best thing to do. The church is open this morning, and will remain so, I assure you."

"Well, I will profit by it, and am now going to pray to the good God for that poor child."

"We have said nothing about her; she is dead, poor little thing! It is wrong to judge her too severely."

"Certainly, certainly. And what did her father say when you gave him—you know?"

"He was very much agitated, and accepted it, blessing your generosity."

"Generosity which he forced from me with his hand on my throat. Well! And the child, where is it?"

"At Marianne's house, where I carried it myself."

"So near here? See how selfish people are! I shall accustom myself to the thought; but at the first moment, it is a painful one. Yet I do not wish the poor little thing any harm. Farewell, M. le curé."

And, wrapping herself in her cloak, she added: "I shall conceal my face, the villagers frighten me."

"Will you pass through the vestry? Then you will not be obliged to go all the way round."

Although there was no one in the church, Mme. de Manteigney took refuge in the darkest corner, and began to pray fervently for the repose of the dead girl's soul. She was embarrassed as she appealed to God in behalf of the poor child, for she could not think of her sudden death without a feeling strangely like relief. She pitied the unfortunate girl, but could not entirely conceal from herself that her death simplified many things, calmed her anxieties, and cut short, at least for the present, the count's follies. It was a misfortune, an accident, a circumstance, which under certain contingencies might prove a benefit. Then, having informed the Lord that she was about to address her prayers to Him for the repose of the soul of Loursière's daughter, she piously recited a number of *Paters* and *Aves*, without any farther thought of her for whose sake they were uttered. But from time to time a shiver ran through her whole frame, and from the depths of her heart she exclaimed: "O Lord! O Lord! turn the count's affection towards me; grant that he may love me; I will strive so earnestly to make him happy!"

While thus absorbed in prayer, she heard an almost incessant noise of footsteps behind her, and when, having concluded her devotions, she turned, was not surprised to see a group of women on their knees before the famous bas-relief presented by Claudius. She cast a hasty glance at the *Flight into Egypt*—the Virgin resembled her. There really was a resemblance, and Saint Joseph, with the exception of his beard, was an excellent likeness of Abbé Roche. She drew down her veil and moved rapidly on. Every head was turned towards her. Several women were eagerly talking together in the porch, but became silent at her approach, and one of them, advancing to meet the countess, made a low courtesy.

"What do you want of me, my good woman?"

"Why! the countess has just been praying for the miracle, of course. I am the mother of the lad, a child who never caused his parents the slightest sorrow. Wouldn't Madame like to speak to my boy? Everybody else has heard his story."

"No, thank you, good mother."

"With all the particulars!"

"I cannot stop, I am in a hurry."

"That is because Madame has heard that it was not my boy who found the spring, and yet he was the one who told everything."

"I do not deny it, but I have not time."

"Then the countess will remember that all they say is only to injure poor people."

Several other women approached. "Let me pass," said the countess, "some one is waiting for me." And she hastened on.

Fifteen minutes later, the whole village knew that Mme. de Manteigney had been praying on account of the miracle. Some persons even asserted that she had placed a bouquet before the bas-relief.

XXIII.

Contrary to the countess's hopes, the excitement in the village did not abate. The wrathful lamentations of mère Ribat, who gradually yielded to the most violent fanaticism, had borne their fruit. All who, for any reason, were jealous or envious of Mayor Baravoux, all who thought his oxen too large, his house too handsome, his fields too green, or his figure too portly, had rallied around the good peasant woman, the devoted mother who so bravely defended the cause of the poor. As usually happens, the question had changed its aspect, and from an individual fact became a general principle, in which every one found food for argument. The Virgin, Saint Joseph, and the poor ass had really very little to do with the matter. The point in question now was to ascertain whether a mayor, merely because he owned a stone house, two pairs of oxen, a tri-colored scarf, and pasture lands, had a right to interpose between Providence and the poor, a right to snatch the bread from the mouths of his subordinates, and intercept the heavenly rays by his huge person. Then other individuals rose to defend Baravoux, and the debates grew so stormy that one evening they actually came to blows.

The mayor, whose nerves, to use a common expression, were strained like the strings of a violin, to expend a portion of his anger, gave orders that the inn of the *Sapin Vert* should be closed at the sound of the *Angelus*. This was pouring oil upon the flames. The excitement increased, some were indignant, others shouted *bravo*. In short, every one was forced to take sides, and declare his opinion publicly. Naturally, the numbers who visited the spring visibly increased, so that after having erected a palisade to protect the miraculous hole, it was soon found necessary to protect the palisade itself, and two gendarmes from the city mounted guard.

If Grand-Fort-le-Haut was greatly excited, the town of Virez was terribly agitated. The question whether Baravoux or mère Ribat would gain the day had, it is true, but a secondary importance; but the discussions were none the less violent. Abbé Vilain, curé of Virez, had not—the avowal must be made, whatever it cost us—had not any great sympathy with Abbé Roche, his brother at Grand Fort. It was not that he had any special cause of complaint against him; but Nature had formed the two men in moulds too widely dissimilar for them ever to understand and sympathize with each other. One was tall, robust, active, grave, fond of long walks, fatigue, and manly exercises; the other, on the contrary, short, fat, careless and indolent, adoring meditations in the shade, calmness, repose, cheerful and dainty meals. Their moral natures were in perfect harmony with their physical temperaments, and traces of this dissimilarity might be detected in the trifling particulars of their lives; they were especially prominent, when the two abbés played a game of bowls together after vespers.

Abbé Vilain, a prudent, skilful player, exceedingly deliberate in his combinations, studied the ground and understood how to take advantage of the slopes: the obstacle of a patch of gravel, the collisions, the rebounds, were to him helps rather than hindrances. He rolled his ball gently and lightly, giving it a benediction, if I may venture to say so, by a final flutter of his fingers, accompanying aud protecting it with a moist, paternal glance, directing it by his wishes. It really seemed as if the fat curé had breathed a portion of his own soul into the ball, to see it rolling cautiously on, wheeling around an obstacle, avoiding a stone, pausing as if to reflect, and taking advantage of a slight declivity that nobody had noticed, approach nearer and nearer the goal, and finally stop in the very best place. During this time the most varying emotions were depicted upon Abbé Vilain's flushed face, with all the more clearness because his pure soul disdained the slightest concealment: hope, fear, ambition, tenderness, anguish, and the pride of success. He advanced and stood before his triumphant ball, with his cassock raised on the right nearly to his waist, his hands on his hips, his mouth half open, and a broad smile beaming for an instant on his flushed face; an instant only, for all eyes, which had at first been fixed upon him, turned almost immediately towards Abbé Roche, and every one seemed to say: "That is very well done—but we shall see!"

And in fact, the curé of Grand Fort drew back two or three paces, tested and patted his ball, measured the space an instant, and then, with a gesture superb in ease and vigor, hurled it, loaded with iron and heavy as a cannon ball though it was, to a prodigious height. It was seen to mount into the air, disappeared amid the foliage of the trees, and then fell back like a bombshell upon Abbé Vilain's ball, which it ignominiously dislodged. Now, I dare venture to affirm, that when a player who is in earnest has a victorious ball—a ball that is very near, and sees it driven away in such a fashion, brutally, without any respect for his clever play—and when the same thing is repeated for ten years every Sunday after vespers, publicly, without truce or mercy, I dare venture to affirm, I say, that the player feels a dull indignation spring up within him that might readily be transformed into an outburst of rage. He incorporates himself, so to speak, with his own ball, and therefore cruelly feels the violent collision to which it is forced to yield.

Abbé Vilain, consequently, could not forget the frightful descent of the iron-shod ball, and the excruciating sound of the heavy mass falling from the skies. Paff, boumm! the sounds had remained fixed in his ears and heart, and when he heard the rumor of the apparition, the miracle, and the spring; when he was told that Abbé Roche indignantly drove the worshippers from the church, and refused all explanation, he murmured between his fat lips: "Paff, boumm! such things only happen in certain parishes."

By these simple words the worthy man regained many lost partisans. As may be supposed, the words, remembered by the notary's wife, who thought it her duty to confide them to the schoolmaster's spouse, spread rapidly through the town, where they were diligently analyzed and commented upon. There was something decidedly ambiguous about this miracle. It was remembered that on the evening of the event the doctor had met Abbé Roche in père Loursière's hut. The curé of Grand Fort must have passed the White Cross at the very hour of the apparition. Why should he have burst into such fits of anger, followed by the most obstinate silence?

The mayor of Virez had vainly sought to elucidate the affair. M. Larreau was impenetrable: Abbé Roche shut his door in people's faces; père Baravoux was in a perpetual state of wild excitement. As to the sous-préfet, he had not even answered the letter that had been sent to him. Was there not some political question, some electioneering manœuvre concealed under this miracle? It was remembered that the stone cross that serves as an object for the pilgrimage of the Seven Sorrows, and the twenty-four little bronze crosses that adorn the highway, had been presented to the public at the time of the last elections. It was evident, therefore, that the apparition of the White Cross had some political signification, but what? What did it mean? Did the government desire the ruin of Virez? The population was greatly excited; it was impossible to employ, or obtain anything whatever from the workmen. The women left their children shut up at home while they went to visit the spring, around which shops of every description had been erected. Peddlers sold caps, stockings, chaplets, and little books; people shot at a mark with the cross-bow to win macaroons; it was a perfect fair-ground. On pretext of being present at a second apparition, bands of pilgrims journeyed towards Grand Fort, and stopped at the inn of the *Sapin Vert*, which had become the official rendezvous of all the drunkards in the country, so that even at midnight the town was disturbed by songs and shouts, and twice in succession Raimbeau the baker had burned his oven-full of bread from returning home at two o'clock in the morning in a state of beastly intoxication. Was such a condition of things to be endured? Was it not to be desired that ecclesiastical authority should take the matter in hand and unravel the mystery?

XXIX.

While Grand Fort and Virez were almost exclusively occupied with thoughts of the miracle and its consequences, the clever Claudius had broached the affair in Paris with marvellous skill. One evening, directly after the Gymnase, he came to Vernon's studio, sure of finding all the journalists of the capital assembled there, and suddenly, without the slightest preparation, as if still excited by a letter which he said he had just received, related the story with inimitable vivacity and animation, describing the scenes, drawing portraits of the personages, depicting, with a warmth bordering upon eloquence, the great excitement rife in this beautiful country. The truth is, that he had studied this impromptu outburst nearly half the day, and just as he entered the carriage, took several glasses of champagne to rise to the height demanded by the circumstances.

It is no easy thing to relate amid certain surroundings a totally new miracle, which has not yet received the stamp of public approval: Claudius, therefore, was extremely careful to advance no personal opinion. In his mouth it was merely a dazzling fairy tale, full of strangely vivid descriptions and piquant details that each could interpret to please himself. The miracle itself he treated with the utmost reverence, for people affected great respect for certain subjects in Vernon's studio. When he had finished his story, he added amidst a general silence : " Well ! I'll wager a hundred to one that you can't guess the name of the owner of the estates on which the very veracious facts I have just related occurred. You can't ? Gentlemen, the scene of this wonderful story is the domain of Manteigney."

"Oh ! come, you are joking, Claudius. Is it a bet ? What does all this mean ?"

"I know nothing at all about it, and M. Larreau, who wrote me this morning, knows no more than you do. The only thing certain is, that there is a mineral spring which no one knew anything about, whose water has been analyzed and found to be extremely healthful. Another fact is, that the whole country is excited about the matter, and Larreau loudly demands an investigation into the subject of this miracle, as he is not willing to assume the responsibility. In short, there it is—it is unheard-of, impossible, but there it is. I have the letter in my pocket."

"My dear fellow, that would make a charming article."

"Do whatever you please, I was not requested to keep it a secret."

The following morning the apparition of the White Cross and the Manteigney spring were presented to the curiosity of the public under the thousand forms that events of this kind always assume. Articles, conversations, Parisian gossip, every-day chat, and daily papers, everywhere one met with the strange occurrence, related and commented upon according to the opinion or fancy of the narrator. Claudius, although he pretended to have a horror of writing, took a sheet of paper and in a delicate hand very unlike his usual chirography, traced the following lines :

"MR. EDITOR,

"Have we not reason to be surprised at the almost

malicious facility with which the irreligious press—it will doubtless take the qualification as a compliment—welcomes and reproduces tales of supernatural events? The account of an apparition, as yet unsanctioned by ecclesiastical authority, seems to be a piece of rare good fortune to these gentlemen. It is one stone the more hurled into the gardens of faith, and these men, blinded by their hatred, cast their little pebbles with a unanimity and ardor that is bewildering and painful. In presence of unaccountable facts which only the clergy can and ought to appreciate, is not the first duty a respectful silence? How is it possible not to perceive that the premature publicity given to such occurrences disturbs the conscience and diminishes the two divine fires, without which modern society would find itself enveloped in the most impenetrable obscurity, I mean, reverence and faith!"

Claudius read what he had just written. "That has not much meaning," said he, "but it will elicit a reply. I will add a few personalities." And he again began to write:

"From their careless and wittily irreverential mode of relating these facts, would not one suppose this apparition to be the clever clap-trap of some anonymous speculation, the shameless advertisement of some mineral spring? It is given to our times, excited by mad speculations and intoxicated with fumes of incredulity, to see such audacious shamelessness welcomed with perfect unanimity.

"And what are the papers that dare to give publicity to such matters? Is it the journal of the man of three moral principles, the famous and absurd *automédon* of the democratic stage-coach, the liberal cuckoo whom we see every morning dragged along by his emaciated Pegasus? Is it the paper of that other conciliatory and meditative harlequin, the high priest of halting between two opinions, the Don Juan of the pros and cons who, surpassing Cadet-Roussel in the art of clothing himself, pulls bits of lining from every passer-by and drapes himself in the grotesque tatters like a new Messiah?"

"Deuce take it!" cried Claudius, "I think I might have made as good a journalist as the next man. Let us continue:"

"Pardon the sharpness of my words, Mr. Editor, but indeed, if we have any respect for our holy religion in our hearts, we must be indignant at such behavior.

"In the name of the most sacred interests we ask for light. We ask the approval or condemnation of an ecclesiastical decision, and that under any circumstances a private speculation should be prevented from seizing upon a divine fact as the basis of its operations, or, taking advantage of public credulity, invest a lie and trick with a sacred character.

"I am, Mr. Editor,

"ONE OF YOUR SUBSCRIBERS."

Claudius, well pleased with his work, made a pen from a goose quill, and taking advantage of his inspiration, wrote upon another sheet of paper without pausing:

"All goes well, and progress is rapidly advancing. We have lately seen the wonders of art applied to industry; the Venus de Milo cast in bronze, and transformed into a hydrant; the Apollo Belvedere entering into the bustle of active life and crowning the roofs of houses in the guise of a chimney; the antique Diana becoming a door latch; the frieze of the Parthenon surrounding clyster pumps; the Acropolis utilized as a mustard pot; and that we may lose nothing of the venerable Past, Olympus is dragged upon the stage, and the gods of ancient Greece take tickets, and amuse the crowd under the wig of Bobèche and the mask of Galimafré.

"Everything has progressed very favorably, but

one noticeable improvement should be mentioned: modern Catholicism feels the necessity of becoming practical. St. Joseph takes a commission, transforms himself into a bath-keeper, administers shower-baths, and, rivalling Calchas, finds no business menial of which God approves.

"The thermal establishment which cures both body and mind is one of the products of our civilization. Is one to hear mass in the bath? will there be a chaplain-chiropodist attached to the institution? All this demands elucidation, and we are impatiently awaiting the decision of some competent authority in regard to miracles, as applied to industry, in order to reply to the questions of every description asked by our subscribers.

"In strict justice, let us be permitted to applaud this prodigious expansion of human activity.

"By courageously placing itself at the head of the industrial movement, striving to rejuvenate these ancient beliefs and extract from their ruins a practical, utilitarian, and fruitful side, Catholicism surely deserves the gratitude of all intelligent people.

"Let us therefore welcome this pious enterprise of Manteigney, whose success is no doubtful matter to us.

"That is quick, brilliant, vivid," said Claudius, rubbing his hands. "The articles are totally dissimilar; now let me find two envelopes, without initials, and of different styles."

After obtaining what he sought, he wrote on the first envelope the name of a democratic journal.

These two articles, published simultaneously by papers most hostile to each other, were the signal for the incredible uproar which is still remembered. The situation of affairs just then was extremely critical. The portfolio of the interior had just been given to a man well known to be excessively partial to the clergy, which had occasioned much discontent, and at the same time aroused eager hopes. There were vague rumors of a change in the faculty of the university. It was said to be certain that our libraries and museums would be re-organized ; absurd reports, which however had gained a certain degree of credence in narrow, malicious minds, thanks to the persistent silence of the government. Be that as it may, the miracle of Manteigney happened at just the time to reanimate the discussion. It was a useful weapon, a very natural pretext for asserting one's opinions, hatreds, or sympathies, and to damage certain elections that had just taken place. Claudius had reckoned upon all this, and it was by no means at random that he had at first written certain political personalities which would not be accepted without noisy retorts to his ill-timed jests. The uproar even surpassed the hopes of the clever viscount. The man of three moral principles, the famous *automédon* of the democratic stage-coach, as Claudius called him, replied with unprecedented violence. Anxious and embittered by a recent and public slight inflicted upon him by the new minister, he saw in this bold attack an opportunity of reinstating himself in the good graces of the government.

The man of three moral principles therefore spoke of "miserable concessions" made to a dangerous and retrograde party. Was our France of '89 to bow her head beneath the holy-water sprinkler of government? The satirical paper burst into shouts of laughter; the religious paper quoted the Fathers of the Church. A duel was the result, and the uproar increased still more. The official papers maintained a decorous, formal attitude that calmed no one.

At this period, a letter from M. Larreau, dated at Manteigney, appeared simultaneously in three or four papers. It was short, and bore that impression of frankness and good faith which instantly attracts the approbation of all worthy people. In the absence of his son-in-law, the count, he considered it to be his duty to answer the report circulating in Paris with the most perfect candor. Then without mentioning his personal opinion, he related the simple facts, confessed that he had suspected the existence of mineral springs in the valley of Manteigney long before, and claimed, with all the energy of an upright man, a searching and immediate investigation of the events that had occurred at the White Cross, in which his own honor and that of his family were involved. No one could have used more dignified or resolute language. While awaiting the decision, irrevocable in such matters, of ecclesiastical authority, he would call into the courts of law any person making insinuations to the effect that either he or his son-in-law had had any thing whatever to do with the affair. The capitalist's conduct was unanimously pronounced to be eminently proper.

During this time Claudius had not been inactive. A constant visitor at Vernon's receptions, he lost no opportunity of influencing public opinion; and when he spoke of the absurd position in which the Count de Manteigney and family were placed, allowed his indignation to burst forth unrestrainedly. Thanks to him, the analysis of the new mineral spring was soon published officially in several papers, and one of them added an extremely eulogistic article.

" Science," it remarked, " has no occasion to trouble herself about the manner in which this spring was discovered ! her mission is only to appreciate its value, and on that point there is no room for doubt. It has tonical and diuretic properties, and an alkaline, magnesian, gaseous, and ferruginous composition, which gives it rare medicinal importance. It strengthens the nervous system without producing the slightest irritation. Obese persons, or those threatened with obesity, obstruction, congestion, or rush of blood, will obtain certain relief."

Claudius had a number of these papers printed and freely distributed, while Larreau sent a letter to Dr. Ferrand, author of the article, inviting him to come to Manteigney, that he might judge of the size of the spring for himself, and give him the benefit of his experience in regard to the best means of making it useful. Claudius was besieged with questions and curious inquirers, and obliged to give every particular concerning the climate of the country, its resources, the way of going there, etc. The Baron de Solernie drew him aside one evening, and with a most charming smile, exclaimed: "Well, my dear Claudius, the Manteigney business is taking a favorable turn; the spring is very medicinal, it appears. They were speaking of it yesterday at the ministry."

"The business, as you call it, will not really take a favorable turn until the count and his father-in-law are entirely absolved from all connection with this miracle, whether true or false. Until the mystery is unravelled the whole affair has an air of trickery which is extremely injurious to my friends. Their situation is positively unbearable."

"No doubt! but these rumors will die away, and the result will be a most lucrative financial operation."

"I don't deny it; but you know Larreau is excessively sensitive."

"That is most praiseworthy. Such noble pride is rarely seen in business matters."

"He values his reputation as an honest man above everything, and is not one of those who— Larreau is a perfect bar of steel, where any tampering with his conscience is concerned."

"And who dreams of accusing him? You know perfectly well that he has the sympathy of all. Between ourselves, I am convinced that he is the victim of some audacious trickster, who wished to grasp a share of the profits of the spring. The people there are very superstitious, I believe."

"More so than you could imagine."

"And the priests must have immense influence! This is a very delicate, even dangerous, affair to elucidate. We must think twice before depriving the people of any illusion whatever. As the writer of that famous article says, all reverence is linked together, all authority mutually dependent; do not hope to touch one without injuring all. A blow from a hammer, dealt on the ground floor, breaks the clocks on the first story. The floors are thin, and the partitions very slight."

"That is a very striking observation, my dear baron."

"It is only common sense. Reverence has become a hot-house flower among the masses. Every time that we permit a discussion, we break a pane of glass; draw aside a straw mat, and the plant becomes chilled. This is what leads me to tell you that the investigation demanded by Larreau is a thing very delicate to exact, and dangerous to obtain. In these times, a pinch of doubt thrown on the ground produces in a month a whole harvest of skeptics. Discuss Saint Joseph to-day, and to-morrow people will discuss the official candidate proposed by the prefect. Discussion is a terrible weapon. I should rather never have a sharp knife in my house than to run the risk of losing three fingers the first time I used it."

"And do you believe the government thinks—"

"As I do? Yes; I should not be surprised if it held the same opinions. You see, my good friend, the question, until now, has not been considered in its true aspect. It is possible, quite possible, so far as I know, that this apparition of the White Cross may really have a supernatural, divine character—yes, divine. I even believe it would be a very fortunate thing if this divine character could be officially recognized and established."

The two speakers exchanged inquiring glances. The baron coughed, and continued: "As to the material, commercial part of the affair, it seems to me that it might prove a matter of great interest, and if Larreau was disposed to give other capitalists a share in the enterprise, which may assume gigantic proportions, he might, perhaps, by that means, obtain valuable aid, whose influence would greatly simplify the present state of affairs. This is a purely personal suggestion, let that be plainly understood."

"We had thought of that," murmured Claudius, with a very confidential expression; "we had thought of it, especially as the improvement of the spring, the necessary arrangements—"

"Which, in case of need, the proper authority could render obligatory."

"Among intelligent people, such means are not employed. We shall never refuse to have the spring made a source of profit; although, to tell the truth, the enterprise would be only a pretext—an excuse for introducing activity and life into a new region."

"Yes, yes; I expected as much"

"We ask only one little railway line, penetrating the heart of these mountains through the valleys of Lindousie and Manteigney, to enable us to put incalculable wealth in circulation. Lend us the key to open the door of this treasure house, my dear baron."

"Suppose we exchange good offices, my dear friend. Speak of this matter to M. Larreau, won't you? For a thousand reasons, he ought to form political friendships. We will talk about this affair again; farewell, my dear Claudius."

XXX.

In spite of the general anxiety, the ecclesiastical authorities could not resolve to interfere. The archbishop, justly alarmed by the enormous and rapid increase of the reports concerning this affair, was in a position whose embarrassment can readily be perceived. The prefect still addressed respectful petitions; M. Larreau and the Count de Manteigney had entreated him, in most urgent terms, to order an investigation. To refuse all interference was to despise aristocratic and powerful influences. On the other hand, to hastily respond to the general curiosity would be compromising ecclesiastical dignity. If the question had been purely a religious one, perhaps the archbishop would have more readily determined to interpose, although such precipitation might be unprecedented; but under present circumstances the miracle was visibly complicated by a publicly avowed commercial enterprise. Was it not to be feared that amid the rumors the investigation of the facts would prove singularly embarrassing? Every detail of the examination would be discussed and commented upon by an excited press. Was it really known what might be concealed beneath this mysterious affair? Several miracles had already been performed in the south of France, it is true; but never had they been so impetuously made public before the decision of the chief of the diocese, who found himself in this case almost driven on to act—an event quite inadmissible.

Very fortunately, the archbishop was intimately acquainted with one of the most attractive and intelligent members of the priesthood. Having taken holy orders on account of a succession of heavy misfortunes, which were formerly widely discussed in certain circles, Abbé Desvialle still retained his refined, elegant tastes. He was a man of slender figure, with a smiling mouth, affable, though searching glance, and a most delightful *blasé* expression. Although his dress was perfectly simple, and precisely like that of the other priests, one could instantly detect the thousand little touches of a man who is careful of his personal appearance, and desirous to please. In the days when sumptuary laws compelled all the gondolas in Venice to assume a uniform appearance, every one was black, without ornament or carving. The cabins were invariably draped with black cloth, and yet the patrician's gondola could be recognized at the distance of a hundred paces. The commands were observed to the letter, but the cloth was fine, the prow glittered like the blade of a razor, and the windows were provided with panes of glass as thick as the finger and as clear as spring water. The gondola itself was black, but the partitions were of ebony; there were no projecting carvings, but elegant designs cut into the wood, were traced with most artistic skill. This explains how it happened that on seeing Abbé Desvialle pass, one instantly supposed that he had a valet, and did not confound him with the common herd.

A man by nature indifferent to ordinary tasks, he had devoted himself particularly to the difficult niceties of his profession. He liked to probe anxious and timid consciences, watch, treat, and cure the ever-grieving and panting feminine souls; he excelled in gently searching the inmost recesses of the heart, and weighing the most intangible sensations with perfect exactitude. He would have found means to apply a dressing to the tiniest prick of a needle; and his scalpels were so minute, his magnifying glasses so powerful, that on the slightest trace of a trifling, venial sin, he would speak for a whole hour, without effort or fatigue, with grace, tact, freshness, vigor, and incomparable intelligence.

Although one of the most prominent men in Paris, I must mention that Abbé Desvialle had never attended any of Vernon's receptions, although a frequent visitor at the painter's studio by day, as he greatly admired the ease and grace of his works, and thus very naturally had made the acquaintance of the principal guests of this famous house. He had been particularly intimate with M. Larreau, even dined several times at his table, and on the marriage of Count de Manteigney with the capitalist's daughter, Abbé Desvialle had consented to perform the ceremony for the young couple. He made a charming little address on the occasion, about as long as one's finger, but most appropriate, a perfect gem. The count and countess had always been on the best of terms with the good abbé, and had made him solemnly promise to come and visit them at Manteigney.

When the archbishop found himself in the embarrassing situation previously mentioned, the priest instantly proposed that he should fulfil the promise made to the count, and after a long conversation, hastily set out for the old château. His mission, it was plainly understood, had no official character; he came as a friend and visitor, and entered with a smile upon his lips. On perceiving M. Larreau, who, crossing the court-yard, received him and helped him out of the carriage, he extended both hands with a friendly gesture, and burst into a little ringing laugh of most cheering augury.

The capitalist felt as if relieved of a two hundred pound weight.

"Oh! how glad I am to see you, my dear abbé! I only received your little note yesterday."

"I keep my promise, as you see, I am a man of my word. The countess—"

"Is perfectly well, thank you; we shall see her directly. But you must be wearied by the heat and dust. Permit me to show you to your room. My son-in-law has not returned, he will be very sorry."

"So am I, I assure you. Is he not near Bordeaux?"

"A little farther south, at the Duke d'Armine's, where he has been detained, much to my annoyance, for you must perceive that under these circumstances the count's presence— I will leave you. This is your room: its windows afford a view of the valley and the famous spring."

"The famous spring," repeated the abbé with a very meaning smile. "I will join you in ten minutes."

"He has been sent down by the archbishop, that is plain as day," thought M. Larreau, pacing to and fro; "after all, I would rather have this worthy Abbé Desvialle than any one else. I have nothing to conceal, I wish to have an investigation. He is very intelligent; we shall understand each other. This absurd story must be put out of sight, there must be no farther discussion."

The capitalist was really disgusted with the supernatural for the time being. His affairs were progressing admirably, the effect he desired had been produced by the Parisian press, the spring at Manteigney was well known, the chemical analysis had been published—appreciated. What necessity was there now for any pretended divine interposition? Besides, he really desired the investigation on account of Abbé Roche, who had thought himself strong enough to act alone—had evidently intended to make use of the spring for his own advantage, slyly, brutally, foolishly, and who, after the excitement caused by his first effort, had neither the skill and courage to pursue his plan, nor the frankness to confess his incapacity. Oh! he desired it most earnestly on account of the curé of Grand Fort; and the longing to revenge himself upon him for his insolence, to place him in an annoying situation, had a large share in causing his sudden dislike of the supernatural.

It must be confessed that the countess had a powerful influence over her father's mind, and wholly dissuaded him from favoring the miracle, by the ever-increasing dislike she had manifested towards the subject. "But, my darling, I cannot understand your horror of this apparition, which could have been seen only by the will of God. I have certainly neglected nothing in your education; I gave you as much religion as any one else has; how does it happen?"

"It is instinctive, dear papa—it is nervous, I know. I cannot account for it, but so it is."

XXXI.

However clear M. Larreau's ideas might be, he was not the man to open his heart without suitable precautions, or to take the initiative in giving his confidence to the archbishop's envoy; so the beginning of the conversation was somewhat constrained, and it was only after exchanging several pinches of snuff, inquiring about each other's health in every variety of phrase, admiring the view, and gazing at the façade of the château, that the two speakers began to talk freely. The capitalist, suddenly assuming the expression of cheerful good-nature which so well suited him, exclaimed:

"Pardon an excess of sincerity, my dear Monsieur Desvialle, but it is one of my faults to be exceedingly frank. May I hope that you come here in the bishop's name? My question is doubtless indiscreet; but that can't be helped—it is my nature, and—"

"Your question is not indiscreet, my dear Monsieur Larreau; it is the natural consequence of your good faith, and I will reply without evasion. I have come here in response to the invitation given me last winter by the countess and yourself."

"So much the better, that is perfectly plain."

"To tell you," continued the priest, laying his hand on Larreau's arm, "to tell you that I feel no curiosity about the event to which you allude, would be—"

"This is perfectly natural, you have no occasion to tell me of it, my dear abbé."

"One cannot conceal anything from you! Curiosity all the more keen, because by satisfying it, I shall perhaps be able to relieve that of another, who cannot and will not manifest it in an official and public manner at present. You see, my dear Monsieur Larreau, that my frankness is at least equal to yours."

The capitalist warily half opened his left eye, and instantly closing it, replied: "Your sincerity makes it a duty for me to conceal nothing from you. In two words, as a Catholic, I am wounded, I can use no other expression, deeply wounded by all that has transpired here. Good heavens! I have reached a time of life when the bustle of business is no longer sufficient, when the ideas and convictions of former days, deadened for years, suddenly awake. Ah! my dear abbé, we must not play with religion! No, no, we must not play with religion!"

He prolonged his sentence by a succession of little nods, impatiently waiting for the abbé, by some word or gesture, to permit him to obtain even the slightest idea of the archbishop's opinion on the subject of the miracle; but M. Desvialle, who on his part was waiting for the rich man to explain himself more fully, replied: "You are perfectly right. From whatever point of view we look at this matter, you are perfectly right. We must not play with religion. The present and future welfare of France demand it — imperiously; but you suppose, then, that some one has been making game—"

"I suppose nothing, oh! good heavens, don't fancy that I suppose anything about the affair. I am wounded, as you yourself must be, by the discussions, the clamor which greets a fact, incomprehensible, it is true, but whose mystery should be respected until the proper authority has pronounced its decree. Until the Episcopal torch—I think the expression a correct one—casts its light upon this adven—hem! hem! this supernatural event, I shall be wounded, M. l'abbé, wounded as a Christian, as the head of a family, as the owner of estates, by hearing some people affirm, with most inexcusable violence, that the miracle is false."

"Do you believe it true?"

"Equally wounded when I hear it proclaimed without the archbishop's sanction that the apparition has a divine character."

"Dear me, your grief is without bounds!" observed the priest with a pleasant little smile that softened the sarcasm of his words.

"I ask for information—I demand a searching, thorough investigation," replied Larreau, somewhat piqued. "I have demanded it orally, in writing, everywhere, and at all— Truth is an admirable thing!"

"Yes, I have read your letter in the papers, my dear Monsieur Larreau, and I think it very clever from a certain point of view; but pray listen to me, I am speaking in all sincerity."

"And I, too," thought the capitalist.

"You must perceive that Episcopal authority cannot compromise its character by studying mere rumors; that it cannot act on account of a vague report that passes on and is borne away by the wind; it must remain cold and deaf to all the tales—pardon the word—that are circulating around it."

"Permit me—"

"Allow me to continue,—and even before deciding upon an investigation, it should wait until public opinion has given more stability to the rumors, more reality to the facts."

"But the deuce! my dear abbé," rejoined Larreau, who was becoming excited in spite of himself, "this rumor has caused a frightful tumult, a universal tempest; all the papers in Paris have discussed—"

"So much the more reason for ecclesiastical authority to wait until calmness is restored. It would be impossible to conduct a trial with sufficient solemnity amid the uproar of eager discussions; and you ought to be the first to wish, as a Catholic, as head of a family, as owner of estates, that the decree should be given with the dignity and prudence befitting so grave a subject. Why, you will admit that the wonderfully rapid spread of this report is well calculated in itself to put the archbishop on his guard. How do you explain this unheard-of, unprecedented speed?"

"The explanation does not appear to me a very difficult one to give, M. l'abbé. The name of Manteigney is well known in Paris, and mine is by no means an insignificant one. As soon as they were known to have some connection with this affair, public attention was excited. That is easily understood. As for the inhabitants of this region, their ardor, enthusiasm, and thirst for the marvellous resemble insanity."

"Indeed? That is very singular. How does it happen, my dear M. Larreau?" And the priest leaned familiarly on the capitalist's arm.

"This is the explanation," replied the latter. "In this mountainous portion of our beautiful France, people, I do not know why, are habituated to the idea of the supernatural. One might say that the miracle has pervaded the whole province, and the mountaineers think of nothing else. It is to them an inexhaustible treasure, ready to open beneath their feet. Thousands of the little books carried about everywhere in the packs of peddlers have taught them the lucrative side of celestial interpositions, and they wish for them just as in Paris you desire to see one of the boulevards laid out which necessitates the removal of a number of miserable buildings. It is the expression of the same feeling in a simpler form: profit without labor, a rapid fortune, a blessing from Heaven in the guise of a shower of gold. The widespread circulation that any fact bordering on the marvellous now has, is the result of former success. The greater the number of these pieces of good fortune, the more the enthusiasm will continue to increase; and at last petitions will be made in the poorer parishes for any miracle whatever—whether true or false matters little—a partial apparition for want of an entire one; and just as in the cities we are obliged to incessantly demolish and rebuild, in order to preserve public tranquillity, so in the mountains it will be necessary to continually perform fresh miracles to satisfy more and more pressing needs. You will tell me that I am permitting myself to be carried away by my feelings."

"I shall say nothing at all," interrupted Abbé Desvialle, laughing heartily, "except that your jests are unseemly. You know very well, my dear M. Larreau, that men do not perform miracles."

"I am aware of that."

"They accept them, that is all."

"With a readiness that is oftentimes very damaging to religion."

"Then you do not believe in miracles, perhaps, Monsieur Larreau."

"Excuse me, I do believe in them, my situation imposes it upon me as a duty—I believe in them as a principle, in general."

"But in particular, you—"

"Oh! bless me! in particular—ha! ha! in particular, I have my doubts."

"So that in the present case, this apparition of the White Cross—"

"In all sincerity, what do you think of it, M. l'abbé?"

"A beautiful view!" observed the priest, leaning

his elbow upon the balustrade of the terrace; undoubtedly he had not heard the capitalist's question. "A beautiful view, a flourishing valley! The laborers that I see down below—"

"They are engaged in works which will greatly increase the value of our spring. We intend to excavate under the mountain, and the black hole you see yonder is the entrance of the passage. It is a great undertaking."

"And the building that is being erected close by?"

"That is a hospital I intend to bestow upon the poor of the country; it is arranged after my own ideas, and designed entirely by myself."

"The thought does you honor. And these new roads that I see laid out in different directions?"

"I planned them myself, and am building them at my own expense—but this is only the beginning."

"You are employing your wealth nobly, and deserve the sympathy of all philanthropists."

"I do as much good as I can. Roads, Monsieur Desvialle, roads are the first necessity. My object is to unite this out-of-the way region with the rest of France; and by and bye, if I have done a useful work by arousing these people to active life, the only reward I shall ask will be the approbation of intelligent, worthy men." He made an almost imperceptible bow to the priest, who just at that moment was looking for his snuff-box.

"And if these intelligent, worthy people should testify their admiration by confiding to you the honorable trust of defending their interests, of being their representative, you would not refuse the recompense—you would have no right to refuse."

The rich man suddenly felt the pleasant thrill that we experience on sitting down to a glittering, well-served table in a warm room. He closed both eyes, and gravely answered: "I have never had anything to do with politics, my dear abbé; I had dreamed of spending the remainder of my days in some quiet, calm retreat, far removed from the pressing anxieties which a trust like the one you mention—"

"Very frequently causes."

"You understand men, my dear Abbé Desvialle!"

"I have seen so many—so many women!" he added in an undertone. "It is on account of these very difficulties that it is honorable, glorious to accept such a mission. You are of the right stuff to make a politician, my dear M. Larreau."

"Eh! well, perhaps I might accept; but it would be after a struggle against my inclinations. And I—why should I—for what reason do I—"

"Those—those are great works—magnificent works!"

"Would you like to go down to the valley?"

"Oh! it is not necessary, I can judge of them very well from here."

"There is plenty of room, as you see, to build as occasion requires." And the capitalist explained his plans in detail. He became animated as he spoke, his gestures grew more expressive, and his face became gradually flushed.

"The hospital, for the time being, will become the bath-house. It is built in such a manner that it can be indefinitely enlarged, and answer all requirements. I will say nothing at present of the house for convalescent patients, the cottages reserved for the clergy, or the—"

"Everything has been foreseen and carefully provided for."

"I have looked into the matter, as you perceive."

"Of course these things do not happen unexpectedly; but in that case," said the abbé, with a most courteous smile, "the famous miracle would not be really—"

"It was accidental, purely accidental. As I have had the honor of telling whoever would listen to me, I suspected the existence of a mineral spring long ago, some time before this annoying occurrence. I had even considered the means of enlarging it, and visited Barèges, Luchon, Uriage, and Saint Sauveur for that purpose. My library is full of books on the subject, for I never do things by halves—I like to investigate matters thoroughly. I was sitting there, studying, and arranging the matter, when this miracle—"

"Fell from the skies."

"Exactly—from the skies, ha! ha! ha! that is just the word, and you must perceive that it was no easy task to make it re-ascend."

"Admitting that it came from thence!"

"Ha! ha! ha! I make no assertions about that." The ice was broken. "You cannot imagine, my dear abbé, how much your frankness and affability cheers me, and what pleasure it gives me to be able to speak to you without evasion. How delightful it would be if all the ministers of our religion had the charming simplicity which you possess in so high a degree! I understand and love devotion, when it presents itself in a cheerful, mild, tolerant form. That is the true aspect of religion, M. l'abbé. People who are unfortunate, who obtain nothing they desire, like to lament; it is very natural, I admit, and I excuse it; but those who, on the contrary, are extremely prosperous, whose efforts have been crowned with success, should not be expected to mourn. Well! I find that people do not think enough of those who have succeeded, and it is a great wrong, for from every point of view, they deserve great consideration. What is admirable under some circumstances becomes pitiful on another occasion. When a miracle attracts attention to some humble spring of fresh water, I understand and applaud it; but in the present case what do we want of one? My spring is among the richest in France; it will cure by the mere power of its chemical virtues. The miracle here is like hairs in one's soup, M. l'abbé, and this scamp, who rushes into my business like a poodle into a game of skittles, ought to be sent to the House of Correction. That is my opinion."

Abbé Desvialle, whose smiling, affable expression had remained unchanged, replied in a confidential tone: "And what is the opinion of your worthy curé, Abbé Roche, if I am not mistaken in regard to all this? He ought to know the country perfectly. He is said to be very energetic and intelligent."

"Yes, yes, certainly—Abbé Roche—ah! there it is—Abbé Roche is very intelligent, as you say, very intelligent—"

At that moment a servant opened the folding-doors of the dining room. "They are coming to inform us that dinner is ready, M. l' abbé," said the capitalist, "and the countess is expecting us."

XXXII.

Mme. de Manteigney had dreaded the coming of Abbé Desvialle, of whose acuteness and penetration she was well aware; but contrary to her expectations he was by no means inquisitorial. During the whole course of the dinner, one would have supposed that the amiable priest had devoted himself to the task of calming the countess's anxiety. There was not the most distant allusion to the events which occupied the attention of the surrounding country. Music was the topic of conversation. The archbishop's envoy was a very tasteful and learned amateur, and talked most delightfully. From profane music, the quartettes of Mozart, they naturally passed on to the *Stabat* of Pergolesi, the Mass of Rosini, and by an imperceptible advance, by the time they reached dessert, began to discuss the unheard-of luxury of women. The countess, relieved from all anxiety, was charmingly gay and bewitching, the abbé dazzling, and Larreau extremely wise and philosophical; so that all three were laughing heartily as they went into the drawing-room to drink their coffee.

It was just at the moment when the young wife approached to offer the priest a cup, that the latter, looking in her face with the expression of a man who has suddenly recollected some forgotten fact, said to her: "But, my dear Madame, how do you explain the position of your good curé in this affair of the miracle?"

Mme. de Manteigney started and turned pale so suddenly that Abbé Desvialle took the cup from her hands, fearing that she might let it fall. "What position? What do you mean? I don't understand you?"

Her embarrassment was all the greater in consequence of her former security. She still smiled, but the corners of her mouth twitched nervously, and her whole countenance expressed the most profound anxiety.

The priest cast down his eyes and played with his tiny coffee spoon, then answered: "Your father and I have been talking about these events, and it was the remembrance of the conversation which induced me to ask that question. Your curé's intolerance, Madame, intolerance whose consequences he certainly did not calculate, has perhaps had a greater influence than would be believed upon public opinion, which he should have left to itself, to be freely manifested. I have heard—it has been everywhere asserted that he drove from the church women who had come to pray. Do you not think that was compromising his position?"

Abbé Desvialle was still stirring his coffee, occasionally glancing at the countess's face, endeavoring to read the meaning of her singular emotion. Strange to say, she instantly calmed herself, breathed freely, and said with apparent restraint: "I did not understand what you meant."

"What could she have imagined?" thought the priest.

She continued, with an ease of manner that was slightly affected:

"M. le curé was doubtless indignant that the story of a little rascal should have produced such an excitement throughout the country, and probably feared the superstition would do religion more harm than good. I do not think he was wrong."

"That was so much the more reason for him to be calm and prudent, my darling," murmured Larreau; "had it not been for M. Roche's stormy violence, all these rumors would have died away of themselves. Religion is above these trifles, and has no need of such Don Quixotism."

"Don't heed what my father says, M. l'abbé; he has taken a prejudice against our poor curé, I do not know why."

"He is a haughty, proud, insincere man; that is my impression, I do not know how to dissimulate."

"Haughty! because his conscience rebelled for an instant? He was rather violent perhaps, I do not —violent it may be; it would have been better if he had controlled himself, but that is not the question. The real point is, that in any other place the little dreamer would have been sent to the police station, neither more nor less. Unfortunately, there are no gendarmes at Grand Fort, that is the whole cause of the trouble."

"I see," said the abbé, playing with his snuff-box and smiling pleasantly, "I see that Mme. de Manteigney is not disposed to believe in the miracle."

"I? Quite the contrary."

"Yet, my dear child, after what you have just told us, it is plain—"

"It is plain—it is plain. Everything is plain to my father at first sight; nothing is obscure, nothing uncertain. It's a very fortunate position to be in."

"Why, what is the matter with you this evening my little countess? I do not wish to vex you; you know very well that I attach no sort of importance to the affair, and Abbé Desvialle has too much intelligence, too much acuteness, not to judge of matters precisely as I do."

"Then why should not I be as indifferent to the whole adventure as you are? What has all this to do with me?" She was becoming more and more excited. "Let this little peasant, thanks to the stir people have made about him, realize a magnificent speculation, I shall be delighted; let him sell his miraculous water by thousands of bottles!"

"Excuse me, my dear, the water belongs to me; he shall not sell a drop without buying it first."

"No matter! Let him become immensely rich, let him be canonized, admitted to the Corps Legislatif,—I will cry bravo. Ha! ha! ha! that will be charming, praiseworthy, funny as possible. How many other intriguers have made a fortune before him, thanks to human folly!"

"Don't let us urge the point," whispered Larreau in the ear of the priest; "my daughter is nervous this evening, and when women have their nerves, you know—or rather you don't know—"

"Oh! I know perfectly well."

The poor lady was aware that she had made a false step, that the warmth of her attack upon the miracle was by no means convincing, but would rather tend to inspire distrust. She well knew that her mode of seeing and speaking did not befit a woman in her position in life, and would be sure to surprise the archbishop's envoy; but unfortunately it was impossible for her to keep cool and appear indifferent.

Meantime, Abbé Desvialle was the first to change the conversation. The subject of profane and sacred music was again introduced, but the countess, dissatisfied with herself and others, and fancying that she detected some allusion in every sentence, was so paradoxical and irritable, that, by M. Larreau's suggestion, they soon separated.

When once more in his own room, the agreeable priest bolted his door, opened a travelling bag, took out some writing materials, and approached a little desk that stood near the window. It was with no small surprise that he perceived on the top of this article of furniture, in the very centre of the desk, in full view, a package wrapped in white paper, on which were these words: "Doubtless forgotten by Saint Joseph on the night of the aparision."

Abbé Desvialle frowned. This coarse paper must have been bought at the village grocer's. The awkward and affectedly sloping handwriting, the word apparition written with an *s* and only one *p*, spoke of the valet and the servant's hall. However, the abbé opened the paper, and saw a carefully folded handkerchief. With the tips of his white fingers, not without an emotion of disgust, he unfolded the article in question, and following the hem, looked at each of the four corners in succession. The last contained the initial R. The archbishop's envoy sat for some time lost in thought. His face had totally changed its expression, and the countess would doubtless have been greatly terrified could she have seen the depth and earnestness of his gaze. After the lapse of a few moments he wrapped the handkerchief again in the paper, and having placed the whole under lock and key, washed his hands, and seating himself at the desk, began to write slowly and thoughtfully, in a large, regular, careful chirography, which could only belong to a man whose imagination would never lead him astray into the kingdom of fancy.

To tell the truth, he felt a little disconcerted, not by the appearance of the handkerchief, which had merely confirmed his previous opinion, but by the evident agitation of the countess, and the strange intolerance she had displayed. The archbishop had already been for some time quietly trying to obtain information in regard to the mystery, and the curé of Virez, a very simple-minded man and a great talker, had been cautiously sounded; the suspicions uttered about the White Cross were soon learned, documents compared, and ere long it was impossible to doubt that Abbé Roche had been in some way, directly or indirectly, concerned in this most embarrassing miracle.

The unexplained but certain presence of a curé in the affair complicated matters greatly; but what would it be if the countess were also implicated. Larreau was very powerful, the count and his wife well known to all Paris. What might not an examination reveal? The priest wrote for some time, and went to bed very late.

XXXIII.

The following day, as soon as Abbé Desvialle rose, he looked in the glass and rang the bell. The free-thinker, whom we have met walking in the vicinity of the White Cross, and hiding something he had just found, instantly entered with the promptness of a man who has been waiting behind the door for the last fifteen minutes. "My friend," said the priest without turning, but watching the servant's face in the glass, "bring me a cup of black coffee."

This valet was a sly-looking person, with a turned-up nose and very wide nostrils; his face had the satirical, aggressive expression peculiar to the natives of Paris. His first glance was directed towards the writing-desk where the package had been placed. The abbé, who was expecting it, maintained a perfectly unmoved expression, stood motionless, and taking up a nail-brush, said: "Raise the window-curtains a little, if you please. Is it damp this morning?"

"The air is very dry."

"Oh! very well. The coffee will be ready immediately, I suppose?" The priest had spoken with the utmost indifference; but just as the valet was about to leave the room, he turned, and looking at him with a winning smile, said: "I was much pleased with the singular token you placed upon my writing-table."

"What token do you mean, Monsieur l'abbé? I—"

"Then you were not the person who put it there, oh! very well. The coffee, if you please. I alluded to a curious pocket-handkerchief I found last evening, and I should have liked to thank—but since you had nothing to do—"

The priest's expression was one well adapted to win confidence. The valet could not help smiling in his turn, and said in a low tone: "It was done for the best."

"That is just what I thought. You have managed very cleverly, my son; I have no doubt your master will be well pleased with you."

The free-thinker was flattered. He closed the door, which had partially opened, and, taking a step forward, seemed to be awaiting permission to say more.

"Have you anything else to confide to me on the subject of—this handkerchief, my good friend?"

"I only wished to inform M. l'abbé that I found it in the place where the apparition was seen, on the following morning."

"What made you suppose that it was forgotten —you are an intelligent person—by some one who played the part of Saint Joseph? Speak freely, my good friend, I wish to ascertain the truth as well as you. Come—"

"Bless me! M. l'abbé, this handkerchief is exactly like the ones used by the curé of Grand Fort."

"Yes—yes. You assert nothing; you merely state a singular and vexatious coincidence, a curious fact, one of those odd resemblances that are sometimes seen in pocket handkerchiefs. It never entered your mind for a single instant that the good, worthy curé of the village had anything to do with the apparition; that would be absurd, and you did well to understand that such an assertion might prove extremely dangerous to you; no, you merely say—what is very true— It is very singular that—"

"Yes, M. l'abbé, that is it exactly."

"It is very singular that it should be found at the foot of the White Cross, or very near there, in a place—"

"Where no one ever passes."

"In a place that is extremely lonely—a handkerchief exactly like—"

"And even marked with M. Roche's initial."

"And even marked with the letter R. Ah! there might have been a cottage occupied by some poor family, some invalid, near by, and the good curé, who is so charitable to all who suffer, might have lost his handkerchief in visiting the hut; but you say the place is very lonely."

"Yes, M. l'abbé, nobody lives there except père Loursière."

And the servant related with great minuteness the facts that every one knows, the death of the poor girl, and the birth of the child, whom the curé had taken under his charge.

"That is all very well," interrupted Abbé Desvialle, "but in the whole story, my son, I see but one thing, and that is, that you have found a handkerchief marked with the letter R, nothing more. You are by no means authorized to suppose that any one has been playing the part of Saint Joseph, which would be a great crime in the eyes of God."

The servant was not at all disconcerted. On the contrary, he answered with a broad smile: "I found the handkerchief a short distance from the White Cross in a little grove of pine trees, on the very spot where a donkey had been fastened."

"How do you know that a donkey was tied—"

"Monsieur l'abbé is aware that the ground under pine trees is soft and smooth, and when a donkey has been stamping for a quarter of an hour under a tree, it leaves marks—marks that are very easy to recognize. In apparitions, donkeys don't leave such traces. That is why I thought—"

"All that proves nothing. Why is it so very extraordinary that a mountaineer should have fastened his beast in that spot, my son?"

"But what reason does M. l'abbé think mère Hilaire would have for going to the White Cross that evening, and tying her donkey to a pine tree?"

"Who is mère Hilaire? How do you know the donkey in question was hers? These are only mere suppositions. It is impossible."

"Mère Hilaire is M. le curé's housekeeper, and everybody in the village is very fond of her, she is such a good woman. Now, to explain the rest to M. l'abbé, I must tell him that the day after the miracle, very early in the morning, as I was passing along the terrace, I heard below me the voice of a donkey complaining. These brutes have a way of saying that they have been kept waiting a long time. Naturally, I leaned over the balustrade, and saw mère Hilaire's ass, saddled and fastened to a bough in front of the little door opening from the terrace. On seeing me, the poor beast began to bray still louder. It was very strange that mère Hilaire's donkey should be there at that hour. It was not market-day at Virez, and besides, the good woman never went there so early. I watched the poor brute dragging at her rope for an instant. The ground was beaten hard all around her; she must have spent a portion of the night at the foot of the tree. It was very extraordinary. Yet I thought no more about it, but as usual at that hour, went to the village to drink some white wine—I mean—"

"Go on! go on! White wine is very healthful in mountainous countries."

"Monsieur l'abbé is very kind. I had scarcely reached the village, when I saw people talking earnestly together, and soon met M. le curé's housekeeper walking along very fast. I stopped her and said: 'Mère Hilaire, do you happen to be looking for your donkey?'"

"Suppose I am, where is it?"

"At the foot of the terrace at the château. Who fastened it there for you?"

"Thank you, I will go and get it."

"And she passed on without saying more. Just at that moment several peasants approached me and related the story of the night before, the apparition and all the rest. As I like to obtain information, I went that very day to examine the place where all this had occurred, and at the first glance saw the hoof-prints of a donkey, which led me to reflect. I naturally looked carefully around, climbed a little slope where the earth was freshly cut, and found myself under the pine tree, where I saw on the ground the handkerchief that M. l'abbé has in his possession."

"Was there any impression of a man's foot among the hoof-prints?"

"I thought of that at once, searched, and soon discovered several. One of them, in particular, was so distinct that I could count the number of nails. There was only one row inside, and two on the outer edge, twenty-seven nails in all."

"You are a close observer, my dear friend."

"It is natural to me; but if M. l'abbé thinks me a chatterer, I will say no more."

"Pray go on."

"Well then, as I left the little pine grove, I saw M. le curé; he was speaking to several peasants who had come to pray before the stone, and was so much excited that he instantly put a throng of suspicious thoughts into my head, each one more strange than the other. I thought of the donkey fastened at the foot of the terrace, and remembered that the good woman did not answer me when I asked who had left the beast before the little door; all these things crowded into my mind so fast, that instead of returning directly to the château, I took a circuitous way to gain the path which M. le curé must take on his return home. On reaching a spot with which I was familiar,—a sunken hollow where the earth is always moist,—I concealed myself, that M. Roche might not perceive me. Ten minutes after, I heard the sound of his steps; he was walking rapidly, and yet it seemed as if he moved slowly, so great was my curiosity. When he had passed, I went back into the path, looked on the ground—and there were two rows of nails on the outer edge and one within, twenty-seven in all."

"But what leads you to think that mère Hilaire's donkey was the one whose foot-prints you saw near the White Cross?"

"I could inform M. l'abbé, only I shall be obliged to confess that I was compelled to tell a lie in order to find out."

"There may be circumstances in which a lie is pardonable. Tell the truth."

"Well, Monsieur, I was very anxious to put the

hoof of the good woman's donkey into one of the prints on the slope; so, after dinner, I went to M. le curé's housekeeper, and said to her: 'Mère Hilaire, the countess has sent me to ask if you will lend her your donkey to ride through the valley. Sophie limps; I don't know what is the matter with her.' M. l'abbé perhaps does not know that the countess's donkey is named Sophie. Naturally, mère Hilaire brought out her donkey at once, and to prevent suspicion, I added: 'Don't saddle her, Sophie's will fit very well.'"

"And you led the animal to the White Cross—"

"And under the pine trees too. I took the beast's hoof more than twenty times and placed it in the prints, which it fitted like a glove. Oh! yes, indeed, I—"

"You seem to be a great talker, my lad," Abbé Desvialle suddenly exclaimed, re-assuming his priestly air and lofty bearing. "I think I asked you for a cup of coffee. Bring it to me at once."

The amazed valet withdrew, not knowing exactly whether to be glad or sorry that he had been so extremely confidential.

XXXIV.

Since the countess's visit, Abbé Roche had suffered deeply. Faithful to the promise he had given, he had avoided all public demonstrations. Besides, what could he have done, what could he have said? Does not one double the strength of a stream by opposing it ever so slightly? But when he was alone in his room, and had bolted the door, he could no longer resist the emotions of his nature, and mère Hilaire often heard the sound of violent sobs.

For fifteen years he had made himself a peasant, a mountaineer, that he might the better understand those whom heaven had entrusted to his care, enter more fully into their lives, win their confidence and affection. He had spent the whole strength of his youth to render himself worthy of his mission, and suddenly, without the power of uttering a complaint, saw himself abandoned by all. They had understood nothing, nor wished to understand anything: they had considered him merely as an official, paid for regularly discharging a duty similar to that of a teacher—a sort of rustic watchman; and when he had addressed them from the old pulpit with tears in his eyes, encircling with his love the whole great family before him, mingling his prayers with theirs, and believing himself beloved in his turn, he had been the plaything, the sport of an illusion!

For fifteen years he had lived without suspecting it in a desert, more isolated, a thousand times more solitary, than on the morning of his birth. "And after all," he thought, "have they not a right to avoid me? They instinctively divined that they could not trust me. Did I not forget them all for her sake on the first occasion that offered?"

He felt overwhelmed with shame as he thought that he had formerly deceived himself in regard to his own feelings, and mistaken the emotion of a passionate temperament for a holy vocation. Had he then loved God because of the absence of a human object? He had taken for an inspiration from on high what was merely the agitation of his pride, seeking to poetize the most profane of all feelings. He had believed himself to be a minister of God, when he was only a sensual, passionate man. Searching his thoughts, he remembered the outbursts of love that he had felt, when amidst his prayers he had pressed his lips to the altar, and recalling at the same time the emotions that other kisses had aroused within him, he compared the two with alarm, believing that he discovered a resemblance between them which made him shudder.

"Then for twenty years I have loved her without knowing it," said he to himself; "all that went before was only a long, accursed preface to the most unworthy baseness! They make way for me, avoid me, fear to meet me. Is it not just? Do I not fear myself; do not I, too, strive to avoid myself?"

It is certain that the obstinate silence of Abbé Roche exerted more and more restraint upon the enthusiasm of this bewitched country. The countess herself—I grieve to say—sought and found pretexts to avoid meeting him. There was a sort of understanding between them that weighed upon her more heavily as the consequences became more serious. Her fate was in the hands of the curé of Grand Fort. Let even a word escape his lips, and a most frightful scandal would result, a scandal of which the count as well as herself would be the victim. Now, after having felt most earnest gratitude to the priest for the promise he had made, she began to question whether he would keep his word; and, in her anxiety, imagined a thousand circumstances under which the poor curé would not have the strength and courage to keep silence and maintain his apparent indifference. She began to suffer from the thought of being at his mercy, and instinctively revenged herself by suspecting him.

Besides, could she place entire confidence in this singular priest, this strange man, who, under the impulse of some unaccountable frenzy, had taken advantage of the darkness and solitude to clasp her in his arms and cover her with kisses. Was it not unheard-of, monstrous? She thought of it again. Had she not reason to be offended and to doubt his promise? The thought that she was obliged to conciliate him, in spite of all this, added to her embarrassment. To her, also, Abbé Roche's presence was a constraint!

She could not think of him without remembering the absurd visit she made to père Loursière: an unpardonable, compromising, dangerous, aimless, foolish proceeding. The horrible man had made sport of her. Why had the curé of Grand Fort aided her in her folly? Ought he not to have prevented it, unless he had anticipated the unpardonable scene which resulted from his yielding to her wishes? These reflections constantly pursued her. Not wishing to enter the priest's house again, she had begged her father to invite the curé to dine at the château; but M. Larreau said decidedly that he wished to have nothing more to do with the priest, and Mme. de Manteigney yielded, very glad in her heart to have a pretext for avoiding the poor man, whose presence most unpleasantly reminded her of her absurd expedition and the various perplexities it had entailed.

XXXV.

The curé of Grand-Fort-le-Haut was breakfasting upon a raw artichoke sprinkled with pepper and salt, when Abbé Desvialle, after a light tap at the door, entered the room. The curé rose, and turning calmly towards the new-comer, said: "What do you wish, Monsieur l'abbé?"

The archbishop's envoy was disconcerted for an instant by the sight of his grave and dignified, almost imposing bearing. This was by no means the sort of personage whom he had expected to meet. We form our ideas of people according to the good or bad qualities we suppose them to possess, and Abbé Desvialle had imagined the village curé to be a little, active, nervous man, with twinkling eyes, thin lips, and red cheeks; he expected an eager welcome; he knew that type of men, and understood what manner to adopt towards them; but at sight of this sad, honest countenance, with the large, clear eyes that steadfastly met his own, and the simple, somewhat haughty bearing, he perceived that he had a thoroughly reliable man before him.

Besides, it was not merely the curé's personal appearance that surprised him; the interior of the humble dwelling revealed a life wholly destitute of all ambition, luxury or human weakness; an existence filled with those austere virtues which the elegant abbé prized all the more because so utterly a stranger to them. He looked at the artichoke, half-stripped of its skin, and remembering the crutch of Sixtus V. said: "I am very sorry, M. le curé, that I have not dined with you at the château as I hoped to do. I have been very anxious to find an opportunity of conversing with you."

"I received no invitation to the dinner you mention, Monsieur; but under any circumstances it would have been impossible for me to accept it."

"Yet I understood the countess to say she expected you."

"You are mistaken, Monsieur. Will you take a seat?"

"This is an intriguer of no common order," thought Abbé Desvialle, as he sat down and instantly made an involuntary grimace, which he quickly repressed, not wishing to show the unusual and disagreeable sensation he experienced at the contact with the hard chairs of the priest's abode.

"Monsieur le curé," he continued, "I have taken advantage of my visit to the château to call upon you. My action, I will at once inform you, is not official. I was very anxious to have your opinion concerning the very singular events that have occurred in your parish, and, as you know, are having a wide-spread circulation. The esteem the archbishop has always felt for you leads him to attach great importance to your impressions in regard to this affair, in which he is compelled to act with the utmost circumspection. Once more, I assure you that I have not come to make an investigation; I repeat that my action is not official; pray be convinced of the fact."

Abbé Roche, still unmoved, looked steadily into the face of his interlocutor, who, despite his usual ease of manner, felt somewhat embarrassed by the earnestness of the gaze. "To whom have I the pleasure of speaking," said he at last.

"Ah! pray excuse me, I forgot to announce myself. I am Abbé Desvialle; perhaps you have heard my name."

"Never, Monsieur."

"The archbishop deigns to bestow his confidence and friendship upon me; and my desire to have your opinion in regard to this apparition of the White Cross is only the echo of your Superior's, Monsieur le curé."

"Question me, as the archbishop has ordered you to do so."

"You give my visit a different character from the one I wished to adopt; but I will do whatever you prefer. I ask you then, Monsieur, if you have any reason for recognizing a supernatural character in the apparition of which every one is talking."

"I affirm that all these facts, which, notwithstanding my efforts, have had a publicity that I deplore, are not in the slightest degree miraculous."

"That is a frank reply. Then I suppose you can explain this pretended miracle, and are not ignorant of any of the details of the affair."

"Yes, Monsieur l'abbé."

"And can you tell me what you know of it?"

"No, Monsieur, that is quite impossible."

The two priests looked each other in the face for a moment.

"You cannot, or you will not, M. le curé?"

"I neither can nor will."

"Remember that this is a very serious matter."

"I am aware of it."

"And that the archbishop—"

"You are not my Superior, Monsieur l'abbé."

"That the archbishop, I say, can command you to speak, compel you to make a full confession."

"It is his place to give me his orders verbally, and mine to decide how far my conscience will allow me to obey."

"You carry matters with a very high hand, M. le curé."

"And you judge from a very low standpoint, Monsieur, if you suppose that fear would make me utter what I had decided to withhold."

Abbé Desvialle was an extremely gentle and wary man, skilful in mild persuasions, and fond of diplomatic strategems; but he felt ill at ease when opposed to this bar of steel, and was actually somewhat intimidated by the curé's quiet firmness. He continued:

"The words which have just escaped your lips will not be repeated to the archbishop, I assure you. You are evidently under the influence of some excitement."

"I am perfectly calm, and have said exactly what I mean."

"But you have not thought of the deplorable consequences that this extraordinary affair may entail upon our holy religion! Do you not know that the papers have taken up the matter, that it is everywhere discussed, analyzed, sifted, perverted?"

"I know all that, and was the first to suffer."

"Yet there is one infallible method of calming all this uproar; namely, by publicly and frankly explaining the natural facts which gave rise to this unfortunate event."

"I can explain nothing."

"Come, my dear curé," said Abbé Desvialle, drawing his chair forward, "let us speak freely to each other. No doubt you are prejudiced against me. Must I repeat once more that my intentions are perfectly friendly, that your firmness interests me, and that I have the most earnest desire to conciliate all parties. Speak to me frankly, tell me what you know; remember that the honor of the priesthood is at stake, that your contumacy may furnish the enemies of religion, already too numerous, with a dangerous weapon; think that the archbishop is wounded by all that has occurred. You do not answer? Yet surely you must understand that I come to hold out my hand to you, that I wish to find some means of helping you out of this difficulty. Are you aware that your mode of action is interpreted in a manner very injurious to you? I have not sought for information in regard to the affair, it has been given me unasked. We know, beyond the possibility of doubt, that during the night of the miracle, as your parishioners call it, you were wandering over the mountains. For what reason? I believe the motive to be a perfectly honorable one, but what is it? Some one even sent me—no, details are insignificant in such a matter—some one even sent me a pocket-handkerchief that was found near the White Cross, under the pine trees, where a donkey, belonging to your housekeeper, had been fastened." The curé could not restrain a sudden start, which was instantly noticed by his judge. "What reply shall I give to people who have the boldness to assert that the pocket-handkerchief is very much like those you use? Here it is, still wrapped in the paper envelope in which it was sent to me. Read what is written there, and judge for yourself how malicious are the interpretations of the villagers, how important it is to put an end to these reports, to elucidate the affair."

Abbé Roche, as has already been mentioned, grew calmer and more steadfast at the approach of danger. As he saw himself more utterly ruined, the feeling of personal dignity increased. "The handkerchief is mine," he replied without hesitation.

"But the story of the child that you carried away at midnight, and the death of the poor girl without confession, are they fables also?"

"No, they are facts."

"Then all that has been said of you must be taken literally, M. le curé; you do not fear scandal apparently. Must I remind you of the sale of a relic belonging to your church, a sale whose publicity—"

Abbé Roche turned pale, started suddenly from his chair and exclaimed: "That is a falsehood! whoever said it is a scoundrel!"

The archbishop's envoy recoiled a pace or two, and speaking with all the more calmness because he felt somewhat disturbed, said quietly: "Avoid such outbursts, M. le curé, they only aggravate your position. Remember that the purchaser of that relic—that precious statuette—belongs to a circle where there is not, where there cannot be, a scoundrel. I have had the honor of meeting Viscount Claudius frequently, and I never—"

"So much the worse for you, Monsieur, so much the worse. He lied to me, deceived me, robbed our poor church: he picked up the scattered fragments in a corner, and said to me: 'Give me this, it has no value.' I believed him, and he carried it away. That is the truth, Monsieur."

"That is not what he says. What are we to believe?" added the archbishop's envoy with a very meaning smile.

"Do you consider my word as nothing, Monsieur?" murmured Abbé Roche, in a suppressed tone.

"Oh! of course, under any other circumstances, a curé's word would have great weight; but you have placed yourself in such a situation that, for the moment, you will admit that we cannot have implicit confidence in you. It is to be feared—I mean, that your memory might play you false. Keep cool, I entreat you, in behalf of your own interests."

The curé's face had the expression of a man suddenly overwhelmed by some disaster. He crossed his arms upon his breast, sat down again, and remained motionless, while large drops of perspiration trickled down his forehead.

Although Abbé Desvialle's opinion was fully decided in regard to the man before him, he was really touched by the terrible anguish expressed in the curé's countenance. "The unfortunate man," he thought, "has rushed heedlessly into this adventure. Ambition has made him half mad, and he thought himself strong enough to make a second *Salette.* Yes, he is a man of energy, but that is not sufficient." He continued more mildly: "Do not attempt a useless resistance, M. le curé, you would only be crushed. You perceive that these juggleries must cease. Go without delay, and throw yourself at the archbishop's feet; implore his paternal indulgence. As for me, I no longer wish to know what part you have played in this deplorable business; I will close my eyes, stop my ears. However guilty you may be, however forgetful of your duties as a priest, your dignity as—"

"But who gives you a right to judge me?" cried the curé. "Who gives you a right to force your way into my house and insult me thus? Is not your task completed, Monsieur?"

Abbé Desvialle grew pale in his turn, and changing his tone, replied: "I can now inform you, Monsieur, that I am here by the orders of the archbishop, who, in his prudence, did not wish to commence an investigation before having studied the question. You yourself assure me that this first duty is completed; then nothing more remains for me to do except to read this letter, whose entire contents were written by the archbishop's own hand."

Abbé Desvialle drew a folded paper from his pocket, and having opened it with the ease whose secret has been preserved by the *Comedie-Française*, read these simple words: "'At the day and hour indicated by Abbé Desvialle, on whom I here bestow full power, the curé of Grand Fort will set out immediately, without delay, and report himself at the archbishopric.' The letter is signed, as you can see."

"I will obey my archbishop, Monsieur."

"It is better for you—for every one, that your departure should not be too much noticed. You might leave this place to-night, for instance, you have the whole day to make your arrangements. By leaving on foot, about ten o'clock in the evening, you can reach Virez in time to take the coach, which passes, I believe, at eleven. I do not know what the archbishop's decision concerning you will be, but I advise you to arrange everything for an absence which may be prolonged."

"Very well, Monsieur."

"You grieve me, M. le curé, you really grieve me."

"I wish you good-morning."

"May God watch over you."

XXXVI.

Evening had arrived. Mère Hilaire, kneeling in the middle of the room, was packing her curé's books and clothing in a large trunk. From time to time she stopped, silently wiped her eyes, and resumed her work. "Monsieur le curé," said she timidly, without turning, lest he might see her red eyes and troubled face, "Monsieur le curé, have you taken your woolen stockings?"

Abbé Roche, who was buckling a little portmanteau similar to those that horsemen formerly carried strapped to their saddles, seemed not to have exactly comprehended the good woman's question. "It is very well," said he, "it is very well!"

And mère Hilaire dared not say more.

Meantime the priest took the light, approached the crucifix hanging on the wall, and taking it down placed it on the table, carefully wiped away the dust that had lodged in the corners, raised it as if to examine it more closely, and, while mère Hilaire's back was turned, noiselessly kissed it, then rubbed the ivory several times, doubtless fearing that it might have been sullied by contact with his lips. He next took a clean white napkin from the great trunk, wrapped the crucifix in it, joined the edges and tried to fasten them with pins; but as his hands trembled and his eyes were filled with tears, he could not see very clearly, and said to the housekeeper in a voice that he strove to keep firm: "Mère Hilaire, will you put in these pins? I cannot manage them with my big fingers."

While the old woman did as she had been requested, Abbé Roche seated himself at the little table, took a sheet of paper and wrote: "Madame la comtesse, you thought my ivory Christ worthy of your notice, permit me—"

Crushing the paper, he took a fresh sheet and began: "Madame la comtesse—"

He sat for a few moments with his eyes fixed on the words, then rose and approaching his housekeeper said: "Mère Hilaire, to-morrow morning you will go to the château."

"Yes, Monsieur le curé."

"You will ask to speak with the countess in private, give her this crucifix, and tell her it comes from me."

"Then you won't take it with you, M. le curé.

You will be sorry not to have it, my child. She doesn't need it."

"You will do as I tell you, will you not?"

"Of course I will; but when you come home and find it gone—"

"Perhaps I may not come back for some time; that depends upon what the archbishop—"

"Yes, yes, if the archbishop should give you another parish, for instance?"

"Perhaps, yes."

"You are no longer contented here, these people are not worthy of you. I don't know what notion they have taken into their heads, but they are not good for much, they are ungrateful wretches, all of them—yes, all. I have heard them, I know them. God will punish them. They have grieved you, made you unhappy! Ah! the archbishop knows all that, I am sure; he will give you another parish and I shall join you—and we will begin over again. You will see the archbishop to-morrow; then write to me immediately and I will set out with the trunks. If we go far away, well! so much the better, perhaps the people will be kinder than they are here. When you arrive— When you arrive—write only these words: 'Mère Hilaire, come.' That is all I shall ask. Oh! if I could only go with you! but you are right, M. le curé, I should be in your way, old people like me cannot walk very well."

The poor woman spoke with increasing excitement, clipping her sentences, suddenly interrupting herself. She moved uneasily around the priest, watching him as a mother does her child when about to part with it, and finding no other pretext to approach him once more, began to brush his shabby cassock, patting and caressing it with her old hands. As she did so, she said to herself: "If I should never see him again—oh! God, suppose I should never see him again!—You know," she continued, "I have put fifty crowns in your portmanteau. They belong to you, I saved them from your own money, but did not tell you before because you would have asked me for them and given them to those rascals. They are in the left hand corner wrapped in the handkerchiefs."

And she asked God's pardon for telling a lie; the silver was really her own, but how could she let her child depart without a penny

The curé had been standing motionless looking at the linen which concealed the crucifix. The good woman's words gave a new direction to his sorrowful thoughts, and he murmured: "Thank you, mother, thank you, my good mother!

"It is only a little excursion, nothing more; but you will walk fast and get very much heated. When you reach Virez you will call for a glass of nice, hot wine—promise me, M. le curé. And you will take a seat—not outside, but in the coach, won't you? Inside the coach.

The priest turned slowly towards her, clasped her in his arms, and both sobbed aloud: "I am unhappy, my dear mother," said he; "do not forget me, I have no one but you—pray for me—I am very unhappy."

Suddenly he drew himself up to his full height, and looking at his watch, exclaimed: "It is ten o'clock, I must go lest I should lose the coach.

"Certainly, my child, certainly, you must go.

She ran to a closet, took out a glass, poured some wine into it with a trembling hand, and weeping and smiling at the same moment, held it towards the curé: "Drink it, drink it. Now go—go quickly." She threw his cloak over his arm and handed him his portmanteau and cane, saying: "Walk straight on without looking back—you will write to me; I love you, my child, I love you. May God and the Holy Virgin protect and be with you. You will write to me to-morrow evening?

"To-morrow evening."

She had taken his hand again, and while kissing it, although he made no attempt to withdraw, said: "Pardon me, M. le curé, pardon me."

He left the house. The air was heavy; a fine, penetrating rain began to fall. Abbé Roche looked at the old belfry and dark porch, raising his hat as if to salute his past, then turned into the path that winds along behind the village. It was not a departure, but a flight. He had been ordered not to attract attention, and he obeyed by avoiding the village. The confused murmur of the shouts of belated drunkards rose from the inn; he walked on more rapidly. When near the château, he heard the stamping of horses, and through the great door that stood open, saw by the light of the lanterns the servants removing the trunks from a travelling carriage. It was the equipage of the Count de Manteigney, who had just returned to the castle of his ancestors.

While in the vicinity of Grand Fort, Abbé Roche, thinking only of avoiding every one, had walked on with a firm step and courageous bearing, but when he descended into the valley, and found himself alone, lashed by the wind and rain; when he saw overhead long black clouds that gave an example of flight, and seemed to wish to drag him with them, his limbs tottered, despair overwhelmed him, and wrapping himself more closely in his cloak, he sat down upon a rock.

The mountains looked dark and gloomy, the dear mountains he had loved so much, and so often explored. Down below, the torrent was flowing beneath the pine trees; there was the village, the church, his own dwelling, where mère Hilaire was weeping and thinking of him, saying to herself: "Where is he now, where is he?" And farther on, towards the left, in the ancient château whose outline was scarcely visible against the lowering sky, the countess was singing to the accompaniment of the piano, or talking and laughing. The lighted windows might be plainly seen. He felt her presence, saw her leaning back in her large arm-chair, gay, coquettish, eccentric, as on the day of his first visit; then anxious, passionate, imploring his aid, confessing her sorrows to him, and, too, pulling him by the sleeve and murmuring: "I am afraid, M. le curé; what is that I see yonder? I am afraid."

What was she doing, what was she saying now? He had not seen her for a long time! She had not vouchsafed him a single word! She no longer remembered him; but he could never forget the rapture, the insults, the shame—nothing, nothing!

He rose, took up his portmanteau, and resumed his walk.

"Eh! who is that?" cried a voice; "you will fall into the ditches!"

The priest then perceived a man holding a lantern walking towards him. "Why, it is you, M. le curé," said père Loursière when within a few paces, "and what are you doing among the works at this hour?"

"I am attending to my own affairs; and you, what are you doing?"

"I'm doing just what you are, M. le curé, minding my own business, since I am keeper of the spring."

"You are right," said the abbé, forcing himself to speak gently; "forgive me if I was harsh to you, but I am in haste; I am on my way to Virez to take the coach that passes at half-past eleven."

"Faith, M. le curé, you are not wrong to take a little trip just now; during your absence people's heads will have time to cool." (He laughed in his red beard.) "The country isn't particularly well disposed towards you just now. When tongues begin to wag, it is no little— It has been said that you were the father of my dead daughter's child! And I never suspected it! Oh! you do well to travel for a time."

"But you know very well that it is a slander, Loursière," cried the curé.

"Well, I really think they do exaggerate a little."

"What, knave, you think! Have the courage to speak the truth. You know perfectly well to whom the child belongs. Do you forget that I paid for your silence myself."

"Faith, M. le curé, I don't remember anything about it. When people grow old, they lose their memory. Besides, I haven't time to think of all that. M. Larreau has appointed me keeper of the spring, and I watch the spring. May I be hung if any one obtains a single glass of water without my consent. I don't remember anything but what M. Larreau told me. I did not hear you coming; I was in my shop, opening a box of chaplets that arrived to-day. Are you going right away, M. le curé Take care, you will fall into the ditches.

"Yes," replied the priest, who had already walked several paces forward.

When Abbé Roche was a little farther away, Loursière muttered:

"There goes a person I shan't miss! One cowl the less, that's all;" then raising his voice: "A pleasant journey, Monsieur le curé, a pleasant journey!

XXXVII.

All the world knows how rapid and brilliant was the success of the Manteigney springs. If the present state of the country is compared with what it was formerly, one feels amazed by the marvellous transformation. "Indeed, gentlemen," as Count de Manteigney himself said a few days ago in an agricultural assembly, "modern industry offers to human activity new horizons, whose immensity would formerly have made the brain reel. The genius of man is only beginning to spread its wings. The conquered earth yields her treasures; the mountains are levelled and disappear, the precipices are filled up, obstacles crumble and vanish. Progress touches the rock with her divine foot, and suddenly forth springs the fruitful trinity, which, from a certain point of view, I might call holy, and which gloriously symbolizes the future of modern society—I mean science, art, and capital." I quote this passage because it was highly praised, and has been reproduced in many places. The Count de Manteigney, as is very evident, had gradually returned to healthful, serious life, and was devoting the political and moral powers which had hitherto slumbered within him to the service of his country; but the other wonders resulting from M. Larreau's efforts must be mentioned.

A large portion of the valley has been transformed into a park, dotted with comfortable cottages designed with the most exquisite taste. These innumerable little villas, half concealed in verdure, with their pink or blue blinds, red vases, fragrant little garden plots, and tiny fountains playing in their limpid basins, produce a most beautiful effect. Works of art have risen on every side, as if by magic, and surprises, as charming as they are dainty, await the promenader at every turn in the walks: here an Egyptian tomb occupied by a pastry cook, there a temple of Vesta, beneath whose pillars handsome donkeys with showy trappings are constantly standing. Farther on is the Parthenon itself, admirably reproduced in *simili-marbre*, and containing a gymnasium, fencing and boxing school, pistol-gallery, billiard-room, and Holland spinning tops. Above the immortal frieze of the divine Phidias, a colossal veranda has been erected, which, while completing the ancient structure, forms the longest photographic establishment in the world; an immense casino, copied from that of Arcachon, dazzling in the purity of its Oriental forms and the richness of its domes, occupies the centre of this earthly paradise, in which the elegances and refinements of the most aristocratic Parisians find suitable surroundings: concert-halls, reading-rooms with a library attached, gambling establishments, an electric telegraph communicating with every part of France and giving each item of news as soon as it is known; there is not a bit of gossip, a change in the stock market, a vote of the chambers, a decision of any noted law-suit, of which Manteigney has not the earliest intelligence. The theatre, where the most celebrated artistes consider it an honor to appear, is most admirably arranged, beyond all criticism from an architectural point of view, and in most perfect harmony with that ardent worship of art for which our times are renowned. The building, standing at one end of the lawn, presents on each of its four façades a specimen of the most fashionable styles of architecture. One is Japanese, another a most successful restoration of the Etruscan mode, while those of the Middle Ages and the Renaissance are reproduced on the third and fourth. It must also be mentioned that all the ornaments, carvings and projections upon this building, which are made of iron, painted in various colors, may be removed with the utmost ease and again replaced, thus affording an opportunity for the most surprising, instructive, and often happy combinations. The idea was M. Larreau's.

The edifice at the springs is, with good reason, considered the beau-ideal of its kind, and offers science an opportunity of observing the most varied and novel modes of treatment. Swedish shower-baths, Polish immersions, Egyptian baths, Roman pools in marble basins, galleries for inhalation, halls for pulverization, Oriental refreshment rooms—Vichy, Luchon, Plombières, and Barèges united together could not form so complete an assortment. The

Virez doctor, whom we met one evening wearing a cap on his head, now never leaves the house except in a black coat and white cravat, having been appointed sub-inspector of the springs, the honorary direction of which Dr. Blavoux, a homeopathic physician from Paris, has consented to accept at the request of the archbishop. New and colossal edifices will add fresh splendor to this thermal establishment, which already defies all rivalry. A gasometer, constructed according to the plans of an English engineer, affords means of lighting the roads, park, cottages, casino, thermal establishment, in short, the whole region.

The first spring, although of great value, would not have been enough to supply all wants; but others of incalculable wealth did not long evade the search of savants and physicians. They are now five in number: the Archbishop's spring, the Larreau spring, the Jean spring, the spring of the Countess, who has given the name of Manteigney an heir, and lastly the St. Joseph spring, the first discovered and least prized of all. The Claudius pool, and the Desvialle pool, the former fed from the Larreau, and the latter from the Jean spring, may also be mentioned.

After all, the principal cause which makes Manteigney a unique thermal establishment is, besides the excellence of its waters, the natural beauty of the country, the purity of the air, and the union of all these attractions in a delightful valley, the aristocratic social position of the persons who meet there. In that respect, M. Larreau was greatly aided by a lucky accident. The first bathers who arrived at Manteigney, even before the arrangements were fully completed, were friends of the count, and belonged to the cream of Parisian society. Men of pleasure, artists, authors, were received at the château. They drank a little of the water and an immense quantity of champagne; most delightful entertainments were given. Narboy finished his last novel during his stay, and dedicated it to the countess. Hunting-parties and races were arranged with an informality very appropriate to the mountains; dukes and marquises prepared fireworks with their own hands, while the Parisian papers made room in their columns for articles from Manteigney, filled with most delightful imprudences. This was the beginning—an admirable opening, which Larreau understood how to turn to the best advantage. The following season there was a rush for the cottages, and the success of the Springs was established. I will not deny that rumor says M. Larreau is not the only one to bear the immense outlay necessary for such a magical transformation. He is said to be in partnership with very great and powerful personages whose names I am not at liberty to mention. Besides, of what consequence are such reports? The result accomplished is a most admirable one.

The famous apparition, the first cause of this unprecedented success is not wholly forgotten; but it seems as if the event had occurred a century ago; it now exists only as a confused legend, which is smilingly related when people go to breakfast at the hermitage of the White Cross. On the very spot where the miracle took place, a little restaurant has been erected, whose platform, built of the trunks of pine trees, projects over the path, covering it like a roof, and affording a most beautiful view to the ladies who come there to breakfast in the open air. Loursière, who keeps this mountain restaurant, has a very fine cellar, and a cook who excels in the composition of certain dishes. When you go there, ask for a *poulet renaissance*, or simply a *manteignaise aux champignons*, and you will not forget it. To complete the moral and physical regeneration of this region, it must be mentioned that the village of Grand-Fort-le-Haut is totally changed in appearance. Within the space of two years, it has been entirely rebuilt on a regular plan and bears some resemblance to the towns inhabited by English laboring men; brick and cast-iron are the principal materials used by Larreau in the construction of these neat, symmetrical houses, which provide every family with a comfortable, almost elegant abode, in perfect harmony with the new customs of the country. Prosperity has been very generally diffused over the mountains; there is no longer a single peasant who does not act as guide, donkey-driver, bath-tender, or dog-keeper, and they have acquired a taste for their new mode of life so rapidly, that in passing through the new village, one might imagine one's self transported into some beautiful suburb of the capital. The livery of the bath-tenders is gray and blue, of elegant cut, and most convenient design. That of the guides is of course more showy, but also in perfect taste. From time to time the countess, or one of the other ladies, adds an ornament or a band of trimming, but without changing the style of the original model, which was designed by Vernon himself. The huntsmen's uniform is very peculiar: the stockholders thought very justly that stout boots and cocked hats would be uncomfortable to wear among the rocks; they therefore adopted the Scotch costume, and it would be hard to imagine anything prettier.

The ancient village church, a very curious edifice, but extremely incongruous amidst the present surroundings, was torn down and rebuilt during one Spring, and Abbé Desvialle consented to be appointed curé, on the express condition that his vicar should take his place during his frequent absences. The famous religious concerts, whose fame has spread throughout Europe, take place in this new church, which is perfectly adapted to the requirements of the fastidious congregation that assembles within its walls; but this lengthy enumeration must be brought to a close: things having been described, let me be permitted to say a few words about men. The Count de Manteigney, who had held aloof from his father-in-law's first efforts, who had even by his prolonged absence protested against the apparition, was deeply impressed when he saw with his own eyes the first advantages of the enterprise. He then suddenly perceived what the future might hold in reserve, the immense benefits which the enlargement of this wonderful establishment would procure for him. Under the wise counsels of his father-in-law, who saw the whole bearing of any matter, as we know, he gradually began to study the affair, and acted as mediator between Larreau and the different persons who wished to join him in the speculation. The stables for the stud were rapidly completed, the grounds for training horses arranged according to the count's directions, and he at last felt that he had a definite object in life. He became acquainted with one of the ministers, who being very anxious to win a man whose name had great influence in the department, welcomed him with most attractive cordiality. The prefect completed the task of making a conquest of the count, and one day M. de Manteigney felt an emotion of regret and indignation at the thought of his past life. Besides, he had attained an age when ambition first begins to awake within the mind. Hitherto he had looked upon his father-in-law as merely a vulgar rich man, a nobody, separated from himself by an impassable gulf. Now, for the first time, he wondered whether his wife's father might not prove to be a man of genius; and wishing to have the matter settled, asked him a few vague questions about his plans and means of action, and was amazed by the acuteness, penetration, and accuracy of the perceptions of the capitalist whom he had despised. As he became more intimate with the spout-maker, he was surprised to find that there was great similarity in their ideas. What he had only vaguely dreamed, his father-in-law translated into clear, precise, practical words. "Let me do the work, my dear Jean," said Larreau, leaning upon the arm of his son-in-law, "only give me the moral sanction of your name, and I will be the architect of your prosperity and fortune. You can and must attain complete success, my dear friend, you have only to allow me to act. Manteigney will soon become the real centre of the department; the frequent visits of the prefect, the excessive graciousness of the archbishop, prove the fact. Is it not evident that every one perceives the immense power we shall wield? Keep calm and cool, as beseems your rank. By your manners, by—permit me to enter into these particulars—by your very dress, inspire confidence, win the sympathies of all. How many political fortunes have been lost on account of the tie of a cravat!"

"You are not so far wrong."

"Do not lose sight of Vernon's studio."

"Oh! Vernon is—"

"In my opinion, Vernon is a knave. As the occasion has presented itself, I am not sorry to tell you so frankly; but after all, he is a clever fellow. If the man himself is of no great worth, the means that he has at his command are none the less valuable, and I don't see why respectable people should deprive themselves of these weapons, which are just now the only efficacious ones. What do we ask of a man who wishes to be a centre, a pivot? We ask him to be amiable, amusing, truthful and sincere; but he ought, notwithstanding this sincerity, to modify his bearing completely, as the circumstances, ideas and impressions around him change their colors and appearance. We are pivots only upon condition that we turn with the rest of the world, my dear fellow. The objectionable thing is not to revolve fast enough, to fail in agility, to creak like an old wine-press, and at last to be crushed by the very power which should keep us upright. I do not mean that in order to do this we are compelled to give up our own tastes and individuality. You, for instance, like horses, and wish to make money by racing: very well, give the thing a different color, present it in a social aspect, speak of free interchange between nations, of taking precedence of government, make it a dynastic question. No one will be the dupe of your theories, but nevertheless, you will inspire confidence; for people will say: 'Here is a man who understands our language, we can rely upon him.'"

"Yes, it is true, we must get a smattering of all this."

"No, it is not at all necessary; on the contrary, it would be a pity to have you initiated into these special questions, for then the reality would triumph over the form, and you would no longer have the brilliancy, the glitter, the tinge of the unexpected, which are indispensable. To make yourself understood you must be perfectly clear, and you can be clear only when you know no more than those who are listening to you. Besides, all that has no real importance: they are only the minutiæ of the moral toilet; but we must not neglect them any more than we should omit fastening our collars with a gold button when we appear in public."

"Yet you must admit that there are certain established convictions which we cannot shake off as easily as we would throw an old garment aside."

"Do not satisfy yourself with mere words, if you have convictions, what you term convictions, keep them for yourself and to yourself, like the old generals who bear within them the bullets they received when they were ensigns. It is a matter relating solely to the health, and only to be mentioned among intimate friends! Sometimes you sigh as you sit by the fireside. 'What is the matter, my dear Jean?' says papa Larreau, who perhaps may be there. 'My bullet hurts me.' 'Oh! then it will rain to-morrow.' We speak of something else and think no more about it. The echo of these little infirmities should never be permitted to cross one's threshold. That is the plain truth. If you will allow me to open my old heart to you, I shall say frankly: 'As regards moral theories, convictions are the false noses that papas and nurses inflict upon us, and by which we are duped all our lives.' Do not be surprised. Suppose one has a conviction about a material fact: my vest is white, your cravat is blue, these are certainties—and yet! Open Chevreul's book for a critical investigation, wholly uninfluenced by anything else, and when you have ascertained what the optic nerve really is and to how many errors and mistakes its sensations are subject, you will say to yourself: 'It is certain that my father-in-law's vest seems to be white, that my own cravat appears sky blue: but deuce take it if I would risk two hairs from my head to affirm this almost certainly.' If, then, we are so liable to error in the matter of physical sensations, what will it be in the domain of feeling? Everything is open to doubt, my dear friend, everything, absolutely everything. In the most hostile camps there are persons who, in good faith, treat each other as knaves and impostors. I will even assert that faith—whether political or religious, matters little—has for its source, its support, and it said, incredulity, and reciprocally comes under the same head. Deists and atheists, materialists and spiritualists, republicans and monarchists, render each other mutual services without suspecting it: they maintain their ground, argue together, and are unconsciously comrades, all the more valuable to each other because totally unaware of the invigorating action of the wounds they bestow."

"What you say, my dear father-in law, is the argument of a profound thinker; but it requires a peculiar temperament to reduce your theories to practice.

To perpetually play a part; to sustain, if occasion requires, an opinion exactly the opposite of what one really thinks—"

"You are a child! you must always think what you wish to sustain."

"But is that possible?"

"Certainly, if one has a mind sufficiently superior to remain unbiassed by any question. You are the same man that you were ten years ago; yet see how much your ideas have changed. Did you not at first believe that your birth compelled you to remain inactive, and have you not honorably and piously led an idle life merely that you might not dishonor your ancestors?"

"I grant that I was foolish—I did wrong."

"By degrees, you began to realize that these ancestors, in bestowing their name upon you, had bequeathed a certain amount of capital, thereby imposing the moral obligation of using this wealth, and drawing from it the revenues necessary to maintain the dignity of your birth, and gratification of your aristocratic tastes. They placed a wonderful tool in your hands; ought not gratitude and respect to induce you to use the instrument skilfully?"

"Undoubtedly, from a certain point of view."

"At the present day it is a disgrace not to reap the full value of everything; we do not, on any pretext, excuse or pardon it. You have estates; make them profitable, or you will be deprived of them. You have a name, a title, moral virtues, physical beauty; reap some advantage from these things; it is the only way to maintain your position as one of the privileged classes. The French nobility, at first, established its authority at the sword's point. Now, when people began to fight with cannon and pistols, did they remain inactive because there was a change in the weapons employed? At the present day, pistols and cannon are replaced by commerce and manufactures. Defend your shield, therefore, with bank-notes, according to the demands of the times in which you live! I assure you that you would not gain a single vote by presenting yourself at the next assembly in the damascene cuirass worn by Raoul de Manteigney, which is now at the end of the corridor. In 1550, the mere sight of that piece of armor would have made your vassals bow their heads, and all would have followed you with the greatest enthusiasm. Zounds! continue to be an aristocratic nobleman, desire and love the same things that your ancestors did, that is, wealth, prosperity and success; only do not fancy you must put on their old worm-eaten clothing to obtain it. Employ different means to secure the same object."

Such were the friendly conversations maintained by Larreau and his son-in-law. The latter, who at first had been shocked at the rude form in which the capitalist expressed his ideas, gradually acquired a taste for them, soon became a convert to his views, and boldly entered upon his new career. From that time nothing appeared useless to him. He organized agricultural meetings, attempted to work the marble quarries in the mountains, and established relations between himself and various important undertakings. His activity became amazing: for many years he had been extremely saving of exertion. He tried experiments, advanced new ideas, proposed a hundred fresh expedients, and became the friend of the prefect, who, one evening, concealed under the count's napkin a bit of red ribbon that he had just obtained for him.

The countess could find no words to thank Heaven for her happiness. She possessed her husband's love, had won his heart, and was, at last, in the position of which she had often dreamed—that is, surrounded by a gay circle, caressed, wealthy, able to gratify all her wishes, the mistress of a luxurious and elegant home, bearing with dignity and honor the great name of

Manteigney. On his side, Count Jean had quickly perceived that his wife's assistance was of no trifling importance in the task he had undertaken, and as he no longer did things by halves, became a model husband, and very quickly acquired a taste for the conjugal virtues which so greatly strengthened his position. The red ribbon made him the countess's devoted lover: perhaps he was not unaware that she had exerted a powerful influence in obtaining the honor.

XXXVIII.

A few days ago, the count having left the room directly after dinner to attend to one of his mares that was very sick, M. Larreau, the countess, Abbé Desvialle, and the prefect were left to themselves in the little blue parlor, chatting together very merrily. After a few moments spent in conversation, Mme. de Manteigney slowly arose from the cushions among which she had been reclining, went to the piano, removed a half dozen bracelets that might have been in her way, and began to play the overture of Don Giovanni.

If there is a time when music is especially delightful, it is surely after dinner, when, comfortably seated among a few friends, we can enjoy it at leisure, without thinking of our neighbors. Under such conditions, music becomes a most exquisite pleasure. Abbé Desvialle and the prefect, who greatly enjoyed it under such circumstances, sank back in their armchairs and permitted it to pervade their whole consciousness. The capitalist, less affected by these dainty luxuries, had drawn a light towards him and was looking over the papers and magazines piled upon the table. One of these pamphlets undoubtedly contained an extremely interesting article; for when the countess stopped, M. Larreau continued to read without raising his eyes. This was by no means his usual custom; he was always the first to compliment his daughter, and though by no means a lover of music, usually appeared to be exceedingly enthusiastic at the conclusion of every piece. "Is papa pleased?" said the countess, touching the capitalist on the shoulder.

The latter started suddenly, like a man roused from a dream, "Excuse me, darling, I heard nothing; I was reading a very interesting article."

"That is very polite; may I know the name of the magazine?"

"The '*Annals of the Propagation of the Faith.*' There are five or six numbers whose leaves have not yet been cut, but this one contains a very remarkable letter."

"What is its subject?" asked Abbé Desvialle; "some martyrdom, probably, some of the heroic actions common among our missionaries?"

"I will read the letter to you," murmured Larreau, adjusting his eye-glasses. "Dear and venerated colleague, etc., etc. I will omit the beginning. Here it is:

"KUEN-TING-PACO,
Dec. 6th, 18—

"Universal alarm prevailed. The bandits, pursued by the imperial soldiers, but rather guided by them, entered the province, yet I did not omit to conduct the holy services of mass as usual, asking the divine protection of God, who alone can save us. At its close, we carried the consecrated vessels, books, and records to a secluded spot, and buried them about a hundred and thirteen yards within the borders of a wood; after which we prepared to fly towards the mountains, carrying the children and old men in the hammocks used as litters in this country. My mind was filled with the greatest anxiety. We had been able to collect only a scanty store of provisions, which would surely prove insufficient, but the most important matter was to reach the mountains in time; and all the rumors caused me to fear that we might be stripped by the bloodthirsty bands in the very heart of the long valley we were compelled to cross. Our only hope was—"

"That is not a very lively article," murmured the prefect, with the music of *Don Giovanni* still ringing in his ears.

"The heroism of these holy martyrs to the faith is really sublime," remarked Abbé Desvialle, pushing a little cushion under his polished boots.

"All these missionaries are sent from the Rue du Bac, are they not, M. l'abbé? That is their central station?"

"Yes, Madame. What a beautiful church it is!"

"Isn't it? so cosy, so warm, so well filled! Oh! if I had been obliged to be married anywhere else, I really believe I should have remained an old maid. Ha! ha! perhaps that is a slight exaggeration, but I only said so by way of emphasis. I have but one fault to find with the Church of the Missions, and that is, the interminable corridor leading to the vestry; it is a perfect labyrinth, enough to make you fancy yourself in the catacombs; little chills pass over you; you are afraid of being attacked. Ha! ha! ha! I am exaggerating a little again, but—"

"I beg you to allow me to continue," said the capitalist; "you cannot help being interested in this article."

"Our only hope, the safety of my dear flock, depended wholly upon the energy of a new missionary, who had joined us only a few days before. This estimable brother, who, listening only to his religious zeal, gave up the parish in France of which he was the incumbent, and obtained permission to become a missionary, is a tall, powerful man, endowed with rare courage and firmness. Scarcely had he been apprised of the danger that threatened us, when he strenuously insisted upon our leaving the village. 'I will take charge of everything,' he added eagerly. 'I will guard the houses.'—'But you will be massacred, my dear Roche,' said I, 'your life is precious to us, and—' "

"What?" interrupted the countess, "Roche—Roche! Is it Abbé Roche, the former curé of Manteigney?"

"I should not be surprised if it were," replied Abbé Desvialle. "I think I heard the archbishop say that Abbé Roche was now in China, or somewhere in that part of the world. He is just the right man to be in the vanguard, and I do not doubt that he has rendered valuable services there. Go on, M. Larreau, this is really by no means uninteresting."

"It is simply magnificent, as you shall see! I will continue: 'But you will be massacred,' etc. 'That is by no means certain; but under any circumstances, I shall be able to keep these savages at bay long enough to give you time to reach the mountains.' I embraced him with tears in my eyes and we set out.

"Our poor hamlet has only one entrance, which is extremely narrow. The brave missionary collected everything that he could carry, furniture, boards, etc., and piled them up there, not with any expectation of opposing a serious impediment to the brigands' progress, but to lead them to fear a sturdy resistance, and thus delay their attack. Having accomplished this task, he shut himself up in one of the nearest huts, barricaded it as well as he could, and waited about an hour, when a small detachment of bandits appeared at the entrance of the village, evidently very uneasy on perceiving the defences that barred the way. Courage is not their strong point; they consulted together, then slowly, one by one, picked their way through the pile of furniture and entered the hamlet, sword in hand, and listening intently. Then they again stopped and hesitated; the silence which reigned round them seemed more alarming than resistance. During this time our revered Roche, while counting the minutes, was with us in thought, and believing that we had not yet reached a place of safety, addressed the most fervent prayers to Heaven. The bandits at last decided, and either by chance or because they had seen the head of the missionary, who was watching them through a chink in the roof, went directly towards the hut in which he had taken refuge, and beat upon the door uttering loud cries.

"Finding that no one answered, and the entrance was still closed, they attempted to force a passage, and soon succeeded. Seven or eight of these fiends then rushed into the house ready to exterminate the unfortunate Christians whom they hoped to find there; but our brave colleague, whose most earnest desire was to gain time, sprang through an opening in the rear of the hut, and passing around it, suddenly attacked three or four of the bandits who had prudently remained outside, threw one of them to the ground, wrested his spear from him, and like a new Samson charged upon the others with superhuman vigor. The Philistines who had remained at the door were soon disabled, imploring for mercy amidst shrieks extorted by the pain of their wounds, while those who had entered the house terrified by the clamor without, believed themselves to be surrounded, lost, and took to flight in every direction as fast as possible.

"Our heroic brother was left master of the field of battle. The scoundrels had probably not dreamed that a black robe could cover so stern a warrior. Wounded, suffering, and unable to rise, they expected the conqueror, imitating their ferocity, would give them a death-blow; but the mercy and charity of a soldier of Christ are equal to his courage. Our dear brother at once sought to relieve them, hastened in search of water, and helped them to moisten their lips. The soldier was transformed into a sister of charity, and it was not until he heard the rapid approach of a more numerous band, that the missionary took refuge in another hut and again barricaded himself, hoping to renew the stratagem which had proved so successful; but this time the assailants came in hundreds; the village was captured in an instant, and the doors were forced or dashed in pieces. Our unfortunate friend, driven into one corner of the room to which he had retreated, defended himself bravely, thinking, even in this moment of peril, of gaining time for us and concentrating the rage of the Pagans upon himself. He killed the nearest, who, pressed forward by the crowd, could not escape his terrible blows by flight; but at last, overwhelmed by numbers, severely wounded, covered with perspiration and blood, was borne down, tied hand and foot, and dragged out of doors.

"It is very probable that if our dear brother had encountered the bloodthirsty mob of rebels, as in the first instance, he would immediately have atoned for his bold resistance with his life; but this second troop was no other than a detachment of the imperial army, with whose banners the newly-arrived missionary had not yet become familiar.

"They led him to the next city as if he had been a malefactor. On the way, the soldiers who surrounded him pricked him with their weapons to accelerate his pace, rendered slow and feeble by his painful wounds. Yet from the memory of our divine Saviour he obtained superhuman courage, did not utter a complaint, and entered with a smile the miserable dungeon, where he was surrounded by wretched criminals, who overwhelmed him with scorn and insult."

Larreau paused an instant to take breath.

"The account is highly dramatic," murmured the prefect, "rather long, but very well written."

"It makes the tears come into my eyes," cried the countess; "poor, poor curé! it seems as if I could see him among those fiends!" And she instinctively glanced towards a Chinese screen on which two warriors of the Celestial Empire were embroidered in gold thread upon scarlet satin. The capitalist, with evident emotion, resumed his reading:

"The very next morning he was removed from this disgraceful cell to be dragged before his judges. It was on this occasion that our revered brother showed a heroism beyond all praise. He was accused, ostensibly at least, of having resisted the imperial army, made common cause with the rebels, and opposed the will of the emperor; but in reality his title of Christian was the true cause of the atrocities inflicted upon him. They pretended to believe in the existence of a conspiracy, a political plot, and insolently accused him of being one of its chiefs.

"I will relate the particulars of his last examination; it is well calculated to inflame the zeal of the young priests belonging to the missions. The following details I received from an interpreter who, belonging to a Christian family, and being himself, through the mercy of God, anxious to become a convert, sent them to me:

"All the princes of the blood were seated at the tribunal. On their right were the civil, on the left the military, mandarins. The hall was filled with soldiers, and behind them struggled a crowd of eager spectators. The executioners, with their instruments of torture arranged before them in regular order, stood at the foot of the tribunal.

"'Do you recognize any of your accomplices among these persons?' asked the president, directing his attention towards several prisoners.

"'I have no accomplices, why should I?' he replied.

"The mandarins looked at each other and one of them gave orders that he should be fastened to the stake and receive ten blows from a bamboo rod to compel him to confess the names of his accomplices.

"He endured the blows without uttering a word, or even changing color.

"'He is obstinate,' said the mandarin. Then addressing the martyr, 'Come, tell the truth, and you shall be pardoned; but if you continue to deny your crime, we shall treat you with still greater severity.'

"'Do I seem like a man who is afraid?' he answered.

"And he said the words so proudly, gazed so boldly towards the tribunal, that the mandarins caused him to be again bound to the stake and scourged anew.

"Two executioners relieved each other, and when he was removed without having uttered a complaint, he said: 'I struck harder than that, you are children.'

"Then all the mandarins began to speak at the same time, in an outburst of fury. One said: 'Your flesh shall be torn with red-hot pincers.' Another: 'He must have swallowed some potion which saves him from pain.'—'Will you resist the whole tribunal?' vociferated a third.

"'Why do you not scream when you are lashed, proud, obstinate fool?'

"'I keep silent because I should ask you in vain to spare me even a single stroke of the bamboo. Why should I weary myself with useless shrieks? I suffer greatly when you scourge me, but I wish to show that the great God whom I adore gives his children strength to endure pain.'

"'You shall die under the pincers!'

"'I have no more fear of the pincers than of the

rod. If I were afraid of anything, I should not be here.'

"'And you will not confess?'

"'I have told you I have nothing to tell.'

"They again fastened him to the stake and began to beat him most brutally. All eyes were fixed upon him; there was a great tumult in the hall, and the judges, excited by the heroism of this holy man, considering his silence as an insult, and urged on by dull hatred of the Christians, shouted to the executioners: 'Strike harder! strike harder!'

"And he, gaining fresh courage under the blows, with his face illumined by a light imparted from on high, also shouted in his powerful voice, which rose above the noise of the crowd and the insults of the mandarins: 'Strike! Have you lost your strength? My God, pardon my sins!'

"Beneath his bleeding skin the muscles of his herculean limbs could be seen contracting, so that the cords seemed to cut into his body, and the stake to which he was bound creaked like the mast of a ship in a tempest.

"This lasted a long time, then he was unfastened and laid upon a mat. His flesh was frightfully lacerated, he was covered with blood, and in his face, from which life seemed to have departed, nothing was visible but his sparkling eyes. He was carried back to a dungeon, where he was left alone, a hideous, yet sublime object. Women recoiled in terror as he passed.

"Meantime, I had been informed of all this by a proselyte, and without reflecting upon the dangers which the step might involve, instantly went to the place and urgently entreated permission to enter the martyr's prison. The fear of incurring the just anger of the French authorities prevented the tribunal from refusing my request, and the door of the dungeon was opened to admit me. Alas! my pen refuses to describe the scene. I beheld our dear brother stretched upon the ground, the death rattle sounding in his throat. Doubtless his wounds had re-opened and a hemorrhage followed, for he was lying in a pool of blood.

"I approached him, tried to speak to him, kissed his icy forehead, but he was perfectly unconscious, his soul was about to ascend to its God, and he expired in my arms a few moments after my arrival, just as I gave him my benediction.

"Such, gentlemen and respected colleagues, was the exemplary death of this generous martyr of the Faith; his fate is to be envied; may Heaven reserve a similar one for us! May this heroism at last enlighten the Heathens and make them comprehend that such courage comes from God alone. It is He who has done all, to Him be the glory.

"*Non nobis, Domine, non nobis, sed nomini tuo da gloriam.*"

The close of the reading was followed by a long, silence, which was first broken by Abbé Desvialle, who had been turning his snuff-box in his fingers for the last ten minutes.

"That is an admirable death," said he, "really admirable, and early to-morrow I shall celebrate a mass. You will come to it, will you not, Madame?"

The countess made no reply. She had turned very pale, and was leaning back in the depths of an arm chair, as if fainting. "I ought not to have read all these horrors before her," cried M. Larreau, hastening towards his daughter.

"Salts, a glass of water!" exclaimed the prefect.

"It is nothing, I am quite well again," said the countess, rising. "Poor curé—poor curé! That horrible death has upset me, and to think that I have left the souvenir he sent me on his departure almost forgotten in the depths of a closet."

"What was it, my child? You never told me of any souvenir."

"Oh! no doubt, because when I received the gift people were so ill-disposed towards the poor curé that I thought it best not to speak of it. It is a magnificent crucifix; I will go and find it; I locked it up and then thought no more about it."

"Not yet, dear child, you have not entirely recovered from your emotion; you need not trouble yourself, I will ring for your maid."

"She would not know where to look for it. Besides, it will do me good to take a little exercise."

When Mme. de Manteigney had left the parlor, the capitalist resumed the conversation: "But what the deuce was that dear Abbé Roche doing there? When I say dear— In short, I wished him no harm, although he left the country in the most unbecoming manner, without even a formal leave-taking, when I had shown him a confidence, a friendship— Fortunately, I am prepared for such things, I have seen so much of it in the course of my life! Besides, he was a rough man, unaccustomed to the amenities—"

"His vocation had a powerful influence over him," observed M. Desvialle with a seriousness full of unction. "The mission of a priest is one of sacrifice, my dear M. Larreau; you cannot understand it. And the prospect, the almost certainty of martyrdom, is a divine allurement which arouses and excites the soul."

"You make my mouth water, my dear curé, pray give me a pinch of snuff. The truth in regard to Abbé Roche is simply this: I can venture to say that I know men thoroughly, and I believe my judgment of him to be perfectly impartial. With all his apparent simplicity, the dead man was a very clever fellow; but he was seeking his path, his goal in life—he had not found his object: hence his hesitations, his inconsistencies. Do not imagine that he went to China without some important motive."

"You surprise me," murmured Abbé Desvialle.

"Some enterprise, some bold stroke tempted his ambition, I assure you; stop, now I think of it: the Chinese accused him of being at the head of a political conspiracy. Eh! eh! that does not appear so very incredible to me. Don't smile, my dear curé, do we ever know what thoughts may be passing through the brains of others?"

"Here is the ivory Christ," said the countess, entering the parlor, followed by her maid. "Put the crucifix on the table, Marie. That is right, you can go. Is it not beautiful, my dear curé? What do you think of it, M. le prefect? How exquisite the carving is, how much feeling is expressed in the countenance of the dying Christ! Look at the head, it is superb."

"Even the frame is wonderful."

"It is a beautiful piece of workmanship, and must certainly be of great value."

"But how did such a masterpiece fall into the hands of a poor country curé, who certainly could not have saved its price from a few farthings?"

"I remember," said the countess, "that poor Abbé Roche told me how it happened, in a very touching manner. This wonderful carving fell into his hands from the skies, one might almost say, just as he left the seminary. The box containing the crucifix was brought to his house in a wagon, and in spite of all his efforts, he had never been able to discover the name of the person who sent the gift."

"Our excellent Abbé Roche was different from the rest of the world in everything," observed Larreau.

"This is no time for jesting, father. He spoke of it with so much feeling! Perhaps there might have been some family tie connected with it, which he guessed, though unable to explain. In some men's lives there are mysteries—"

"Oh! M. Roche's family—" Abbé Desvialle, who had spoken the last words, suddenly stopped. "This is carved with wonderful skill."

At that moment Count de Manteigney appeared, pushing aside the curtain that hung over the doorway. His face expressed great annoyance. "She is dead!" he exclaimed, pulling off his red gloves, "she is dead! Oh! I am so sorry."

"You mean he is dead, my dear Jean. Ah! yes. It is true."

"No, the colt is doing very well, it is my poor mare that is dead! Why, where did you get that crucifix? It is a superb thing! But I know that carving; I have seen it a hundred times." He turned the crucifix in every direction; as he looked at it more closely, his recollections seemed to become more exact. "I recognize this red velvet. I remember this gap you see in the frame. How long ago it seems! Stop, here at the bottom there used to be a silver shell to contain the holy water; has it been lost? But where was this crucifix discovered? I gave orders that every corner of the château should be searched. How glad I am to find it again! It hung beside the bed in the large yellow room where my mother died." Then turning to the countess: "You will have this relic placed in the spot where it belongs, and from which it should never have been removed, won't you, my love?"

"Certainly, my dear," replied the young wife, who was trembling with emotion, "certainly."

No one dared to resume the conversation which had been interrupted by the count's entrance. Not a word more was said about the heroic martyr.

M. de Manteigney, seeing that all were silent, eagerly continued: "Did you ever hear of such fools! When they saw the poor beast was ill, one would have supposed they would have told me at once! Not a bit of it! On pretence that I was just going in to dinner, they sent for the veterinary surgeon at Virez! Poor beast!"

"Are you talking of the veterinary surgeon?"

"No, I am talking about my mare. Ha! ha! ha! Yet I am by no means in the mood for laughing."

"It was a natural mistake. Ha! ha! ha!"

"Gentlemen, tea is ready."

THE END.

www.ingramcontent.com/pod-product-compliance
Lightning Source LLC
LaVergne TN
LVHW020237110826
845151LV00003B/947

* 9 7 8 1 4 2 5 5 3 0 6 8 6 *